ISSI

Political Theory has undergone a remarkable development in recent years. From a state in which it was once declared dead, it has come to occupy a central place in the study of Politics. Both political ideas and the wide-ranging arguments to which they give rise are now treated in a rigorous, analytical fashion, and political theorists have contributed to disciplines as diverse as economics, sociology and law. These developments have made the subject more challenging and exciting, but they have also added to the difficulties of students and others coming to the subject for the first time. Much of the burgeoning literature in specialist books and journals is readily intelligible only to those who are already well-versed in the subject.

Issues in Political Theory is a series conceived in response to this situation. It consists of a number of detailed and comprehensive studies of issues central to Political Theory which take account of the latest developments in scholarly debate. While making original contributions to the subject, books in the series are written especially for those who are new to Political Theory. Each volume aims to introduce its readers to the intricacies of a fundamental political issue and to help them find their way through the detailed, and often complicated, argument that that issue has attracted.

PETER JONES
ALBERT WEALE

ISSUES IN POLITICAL THEORY

Series editors: PETER JONES and ALBERT WEALE

Published
David Beetham: **The Legitimation of Power**
Tom Campbell: **Justice** (2nd edition)
John Horton: **Political Obligation**
Peter Jones: **Rights**
Albert Weale: **Democracy** (2nd edition)

Forthcoming
Raymond Plant: **Equality**

Issues in Political Theory Series
Series Standing Order

ISBN 978–0230–54393–5 hardback
ISBN 978–0230–54394–2 paperback
(outside North America only)

You can receive future titles in this series as they are published by placing a
standing order. Please contact your bookseller or, in the case of difficulty, write to
us at the address below with your name and address, the title of the series and the
ISBN quoted above.

Customer Services Department, Palgrave Ltd
Houndmills, Basingstoke, Hampshire RG21 6XS, England

Rights

Peter Jones

Published by
PALGRAVE
Houndmills, Basingstoke, Hampshire RG21 6XS and
175 Fifth Avenue, New York, N.Y. 10010
Companies and representatives throughout the world

PALGRAVE is the new global academic imprint of
St. Martin's Press LLC Scholarly and Reference Division and
Palgrave Publishers Ltd (formerly Macmillan Press Ltd).

ISBN 978-0-333-36135-1 hardcover
ISBN 978-0-333-36136-8 paperback

This book is printed on paper suitable for recycling and made
from fully managed and sustained forest sources. Logging,
pulping and manufacturing processes are expected to conform
to the environmental regulations of the country of origin.

A catalogue record for this book is available
from the British Library.

Transferred to digital printing, 2005

Printed in Great Britain by the MPG Books Group,
Bodmin and King's Lynn

To Pat

Contents

Contents

Acknowledgements

I have acquired many debts in writing this book. I owe a great deal to my colleague, Albert Weale, both for his very valuable and helpful advice on the text of this book and for the encouragement and intellectual stimulus he has given me over very many years. Steven Kennedy has been immensely helpful as publisher of this book. I am indebted to him for his advice and for the patience and good humour with which he has tolerated my repeated delays in completing this project.

My colleagues, Simon Caney and Tim Gray, spent many hours carefully scrutinising an early draft of the text. They have saved me from many errors and suggested a great many improvements and the final product is very much better for their efforts. I am also grateful for their support and encouragement to several other of my colleagues at Newcastle, particularly to Hugh Berrington.

Some of the arguments in Chapter 7 were first developed in a paper I wrote for an ECPR Workshop on Needs and Welfare organised by Robert Goodin and Alan Ware; I am grateful to them and to the other members of the Workshop for their helpful comments on those arguments.

I claim the author's customary right to whatever errors and misjudgements remain, particularly since I have sometimes resisted the good advice that I have received.

Finally I must express my thanks to my wife, to whom this book is dedicated, and to my children, Adam and Rachel. For a long time they have seen me retreat to my study when I might have spent my time with them. In spite of the neglect that they have suffered while I have been writing this book, they have constantly given me their support and have shown a tolerance of my academic preoccupations to which I certainly had no right. I count myself very lucky. I know they are as pleased as I am to see my word-processor at last give birth to this book.

PETER JONES

Introduction

The language of rights has formed part of our moral, legal and political vocabulary for many centuries. The history of that language has not been one of unimpeded growth but it is probably true that it has achieved a wider currency in our own age than at any previous time. Rights are now claimed to more things and for a wider range of beings than ever before.

Rights are so common in our world that we might suppose that they are woven into the very fabric of human existence. But there have been worlds without rights. The conventional wisdom is that neither the ancient Greeks nor the ancient Romans possessed the concept of a right. They did, of course, possess ideas of right conduct, but it seems that our notion of a right did not figure in their moral thinking or in their systems of law. There are also some contemporary cultures for which the idea of rights is said to be an alien intrusion. Thus the idea that individuals possess entitlements which it is incumbent upon others to acknowledge and respect is not an inescapable part of the human condition. Quite when people began to think in those terms is disputed. Some scholars claim that the notion of rights did not appear in European thought before the fourteenth century. However, more recent scholarship has pushed that date of birth back to the twelfth century (Tuck, 1979; Tierney, 1988, 1989). Clear and clean 'beginnings' are rare in the history of ideas and the precise moment at which the idea of rights came into the world is likely to remain contentious.

What cannot be doubted is the popularity that 'rights' have achieved since their birth. They are now integral to our legal thinking and are central to our moral and political thinking. Perhaps the clearest manifestation of modernity's commitment to rights is the Universal Declaration of Human Rights adopted by the United Nations in 1948. It is a mark of the ubiquity of rights thinking that a body such as the United Nations, whose member states espoused conflicting ideologies and possessed widely different cultures, should nevertheless have been able to promulgate such a declaration. The Declaration was followed in 1966 by two Cove-

1

nants which provided for the human rights in greater detail, one dealing with civil and political rights, the other with economic, social and cultural rights. The UN has also committed itself to a series of special conventions on rights dealing with matters such as genocide, slavery, torture, the rights of refugees, religious and sexual discrimination and the rights of children.

International concern for human rights has not been limited to the United Nations. Various regions of the world have developed and adopted their own statements of human rights. In 1950, 20 European states signed the European Convention on Human Rights and created the European Court and the European Commission to supervise and enforce that Convention. An American Declaration of the Rights and Duties of Man was promulgated in 1948 and, in 1969, several Latin American states pledged their allegiance to the American Convention on Human Rights and established a court and a commission to give effect to that Convention. In 1981, the Organisation of African Unity adopted the African Charter on Human and Peoples' Rights. Often these international declarations and their associated administrative machinery have had only a limited impact upon the lives of the people for whom they ostensibly provide, but their existence symbolises the hold that the idea of human rights has taken on modern political thought.

In recent decades human rights have also become a much more prominent concern in foreign policy. Several governments have made respect for human rights by other governments a precondition of favourable relations. It is difficult not to be cynical about some of the uses made of the doctrine of human rights in contemporary foreign policy. Its invocation by governments is often too convenient and too selective to carry conviction. Nevertheless it is hard to think of any idea which has achieved a similar stature amongst the international community, except perhaps for the idea of national self-determination which is itself typically formulated as a 'right'. Few states are willing flatly to reject the idea of human rights and few governments are willing to present themselves openly to the world as violators of human rights.

Of course, the idea of human rights is not a recent one. Historically that idea descended from the older idea of natural rights – the idea that people have certain rights simply as natural human individuals. In its radical form, the theory of natural rights was developed to provide political safeguards for individuals. It was a way of asserting that individuals had rights which ought not to be violated by anyone. Protecting and enforcing those entitlements was conceived as the primary task of governments. But, since governments themselves posed the greatest threat to individuals, natural rights were asserted first and foremost as checks upon political power. Those who wielded political power were obliged to do so in a manner which respected people's natural rights. If they did not, they forfeited their right to rule.

Thus the doctrine of natural rights was used (by some) to justify the English revolutions of 1642-9 and 1688. It was also used to vindicate the two great popular revolutions of the eighteenth century, the American and the French. The Virginia Declaration of Rights (June 1776) and The United States' Declaration of Independence (July 1776) both enunciated inalienable rights, including the right of a people to alter or abolish a government which violated its rights. In 1791 a series of amendments, commonly known as the Bill of Rights, were added to the US Constitution which have been of incalculable importance for subsequent American history and immensely influential outside the United States. Likewise one of the chief legacies of the French Revolution was its Declaration of the Rights of Man and the Citizen (1789), which became the most celebrated and influential formal declaration of rights in European history. Inspired by the examples set in America and France, a strong tradition developed of incorporating declarations of rights in the constitutions of states. A catalogue of rights has now become a standard feature of the constitutional apparatus of the modern state.

The significance of rights in the modern era is not limited to their entrenchment in constitutions and their announcement in international declarations. Of equal and perhaps greater significance is the way in which rights inhabit our ordinary moral and political thinking. Claiming or asserting rights has become the common mode by which people seek to promote an interest or advance a cause. That is to be explained, in part, by the special force possessed by the language of rights. If we are concerned that people should be able to speak freely, or to choose their own careers, or to vote, or to marry the person of their choice, or to have an abortion, or to hunt animals, or to determine their own life-style, or to work, or to strike, or not to suffer discrimination, or to receive medical treatment, or not to receive medical treatment, or to live, or to die, it is much more forceful to say that people have rights to do all of those things than to say merely that it is desirable or good that they should be able to do them. In coming to think of these things as rights, we shift them out of the realm of the merely desirable and into the domain of the morally essential. It is not surprising therefore that people have taken so readily to expressing their deepest concerns in terms of rights.

The ascription of rights has also been important for the standing they have given to their holders. If all human beings possess rights merely in virtue of being human, then all humans possess a certain equality of moral standing which cuts across differences of class or caste or race or religion. If the rights of women are identical with those of men, that implies an equality of moral status between the sexes. More controversially, if animals possess rights that implies that they should occupy a place in our moral thinking that they would not if rights were confined to human beings. If foetuses or 'unborn children' possess rights, we cannot regard aborting them as morally no different from clipping a fingernail or getting rid of unwanted hair. If nations have rights, we cannot ignore their existence in the way we construct and reconstruct the political world. These observations are not meant to suggest that, logically, it must be rights that deliver standing rather than standing that delivers rights. Rather the point is that the two have become so closely associated that rights have become significant not just for what they are entitlements to but also for what they say about the moral standing of the beings or entities that possess them.

Yet the readiness with which people have embraced the idea of rights in our age is not symptomatic of a unanimity about their content. The popularity of rights has been achieved at a price. If an idea is promiscuously available to all, it will find itself pressed into the service of every sort of interest, cause and persuasion. And so it has proved with rights. Rights have been invoked both to attack and to defend private property, to attack and to defend the free market, to attack and defend the welfare state; they have been used to require obedience to law and to justify disobedience to law, to justify the majority's prevailing over the minority and the minority's restraining the majority, to vindicate the use of violence and to condemn the use of violence. The point need not be laboured. The merest acquaintance with contemporary political argument is enough to make one aware of the diverse and conflicting claims that are asserted as rights.

If we turn to the philosophers for guidance on how we should determine which rights people really have and which they do not, we find a similar pattern of diversity. There is not a single agreed theory that argues for rights but a whole variety of theories each of which argues for rights in a different way and with different implications for their content. Even when we seem to agree upon rights, our agreement may be more apparent than real. We may all, for example, endorse the right to life, only to discover that, when we confront matters such as abortion, euthanasia, capital punishment and killing in war, we actually have very different understandings of that right. It is sometimes suggested that the United Nations was able to secure agreement upon a declaration of human rights only because it formulated those rights so generally that different countries, cultures and ideologies were each able to interpret them in ways they found acceptable.

Nor is everyone happy with the prominence that rights have achieved in our moral and political thinking. The rhetoric of rights is sometimes said to be out of control (Sumner, 1987, p. 1). Rights are rampant. They seem to increase by the day. Nothing seems to check the enthusiasm with which people discover new rights, nothing seems to restrain the confidence with which they declare that their discoveries are indeed rights. It is not only the chaotic and indiscriminate nature of this proliferation of rights that attracts criticism, it is also the manner in which rights are claimed. Bentham complained that the doctrine of natural rights was 'so much flat assertion' (1952, I, p. 335). Much the same complaint might be made today. People have a way of just 'declaring' rights as though nothing need be said in justification of what they declare. Disputes phrased in terms of rights often present us with little more than assertions and counter-assertions. They seem to exacerbate rather than ameliorate conflict. We are confronted with opposing sets of dogmatic claims which offer no means of resolution and no prospect of reconciliation. Thus debates on questions such as abortion or the treatment of animals or social justice can turn into sterile rituals in which rights are thrown backwards and forwards by the warring parties. The rhetoric of rights can seem to do more to impede than to aid our understanding of moral and political issues.

Reservations and doubts about the very morality of rights are probably more common amongst academic philosophers than amongst people at large. But even outside the academy, the complaint is often heard that people have become too ready to claim rights. People announce their entitlement to this or that without giving sufficient consideration to the burdens or restrictions or sacrifices that these alleged entitlements entail for others. They would do better, it is often said, to give rather less attention to their rights and rather more to their duties. Rights and duties should tally. If there is an imbalance between the rights people claim and the duties they acknowledge, that is prima facie evidence that there is something wrong with their moral accountancy.

The very truculence and assertiveness with which rights are often associated, and which make them attractive to some, has made them unattractive to others. The women's movement has made extensive and effective use of the language of rights, but some of its members now suggest that that language is inappropriate to their gender – that the strident and aggressive language of rights is part of the very male-oriented world that feminism should be seeking to curtail or supplant. Similarly some of those who place a high value upon ideals of community and solidarity see rights thinking as individualistic and divisive and an obstacle to the closely bonded society to which they aspire. For those people, our aim should be not to discover the correct set of rights, but to recast our thinking so that we get rid of them.

The subject of rights is, then, rich in controversy. The friends of rights quarrel over what rights people have, over why they have them, over just who or what has them and over their moral and political significance. Those less friendly to rights would like to find ways of weakening their grip on our thinking, while the outright enemies of rights would have us dispose of them altogether.

This book attempts a comprehensive examination of the idea of rights and of the issues surrounding that idea. Rights vary greatly both in their content and in their importance. Some, such as the rights to life and to fundamental freedoms, are of the greatest significance, while others, such as the right to choose which washing powder to buy, can be quite trivial in content. My concern will be with the 'big' rights – with rights that have been at the forefront of moral and political thinking and that have been claimed as natural rights or human rights or 'fundamental' rights of some other sort. In examining these rights I try to do justice to the full range of arguments that they have attracted, but I do not pretend merely to report those debates since I add my own voice to them.

I share in the sorts of moral and political concerns that rights have been used to express and consequently I approach the subject of rights in a broadly sympathetic spirit. Some modern writers have brushed aside all talk of rights with barely disguised contempt; their dismissive attitude reveals a remarkable insensitivity to the miseries and evils that have led people to claim rights. Ideas of rights have been developed not as mere intellectual diversions but in reaction to the reality of human suffering and to the injustices done by man to man. In our own age, the idea of human rights owes much of its popularity to people's revulsion against the grotesque evils perpetrated by some twentieth-century regimes. There are very strong reasons for taking rights seriously. However, those reasons cannot excuse our ignoring the problems and complications that afflict rights-thinking. In much of what follows I focus on the difficulties and disputes that beset claims of right. Proponents of rights must take those difficulties and disputes no less seriously than the rights to which they are committed, although it is worth stating at the outset that the sorts of problems and complications that beset theories of rights are often not unique to rights but are the common lot of moral and political philosophy.

A study of rights must begin with an analysis of what a 'right' is. Since we speak of rights so frequently and so confidently in our everyday language, we might suppose that we all know very well what a right is. But, like many concepts that we seem able to use unproblematically as long as we do so unreflectively, the concept of a 'right' is one whose precise content is not easily laid bare. We use the single term 'right' to cover four quite different forms of entitlement which are usually described as 'claim-rights', 'liberty-rights', 'powers' and 'immunities'. The beginning of wisdom about rights resides in an understanding of these different forms and consequently I begin, in Chapter 1, by explaining the nature and significance of those different forms of right.

If rights can take these different forms, what is it that makes them all species of a single genus? Attempts to capture the essential defining feature of rights have produced two rival schools of thought. One, the benefit theory, claims that having a right is essentially a matter of enjoying a benefit or of having something addressed to one's interests. The other, the choice theory, holds that having a right is essentially a matter of having a choice; a legal right is a legal option, a moral right is a moral option. In Chapter 2, I examine the strengths and weaknesses of those two interpretations of rights and suggest that, in trying to unearth what is essential to the idea of a right, we might do better to focus upon the idea of a 'title', although that way of understanding rights still leaves a role for the benefit and choice theories.

Claims that people possess legal rights are, for the most part, uncontroversial although claims concerning the legal rights that they *ought* to possess are not. Claims that people possess moral rights have been much more controversial, but it is rights of that sort that have been the pre-eminent concerns of moral and political philosophy. If we turn to rights for instruction on how political power should be used and where its limits should fall, those rights cannot be legal rights. Ordinarily, they will have to be moral rights.

In Chapter 3 I examine the idea of moral rights and the sort of moral thinking with which rights have been associated. Rights have significance for our moral and political thought because of their special status. They constitute titles which others must recognise and respect. I explicate the morality of rights by examining the contemporary debate between rights-theorists and utilitarians – a debate which is emblematic of two fundamentally contrasting approaches in moral and political philosophy. In its simplest form, that debate has been about whether there is good reason for singling out certain areas of people's lives and using rights to make them objects of special moral concern. In its more complex form, it has been about whether consequentialist theories like utilitarianism can themselves provide a satisfactory case for rights or whether only 'rights-based' theories – theories which give a fundamental rather than a subordinate significance to rights – can provide adequately for rights. My own view is that taking rights seriously entails a measure of commitment to rights-based thinking (properly under-stood), although it need not entail that all of our moral and political thinking must be rights-based nor even that all rights must be rights for rights-based reasons. The idea of moral rights also raises the question of who or what can possess rights, and in Chapter 3 I try to indicate what is at issue in deciding whether we should ascribe rights to beings other than adult human beings.

The moral rights that have figured most prominently in political thought have been natural rights and human rights and Chapter 4 is devoted to examining what it is that makes a right 'natural' or 'human'. Some people have found the claim that rights can be 'natural' both fraudulent and bizarre but I try to show that, when understood in its appropriate context, there is nothing extraordinary in that claim. Even so, people nowadays are generally more comfortable with the concept of human rights. The general idea that human beings have rights has achieved widespread acceptance both amongst moral and political philosophers and amongst people generally. Yet that apparent consensus disguises a great deal of disagreement about what human rights people have and why. There are also philosophers who suggest that there is no less reason to be sceptical of human rights than of natural rights.

How then might we defend the ascription of rights to human beings? In Chapter 5 I examine several of the most important justificatory theories of rights offered by contemporary thinkers. The range of arguments dealt with in that chapter should dispel any notion that the idea of human rights is tied uniquely to a single moral theory. On the contrary, different theorists arrive at the idea of human rights by very different philosophical routes and, having converged upon the general idea of human rights, part company again when they begin to detail the rights that human beings have. The thinking associated with rights is therefore markedly diverse. We should also recognise the possibility that different rights may need to be justified in different ways and that a single right may be supported by more than a single reason. We should not take for granted therefore that the justification of rights must be the work of a single comprehensive theory.

In that spirit, each of the next three chapters examines an area of moral and political concern in which claims of right have figured especially prominently. Chapter 6 examines rights as they relate to freedom – the grounds upon which people may have rights to freedom, the sort of freedom or freedoms to which they may have rights and how we are to go about delimiting the freedom to which they have rights. Chapter 7 examines rights to socioeconomic goods, particularly the goods and services associated with the welfare state. It considers how far we can translate needs into rights, whether we should translate human needs into human rights or into citizens' rights, and why some theorists would prefer us not to speak of rights at all in this area.

Chapter 8 examines the relationship between democracy and rights. That relationship is an ambivalent one. Democracy itself can be understood as a system of rights and many statements of rights give explicit endorsement to democracy. Yet rights have also been invoked as constraints upon democracy, particularly when people have been anxious to safeguard individuals or minorities against majorities. We have therefore to disentangle democratic from non-democratic rights and to consider whether those two sorts of rights can coexist harmoniously. We have also to confront the question of whether democracy is 'rights-based'? If people should be governed democratically and only democratically is that because they have a right to be governed in that way? If so, what sort of right is that? Is it a right held by each individual citizen or is it a 'group right' held by a people as a collectivity?

In Chapter 9 I turn to a number of doubts and difficulties that beset all theories of rights. Those fall into three categories. First, there are a number of questions which cluster around the precise status that we should give to rights. The special status possessed by rights is essential to their being rights and to the distinctive role that they perform in our moral and political thinking. But just how special should that status be? Must rights be recognised and respected no matter how great the costs? Some theorists have wanted to give rights, or at least some rights, an 'absolute' status; they have held that rights must be treated as absolutely inviolable in all possible circumstances. However many proponents of rights fight shy of that extravagant claim. Life, particularly political life, often presents us with choices not between good and evil but between competing goods or between competing evils. When we are faced with those unhappy choices, it is not obvious that we should sacrifice all else to rights. But, if we begin to qualify the status possessed by rights, we seem to lose any clear sense of just how much rights should matter.

A second set of questions cluster around the morality of rights. If people have rights, can they use them to do anything other than what is right? If they cannot, rights may seem redundant; but, if they can, we have to make sense of the apparently odd notion that people can have a right to do wrong. In addition, rights-theorists have to consider how large the realm of rights should be. Should we do all of our moral and political thinking in terms of rights or are there values and relationships which belong outside or beyond the realm of rights? Rights-theorists must also confront claims that their morality is not merely limited in its range but also harmful in its effect upon human relationships. Modernity's insistence upon individual rights has sometimes been blamed for eroding the bonds of human community and creating societies peopled by anomic and aggressively self-centred individuals.

A third area of difficulty, which is particularly significant for human rights, is that of cultural diversity. The existence of that diversity is often thought to make the doctrine of human rights both implausible and objectionable. Given the diverse systems of value to be found across the world, can all human beings plausibly be said to possess the same rights? Can ideas of human rights rise above or be made consistent with cultural diversity, or must proponents of human rights resign themselves to replacing cultural diversity with moral uniformity?

Diversity is not only a feature of cultures, it is also a characteristic of theories and conceptions of rights. In the Conclusion I consider what are the implications of that diversity for our thinking about rights. I suggest that that diversity of thinking is much less of a problem for the moral philosophy of rights than critics of rights have often supposed. On the other hand, that diversity does pose a problem for practical projects designed to secure rights for people and it may well affect our thinking about the best way of providing for rights in political systems.

1 Forms of Right

It has long been recognised by legal writers that different sorts of entitlement masquerade under the single term 'right'. Early in this century, Wesley Hohfeld (1919) produced what has come to be regarded as the classic analysis of types of legal right. His analysis has not gone unchallenged either in its detail or in its general form, but it remains a highly enlightening account of how the single term 'right' may be used to describe quite different sorts of jural relation.[1] Hohfeld pointed out that the term 'right' was used to describe four distinct types of jural relation.

1. *Claim-rights*. Suppose A and B enter into a contract in which B undertakes to pay A a sum of money. A then has a right to that sum of money and B has a reciprocal duty to pay A that sum of money. Hohfeld called this sort of right a right 'in its strict sense', but it has been more commonly described as a 'claim-right' since it constitutes a claim that one party has upon another. Because claim-rights constitute claims upon others, they always exist in conjunction with duties.

2. *Liberty-rights*. Suppose now that I assert that I have a right to dress as I please. Here the term 'right' has a quite different import. The thrust of the assertion is not that others owe me a duty (although that may be implied) but rather that I am guilty of no wrong in dressing as I please. I am saying that I am 'at liberty' to dress as I please in that I have no obligation to dress, or not to dress, in any particular way. Hence this sort of right has come to labelled a 'liberty-right'.

3. *Powers*. Consider next the right to make a will or the right to vote. These could be asserted as liberty-rights (people are under no obligation not to make a will or not to vote) or as claim-rights (others are duty-bound not to prevent people from making a will or from voting). However the more likely sense in which these are likely to be asserted is as 'powers'. I have the right to make a will in that the law provides a legal facility which enables me to determine the disposal of my estate after my

death. I have the right to vote in that I am legally 'empowered' to cast a vote in an election; someone who is not enfranchised is not so empowered.

4. *Immunities.* Finally I may enjoy a right in that I am not subject to another's power; that is, I am 'immune' from another's power. In a society where there is no legal provision for divorce, a person has the right not to be divorced by his or her spouse, in that spouses have no power to divorce.

Hohfeld attempted to bring out the distinct character of each of these types of right by identifying the 'correlative' and the 'opposite' of each.

Type:	claim-right	liberty-right	power	immunity
Correlative:	duty	no-right	liability	disability

Type:	claim-right	liberty-right	power	immunity
Opposite:	no-right	duty	disability	liability

Hohfeld characterised a right as a relation between two parties. Thus he held that, for every type of right, there must be a correlative term describing the position of the other party in the relation. If A is the right-holder and B is the other party in the relation, when A has a claim-right, B has a duty; when A has a liberty-right to do something, B has a 'no-right' (that is, no claim-right) that A shall not do it; when A has a power, B has a liability; and when A has an immunity, B has a disability or 'no-power'. Hohfeld's 'opposites' simply describe the condition directly contrary to that of holding the type of right in question. Before examining each sort of right in more detail, a few general comments are necessary on Hohfeld's scheme.

Firstly, Hohfeld thought that the four different usages of the term 'right' caused confusion. He therefore proposed that usage of the term 'right' should be limited to 'claim-rights' or what he himself called 'rights in the strict sense'. However, most analysts have continued to recognise all four as types of 'right', partly because that more generous interpretation of the term corresponds with its use in ordinary language. Secondly, Hohfeld's anaysis is of *legal* rights. Whether it can be usefully applied to the concept of a right in non-legal contexts remains to be seen.

Thirdly, it would be mistaken to suppose that every right that is asserted must belong to one and only one of Hohfeld's four categories. I have already indicated how the assertion of a right to vote may be simultaneously the assertion of a power, a claim-right and a liberty-right. Similarly, if I have a property right in a car, that right is likely to consist of a complicated cluster of Hohfeldian rights. Typically these would include the claim-right that others should refrain from damaging my car or using it without my permission, my liberty-right as owner to use the car, the power to sell the car or to permit others to use it, and my immunity from any power of others to dispose of the car without my consent. In other words, a single assertion of right might, on inspection, turn out to be a cluster of different types of right.

Fourthly, Hohfeld's analysis rests upon the supposition that every type of right, and every actual instance of a right, is ultimately reducible to a relation between two parties. The logic of that position led him to argue that, strictly, we have as many rights as there are people in relation to whom the rights are held. Thus, although we would normally speak of a person's 'right' not to be assaulted in the singular, that person really has as many rights as there are individuals who have the duty not to assault him. He has one right against B, another against C, another against D, and so on. Whether it is always appropriate to regard rights in this way is open to question, but at least Hohfeld's approach serves to make the elementary point that rights may be held in relation to some people and not others. If B is A's debtor, but C is not, A holds a right in relation to B that he does not hold in relation to C. If A has promised B, but not C, not to do x, A has no liberty-right to do x with respect to B, but remains at liberty to do x with respect to C. Similarly powers and immunities can be held in relation to some people but not others. Let us now look more closely at each of the four types of right.

Claim-rights

To have a claim-right is to be owed a duty by another or others. A claim-right is necessarily a right *against* a person or persons who owe the corresponding duty to the right-holder. In the absence of that duty there could be no claim-right. Although the term 'claim-right' is widely used, other labels are sometimes given to this sort of right. Some have followed Hohfeld in calling it a right 'in the strict sense'. It has also been called a 'demand-right' (Radin, 1938; Anderson, 1962) because it constitutes a demand upon others and a 'right of recipience' (Raphael, 1967b, p. 56) because it is a right to receive something from others.

Obviously the content of claim-rights can vary a great deal. One useful distinction is between 'positive' and 'negative' claim-rights. Positive claim-rights are rights to specific goods and services and are so called because they call for a positive response from those who bear the corresponding duties. Examples are the right to be protected, the right to receive compensation and the right to be provided with welfare benefits. Negative claim-rights are rights to non-interference and are so called because they require no more than restraint or 'negative action' from others. Examples are the right not to be assaulted, the right not to be libelled and the right not to have one's property taken.

Another useful distinction is between 'rights *in personam*' and 'rights *in rem*'. The same distinction is sometimes identified as that between 'personal' and 'real' rights or that between 'relative' and 'absolute' rights. None of those labels is very helpful as a guide to the content of the distinction and some are positively misleading. Simply stated, a right *in personam* is a right held against a specific person or persons, while a right *in rem* is one held against people at large. Thus the duty corresponding to a right *in personam* falls upon a determinate person or group of persons, while the duty corresponding to a right *in rem* falls indifferently upon the world at large or, at least, upon all who fall within the jurisdiction of the relevant legal system. (For a more precise treatment of this distinction, see Honore, 1960.) Typically, positive claim-rights are rights *in personam* while negative claim-rights are rights *in rem*. That is, where a right is a right to a positive good or service, the duty to provide that good or service usually falls upon specific individuals or institutions. For example, the right to have one's rubbish collected is a right held against a specific local authority or contractor; the right of an employee to be paid for his work is a right held specifically against his employer. Conversely, where a right is a right to non-interference, it is usually held against people at large. For example, the right not to be assaulted or the right not to be libelled is ordinarily a right held against all-comers. However, although these pairings are the norm, there can be exceptions to them. For example, 'good Samaritan' laws – laws which impose duties upon all citizens to assist anyone in distress – could be said to create positive rights *in rem*: the potentially distressed person has a right to positive assistance against the world at large. And when a court imposes an injunction upon an individual restraining his behaviour in relation to another individual, that other individual may be said to possess a negative right *in personam*: he is owed a duty of non-interference which is special to a particular individual.

Since to possess a claim-right is to be owed a duty, the content of the right is integrally related to the content of the duty. A different duty means a different right. For example, many declarations of rights include the 'right to life'. Those who seem to agree in accepting that individuals have the right to life seem, nevertheless, to disagree over what duties that right entails. Does it entail only the duty of others not to murder, or does it also entail the duty (usually of governments) to protect people from being murdered, or, beyond that, does it entail the duty (again usually of governments) to provide health care and the material essentials of life? But, if there is disagreement of this sort over duties, there must also be disagreement over rights, for the right not to be murdered is distinct from the right to be protected from murder and both are obviously distinct from the right to be provided with health care, food and clothing. The definition of its correlative duty is therefore essential to the definition of a claim-right.

Given the integral relation of claim-rights and duties, this is an appropriate point at which to mention the 'correlativity' thesis concerning rights and duties. That thesis has two elements and one can subscribe to neither, either or both. The first element is that for every right there is a correlative duty. The truth of that proposition depends entirely upon how broadly or narrowly we construe the term 'right'. If by 'right' we mean only claim-right, it is necessarily true, for the existence of a correlative duty is part of the very definition of a claim-right. If by 'right' we mean all four of the types of right that Hohfeld identifies, it is necessarily not true (as will be made clear in due course).

The second element of the correlativity thesis is that for every duty there is a correlative right. Hohfeld would also seem to endorse that proposition. However the truth of this element of the thesis is a more complicated matter and I shall postpone examining it until the next chapter since it raises large issues about when it is appropriate to speak of someone's 'having a right'. One last word on the link between claim-rights and duties. Alan White (1984, pp. 70–3) has challenged the normal idea of claim-rights in holding that *no* right logically implies a duty. Some rights, such as the right to be repaid or the right to be told the truth, are typically 'accompanied' by duties – the duty to repay and the duty to tell the truth – which 'protect' and render them 'effective'. But that, on White's analysis, would seem to be an entirely contingent relation and the rights could continue to exist even if there were no such duties.

If this view were correct, it would undermine the idea of claim-rights as it is ordinarily understood. In fact it seems unsustainable. As we shall, see liberty-rights, powers and immunities do not entail correlative duties, although they may be 'associated' with duties in some looser way. Claim-rights may also be 'associated' with duties which they cannot be said strictly to entail. For example, my right not to be assaulted may be 'associated' with the duty of a government to protect me from assault, which duty may be said to 'protect' that right and to render it 'effective'. However my right not to be assaulted does not logically entail the 'associated' duty of a government to protect me and it could intelligibly exist in the absence of that duty. (The duty to be protected by the government would be 'entailed' only by a right to be protected by the government). However that relation is of a quite different order from the relation between my right not to be assaulted and its correlative duty, the duty of another not to assault me. That *is* a logical relation: my right not to be assaulted would be unintelligible if no-one had a duty not to assault me. A right not to be assaulted is a right to be treated by *others* in a certain way and would therefore be nonsensical if those others had no duty not to assault me.

Liberty-rights

To have a liberty-right is to be free of any duty to the contrary. Thus, legally, I have the liberty-right to do x if there is no law imposing a duty upon me not to do x. Similarly I have a liberty-right *not* to do x if there is no law requiring me to do x.[2] Sometimes liberty-rights are spoken of simply as 'liberties'. They have also been called 'permissions' (Austin, 1911, p. 345; Benditt, 1978, p. 158) and 'rights of action' as opposed to 'rights of recipience' (Raphael, 1967b, p. 56). Hohfeld himself called them 'privileges' but that misleading term is best avoided.

In principle it would be possible for a legal system to exist in which everything that was not expressly permitted was forbidden. In fact legal systems have usually operated the other way round so that people have been legally at liberty to do whatever is not prohibited. For that reason a person's liberty-rights, unlike his claim-rights, are indefinitely many. They would include his freedom to express his opinions, to worship his God and to associate with whom he chooses. They would also include less grand matters such as his 'right' to paint his front door, to paint it whatever colour he likes, to use whatever size paint brush he chooses, and so on. All of the endless array of human actions that are not proscribed by law fall within the compass of liberties, even though it would probably not occur to us to speak of most of them as 'rights' – until, that is, they are challenged. For example, if I were asked to list my rights, the right to paint my front door purple is not the first that would spring to mind. But, if a next-door neighbour upbraided me for using such a disagreeable colour, my response might well be 'I have a perfect right to paint my front door purple'. Stoljar suggests that liberty-rights might be labelled 'defensive rights' since they are most often invoked as defences against the complaints or grievances of others (1984, p. 13).

In large measure, then, liberty-rights exist merely in virtue of the absence of any rule or general duty to the contrary. However liberty-rights can also take specific and express forms. For example, I may own a piece of land and so have a claim-right that others shall not enter it. But if I waive that claim-right to allow you to enter the land without trespass, you then possess a liberty-right with respect to my land that others do not. Liberty-rights may also be provided by law in the form of exemptions. Thus, ordinarily, I am legally forbidden from using violence against others but, if someone assaults me, the law gives me the liberty-right to use reasonable force in my self-defence.

Unlike claim-rights, liberty-rights are not correlated with duties. If I have the liberty-right to do x that means that I myself have no duty not to do x. Of itself, it does not mean that others have a duty not to prevent my doing x. The distinction between liberty-rights and negative claim-rights is one that has often been misunderstood (for example, Stone, 1964, pp. 140, 143; Paton, 1972, p. 291) and one which some have declared themselves unable to accept (for example, Braybrooke, 1972; Buckland, 1945, pp. 93–5; Renteln, 1990, pp. 41–2). If I have a right to do something, surely, it is sometimes objected, others must have a duty not to prevent my doing it. If they do not, how can I be said to have a right? To appreciate how this can be said, consider the following example.

In the game of soccer any player has the 'right' to score a goal. That right is a liberty-right. It means that, under the rules of soccer, each player is at liberty to score. It is not a claim-right. If it were, presumably other players would have the correlative duty to allow the goal to be scored and that, plainly, would be absurd. On the contrary, just as a player has the liberty-right to score a goal, so too his opponents, provided they remain within the rules of the game, have a liberty-right to prevent his scoring. Thus one player's liberty-right to score a goal can co-exist, quite consistently, with other players' liberty-rights to prevent his scoring.

Consider another example, one cited by Hart (1982, pp. 166–7). According to English law, I have the right to look over my garden fence at my neighbour in that I have no legal duty not to do that. However that is merely a liberty-right and does not entail that my neighbour is under a correlative duty to allow herself to be looked at. If she chooses to erect a high fence to obstruct my gaze, she too is legally at liberty to do that. So again, we can see how I may have the liberty-right to do something without its having to be true that others are duty-bound not to prevent my doing it. To express the same point in terms of Hohfeld's correlatives, that B has no claim-right that A shall not do x, does not entail that B has no liberty-right (has a duty not) to prevent A's doing x.

What serves to complicate matters and to promote confusion between liberty-rights and negative claim-rights is that liberty-rights often exist within a context of claim-rights. Thus, a moment ago, I stated that in soccer a player is at liberty, has a liberty-right, to stop an opponent from scoring a goal. However he is not at liberty to use *any* means to impede an opponent. He may not punch or trip his opponent nor, unless he is the goalkeeper within his penalty area, may he handle the ball. These acts are proscribed by the rules of the game. To that extent the would-be goal scorer's liberty-right to score may be said to be 'protected' by a number of claim-rights not to be impeded in certain ways. Nevertheless his liberty-right to score is still distinct from his various claim-rights not to be prevented from scoring by what the rules define as 'fouls'. And, of course, the liberty-right to score is itself circumscribed by the same rules limiting the ways in which that result may be achieved. Similarly, although my legal liberty to gaze into my neighbour's garden may be confounded by her erecting a high fence, there are other ways in which she may not thwart that liberty. She may not do so by shooting me or by poking out my eyes or by threatening to set fire to my house.

Thus liberty-rights often exist within what Hart describes as a 'protective perimeter' of claim-rights (1982, p. 171). A liberty-right may be accompanied by one or more claim-rights which afford partial if not total protection for its exercise. Indeed Hart himself suggests (ibid., p. 173) that it is appropriate to speak of liberties as 'rights' only if they enjoy this sort of protection. However, given the relevance of laws, such as those against assault, to one's ability to do virtually anything that is legally unforbidden, it is difficult to discover any legal liberty that is wholly unprotected by legal claim-rights.

To find a complex of liberty-rights entirely naked and unadorned by claim-rights we have to imagine what might be. The most celebrated example of a condition in which people would have liberty-rights entirely unaccompanied by claim-rights is Hobbes's state of nature. For Hobbes, a state of nature was a condition in which individuals were subject to no legal authority and therefore entirely without legal obligations. It was also a condition in which they were without moral duties to one another as these would ordinarily be understood. Consequently, in his state of nature, individuals were 'at liberty' to do anything, but their comprehensive lack of duties also entailed that they were comprehensively bereft of claim-rights.

Hobbes's state of nature represents little more than a logical possibility. In societies as we know them, liberty-rights are usually associated with 'protective' claim-rights. Yet it is still important that their difference is recognised. Their confusion can result not only in mistaken beliefs about what a particular right amounts to, but also in mistaken decisions, not least by judges.[3]

The negative way in which liberty-rights are defined ('no duty not to') and the fact that, in themselves, they do not entail correlative duties, may lead one to suppose that this sort of right is relatively unimportant. That would be a mistake. It is true that any and every trivial and insignificant action that is not proscribed by law may be claimed as a liberty-right. But so too, as far as law is concerned, may many important freedoms. For example, in English law the right of free expression exists only in that (and to the extent that) there is no law making it an offence to express one's views. Even if the law were to impose upon people a specific duty not to prevent others from expressing their views, that would not transform the liberty-right into a claim-right. The distinction between the two rights would remain and they would continue to have different contents. The liberty-right would be the right to express one's views; the claim-right would be the right not to be prevented from expressing one's views. The liberty-right would concern what one was oneself entitled to do; the claim-right would concern what others had a duty (not) to do. The separateness of these two rights can be seen not only in that liberty-rights can exist with or without protective claim-rights, but also in that claim-rights can exist with or without their kindred liberty-rights. For example, suppose that someone began saying things that she had no legal liberty-right to say. It would not automatically follow that those in her vicinity were absolved of their legal duty to refrain from silencing her (Lyons, 1970).

This points to a fundamental and important difference between claim-rights and liberty-rights. From the perspective of the right-holder, liberty-rights are 'active' in that they concern what the right-holder is himself entitled to do or not to do. From the same perspective, claim-rights are 'passive' in that they concern what *others* are obliged to do or not to do in respect of the right-holder. This again serves to underline the significance of liberty-rights. Whenever we are concerned with what a person has the right to do or not to do, or the right to be or not to be, as opposed to how he should be treated by others, we are concerned with liberty-rights. Indeed, if one inquired why people had rights concerning freedom, the obvious order of justification would be from liberty-rights to claim-rights. That is, the most obvious reason why people should not be prevented from doing something is that there are good reasons why they should be free to do it. In other words, in order of justification, liberty-rights would appear before claim-rights.

Despite the readiness with which, in ordinary language, we speak of Hohfeldian liberties as 'rights', many theorists resist that usage. Sometimes that is simply because, like Hohfeld, they would prefer technical usage to be stricter than ordinary usage and to confine the term 'right' to claim-rights. But sometimes their reluctance stems from the merely negative character of liberties. Does the mere absence of a duty amount to the possession of a right? If I have no duty not to do x, is that really enough, taken by itself, for it to be said that I have a *right* to do x? Some think not. For example, we have already noticed that Hart suggests that liberties warrant description as rights only when they are accompanied by protective claim-rights.

In the next chapter, I shall emphasise the centrality of the idea of a title to that of a right and I think it is that idea which holds the clue to why people sometimes hesitate to describe liberties as rights. Does the mere absence of a duty invest one with a title? Presented in that form, the question invites a negative answer. However it does not follow that we are always wrong to describe liberties as rights. Rather what that question suggests is that liberties are most appropriately spoken of as rights in contexts where there is an *understanding* that, in the absence of a duty not to do something, one is entitled to do it. That is a typical, but not a necessary, feature of systems of law and a characteristic of some, but not all, moralities.

Powers

A legal power is usually defined as the legal ability to change a legal relation. Such powers are usually spoken of as rights. Indeed they are more commonly spoken of as rights than as powers. Each of the following rights constitutes a power: the right to enter into a contract, the right to sell or to purchase property, the right to make a will, the right to marry and to divorce, the right to vote, the right to sue. In each case, the right-holder is legally empowered to effect some transaction. His not possessing such a right would mean that he would be legally incapable of that act. For example, if there were no legal provision for people to make wills, they could still indicate what they wished to happen to their property on their death but, as far as law was concerned, there would be no way in which they could ensure that their wishes would determine the disposal of their estate.

'Power' in the sense of 'legal ability' is, of course, distinct from 'power' in its non-legal senses. Just as I may be legally at liberty to do what, for non-legal reasons, I am not 'free' to do, so I may be legally empowered to do something which, in some non-legal way, I lack the power to do. For example, at one time Black Americans were legally empowered to vote but, in some areas of the United States, various intimidatory devices were used to thwart their real ability to vote.

Each of the powers that I have cited so far is typically held by citizens in general. However very often powers are held by some but not others and the distinct character of rights as powers may be more readily apparent in those cases. A judge has the right to preside over a trial, a Member of Parliament or of Congress has the right to vote on legislative proposals, a doctor has the right to prescribe drugs for patients. I, as an ordinary citizen, have none of those rights, and I lack those rights not because others do not owe me the duties that they owe judges, legislators and doctors, nor because I have a duty not to preside over trials, or vote on bills, or prescribe drugs. Rather I do not have those rights because I am not empowered to do what judges, legislators and doctors can do. I may express my view for or against a bill but, if I am not a duly elected member of a legislature, I am constitutionally unable to cast a vote for or against it. I may write the name of a drug on a piece of paper but, if I am not a qualified doctor, that does not count as a medical prescription.

The same applies to less exclusive powers such as the right to vote and the right to divorce. In a society in which I am disfranchised or which makes no provision for divorce, it is not that, legally, I am forbidden from voting or from getting divorced; rather, legally, I am unable to vote or to get divorced. It is not that legally I 'ought' not to do these things, rather it is that legally I 'cannot' do these things. Thus what people have the legal opportunity to do is affected not only by the distribution of claim-rights and of liberty-rights but also by the provision, or lack of provision, of powers. Rights in the sense of powers are, then, quite distinct from either claim-rights or liberty-rights. Typically, of course, powers will exist in conjuction with claim-rights and liberty-rights. But the distinct identity of 'power-rights' is evident in that, in cases like this, these other rights presuppose the separate existence of a power. For example, in a society in which I am not empowered to vote, the question of whether I am at liberty to vote or whether others have a duty not to impede my voting simply does not arise.

In Hohfeld's scheme, the correlative of a power is a 'liability'. To be 'liable' is to be subject to another's power. In ordinary language, 'liability' connotes something burdensome or disadvantageous, but, in this context, the term does not necessarily carry those overtones. A power may be used to the disadvantage of another, but it may also be used to someone's advantage as, for example, when a person uses his power to alienate his property to make a gift. Thus I may be 'liable' to the conferral, as well as to the removal, of claim-rights, liberty-rights, powers or immunities.

Immunities

To possess an immunity is to be not subject to another's power. In Hohfeld's analysis, immunities stand to powers as liberty-rights stand to claim-rights. To possess a liberty-right is to be free of another's claim-right; to possess an immunity is to be free of another's power. The opposite of an immunity is therefore a liability. The correlative of an immunity is a disability: if A possesses an immunity, B has a correlative disability or 'no-power'.

Perhaps the clearest examples of immunities are constitutionally entrenched rights. The constitution of the United States, for example, places some matters outside the competence of Congress and, in so doing, provides US citizens with immunities on those matters. If Congress attempts to pass a law which the Supreme Court judges to intrude into those areas of immunity, that law will be declared invalid. It will be invalid because the legislature will have exceeded the limits of what it is constitutionally empowered to do. American citizens therefore enjoy certain rights, such as the rights of freedom of speech, press, religion and peaceable assembly, in the form of constitutionally established immunities. Immunities can also take less exalted forms. If I, as the owner of a piece of property, have the sole right (that is, power) to sell my property, I also have the right (that is, immunity) that it shall not be sold by anyone else. In a society, like the Republic of Ireland, which makes no provision for divorce, people may be said to lack the right (that is, power) to divorce but they may also be said to enjoy the right not to be divorced in that spouses are 'immune' from divorce by their partners.

Immunities, like liberties, are defined negatively – they exist in virtue of absences of powers. Therefore, like liberties, they constitute an open-ended category. Just as my liberties include anything that is not proscribed by a duty, so my immunities include every respect in which I am not subject to another's power. Just as, without prompting or provocation, we may not think of any and every trivial liberty as a right, so it may not readily occur to us to think of all of the indefinite number of our immunities as rights. But we do take to describing even trivial liberties as rights when they are challenged and, similarly, we are likely to assert even trivial immunities as rights when we find others trying to make us do things that they are not empowered to require of us.

Hohfeld's analysis shows us, then, that when we are confronted with a right we have to think carefully about what sort of right it is. Is it a claim-right or a liberty-right or a power or an immunity, or some combination of two or more of these? Different rights entail different things, and when we consider rights, such as the right to work or the right to strike or the right to self-determination or the right to self-fulfilment, much of practical significance turns on what form or forms of right we understand those to be. Yet, although these differences in forms of right are very important, they still seem to be different species of a single genus. Hohfeld's analysis enables us to identify what distinguishes different forms of right, but we have still to discover what they have in common.

2 Benefits, Choices and Titles

If rights can take such different forms, what is it that makes them all 'rights'? In virtue of what do laws and other sorts of rules give rise to rights? People have generally divided into two schools of thought in answering these questions. On the one hand, there is the 'benefit' or 'interest' theory of rights; on the other, there is the 'choice' or 'will' theory. The difference between the two is best explained by returning to the issue of 'correlativity'. We have seen that claim-rights entail correlative duties but that other sorts of rights do not. But what about the obverse relation? Do duties always entail correlative rights? If not, what distinguishes duties that are paired with rights from those that are not?

Rights as benefits

Hohfeld himself says little on this issue but, since he presents rights and duties as correlatives and since his correlatives are supposed to work both ways, he would seem to hold that for every duty there is a corresponding claim-right.[1] Others have shared that view. Bentham, for example, although he was hostile to the notion of moral rights, was generous in his interpretation of legal rights. He often wrote as though every law created simultaneously both rights and duties. Every law imposed a duty, every duty was a duty to render a service or benefit to someone and that someone, as the beneficiary of the duty, possessed a right; 'consequently there is no law whatsoever that does not confer on some person or other a right' (1970b, p. 220). In fact Bentham made two qualifications to that generalisation. First, he recognised that a law might be designed to benefit the very person on whom it imposed a duty; such self-regarding duties could not be said to give rise to rights (1970a, p. 206). Second, while legislators ought only to make laws which are of benefit to somebody, they might make laws which are of advantage to no-one. The 'ascetic' or 'barren' duties created by such laws would not yield rights. (1962, III, pp. 181, 221). But, with those two exceptions, Bentham held that all legal duties entailed corresponding rights.

In Bentham's thinking rights were essentially 'benefits' and whoever benefited from a duty possessed a right. There is considerable appeal in that idea. That, for example, seems why it would be unexceptional to speak of a right to be rewarded or a right to the essentials of life, but distinctly odd to speak of a right to be punished or a right not to be fed ('a right to starve'). It seems that people can have rights only to what is in their interest; it may be 'right' that people should sometimes suffer things contrary to their interests but it would be odd to say that they had 'a right' to be so treated. In fact, there are occasions when we might speak of punishment or starvation as the objects of rights but those serve only to confirm the general point here. It might be said that a criminal has a 'right' to be punished because otherwise he has no way of expiating his guilt and will remain saddled with that burden for the rest of his life. Or the criminal might protest that he has the right to be punished rather than be compelled to undergo a course of therapy which treats him as less than a person who is fully responsible for his actions. In both of these cases punishment becomes a sort of benefit, if only a 'relative' benefit, for the criminal. Similarly, although the 'right to starve' would normally be a nonsense or a piece of sarcasm, it would not be if what was at issue was one's right to go through with a hunger strike rather than be subjected to forced feeding. In both of these cases, special circumstances or considerations make something a 'good' that would ordinarily be a 'bad' and only that seems to render the assertion of 'a right' intelligible.

However most of those who have followed Bentham in identifying rights as benefits have held that he was over-generous in his ascription of rights. Bentham divided offences to others into three types: 'private' offences, which were offences against 'assignable' individuals; 'semi-public' offences, which were against unassignable individuals who formed a neighbourhood or who constituted a 'class' in some way, for example, a religious group; and 'public' offences – those which threatened a 'distant mischief' to 'an unassignable indefinite multitude of the whole number of individuals, of which the community is composed' (1970a, pp. 188–90). The laws creating those offences imposed duties, and the beneficiaries of those duties – be they assignable individuals, classes of individuals or the public at large – possessed corresponding rights. But can we really think of duties to 'unassignable individuals', duties directed at some diffuse public benefit, as creative of rights? That seems extravagant and unwarranted. Duties such as the duty to pay taxes, or the duty to observe traffic laws, or the duty not to sell certain sorts of drug are designed to benefit a population in a general way but they are not directed towards specific, or 'assignable', individuals. Those are duties which are 'due from' specific individuals without being 'due to' specific individuals. It seems inappropriate therefore to regard those duties as conferring rights upon individuals.

Most contemporary writers who subscribe to the benefit or interest theory of rights would, therefore, hold that duties give rise to rights only when they are duties specifically directed towards the interests of determinate individuals. The crucial point is not that duties create rights only if they benefit some rather than all individuals. A duty may be a duty to all members of a society and still give rise to rights. What matters is whether the duty is a duty to benefit individuals severally, in which case it gives rise to rights (for example, the duty not to assault and the correlative right not to be assaulted) or whether it is a duty designed to benefit individuals only as members of an undifferentiated collectivity, in which case it does not (for example, the duty to pay taxes). Thus Neil MacCormick holds that 'the essential feature of rules which confer rights is that they have as their specific aim the protection or advancement of individual interests or goods' (1977, p. 192, 1982a).[2] Similarly David Lyons, in his qualified version of Bentham's theory, holds that one has a right in respect of another's duty or obligation only if one is 'the direct, intended beneficiary of that duty or obligation' (1969, p. 176). It is this combination of benefits or interests with determinacy and intentionality that enables us to speak of rights corresponding to duties not to assault, rape or thieve and duties not to libel, trespass or damage.[3]

Similarly Joseph Raz holds that an individual, X, has a right 'if and only if X can have rights, and other things being equal, an aspect of X's well-being (his interest) is a sufficient reason for holding some other person(s) to be under a duty' (1986, p. 166). Like MacCormick and Lyons, the notion of being benefited, of having an interest, is central to Raz's definition of a right, but his definition has two further features which require special note. Firstly, he is keen to stress that rights do not entail duties which merely correlate with, or correspond to, those rights. Rather rights are to be understood as *grounds* of duties. Rights and duties are not merely two sides of a single coin; rather rights are the *reasons for* the duties to which they give rise. (Which is not to say that it is *only* rights that can give rise to duties.) Secondly, for Raz, one has a right not merely if one is an intended beneficiary, but only if one's interest is a sufficient reason for holding another to be under a duty. Thus Raz takes a rather more discriminating view of the relationship between interests and rights. To possess a right, it is not enough that a duty should promote one's interest directly and intentionally; the relevant interest must be such that it justifies another person's having a duty.

Thus if we return to the question of when it is appropriate to pair duties with claim-rights, the answer offered by modern benefit theorists is: only when those duties are designed to benefit specific individuals. The idea of benefit or interest has also been used to elucidate the idea of rights more generally. Law may secure benefits to people in the form of claim-rights, liberty-rights, powers or immunities. According to the benefit theory, what distinguishes each of those as a 'right' is that, in each case, law secures a benefit or good to those whom we identify as the possessors of the right (for example, MacCormick, 1977, 204–5). Hohfeld himself gave 'advantage' as the common ingredient of the four types of right. However the benefit theory may entail some winnowing of Hohfeld's 'rights'. For example, if a liberty is not beneficial, it will be inappropriate to describe it as a right. People are 'at liberty' to starve themselves to death but, outside of the sort of special circumstances I described earlier, starvation could not be represented as a 'good'. It would therefore be inappropriate to speak of the liberty to starve as a right even though, legally, people have no duty not to starve themselves. On the other hand, if one were prepared to argue that the existence of *any* option merely *qua* option was a benefit, all liberties would be describable as rights. Similarly, and plausibly, the benefit theory would imply that an immunity that was not in one's interest would not be a right. If you have no power to vote me favours, I am immune from the receipt of those favours but it would be odd to describe that immunity as a 'right' not to receive favours – unless, that is, one was prepared to

appeal to an ideal of autonomy or independence and argue that
every immunity is a good.

Not everyone is persuaded that rights are satisfactorily analysed
as interests or benefits. Some complain that the benefit theory does
not provide an adequate account of the relation between rights and
duties since it presents rights as mere 'reflexes' of duties, so that 'all
that can be said in a terminology of such rights can be and indeed is
best said in the indispensable terminology of duties' (Hart, 1982, p.
182; cf. Donnelly, 1985, p. 12). In other words, the benefit theory
fails to give a sufficiently distinct meaning and role to rights in our
legal and moral vocabulary. Indeed it is sometimes suggested that
the notion of rights *is* redundant, since a right and a duty are but
two sides of a single relation and that relation can be fully described
in terms of duty (Arnold, 1978). Even if true, this is somewhat odd
as a criticism. 'South' is merely the opposite of 'north' but that does
not lead us to worry about the legitimacy of the term 'south' in our
geographical vocabulary. However there is also reason to reject the
claim that a benefit theory must reduce rights to mere reflexes of
duties. In moral argument there are many occasions when an
interest theorist might hold that rights are the grounds of others'
duties and therefore distinct from, and logically prior to, those
duties (Raz, 1986, pp. 166–71, 184–6; Gewirth, 1982, pp. 14–15).
Even in law there are cases in which claim-rights are both logically
and temporally prior to their correlative duties, such that those legal
rights cannot be represented as mere 'reflexes' of the legal duties
they entail (MacCormick, 1977, pp. 200–2; Raz, 1984, pp. 14–15).

A second criticism of the benefit theory is that there are cases in
which rights and benefits appear not to be conjoined. Hart has made
this point in a well-known example concerning promises and third
party beneficiaries (1967, pp. 57–8; 1982, pp. 187–8). Suppose that X
promises Y that, in Y's absence, X will look after Y's aged mother,
Z. This sort of arrangement poses two difficulties for the interest
theory. First, the person who holds the right against X here would
seem to be not the beneficiary of the promise, Z, but the promisee,
Y. It is Y to whom X's obligation is owed, who can waive or insist
upon X's keeping his promise, and who is wronged if X fails to do
what he has promised. Second, although Y's mother, Z, is a specific
and intended beneficiary of X's duty to do what he has promised,
she does not obviously hold a right against X since X has given his

promise not to her but to her son, Y. Thus it would seem both that there can be right-holders who are not beneficiaries and that there can be beneficiaries who are not right-holders.

How might the interest theorist deal with this case? As far as the third party beneficiary is concerned, some interest theorists would simply reject what Hart contends and hold that, where a promise or contract is clearly directed towards the benefit of a third party, that party can be said to possess a right. Y's mother, Z, could therefore be said to have a right against X to be looked after (Lyons, 1969, pp. 180–82; Marshall, 1973, pp. 229–31; MacCormick seems unwilling to join them, 1977, pp. 208–9; cf. Hart, 1982, p. 187n91.) That sort of straightforward counter-assertion would seem implausible as a response to the second objection contained in the example. That is, it would not seem plausible to argue that, since the promisee, Y, is not a beneficiary of the promise, he has no right in virtue of X's promise. Surely all would agree that Y, as the promisee, must possess a right in relation to X, the promisor. If the interest theorist is to deal adequately with this leg of the objection, he has somehow to represent the honouring of a promise as a benefit to the promisee even when the specific promise is designed to benefit the condition of someone other than the promisee. He might, for example, argue that it is in a person's interest that promises made to him should be kept and that that general interest in promise keeping is quite distinct from any further interest a promisee might or might not have in the content of any particular promise (cf. Raz, 1986, pp. 175–6; Hart, 1982, p. 187n92).

As for rights other than claim-rights, the benefit theory has least success in describing some sorts of power. Very often the possession of a power will be in the interest of the possessor as, for example, in cases such as the right to make a will or the right to acquire property. But consider powers that people possess in official capacities such as rights that are special to judges or doctors. Those powers are intended to be exercised disinterestedly, or at least not in the interests of judges and doctors themselves, and it is not easy to see how the right of a judge to decide a civil suit, or the right of a doctor to prescribe a drug, can be represented as benefiting, or promoting the interests of, either the judge or the doctor. Similarly suppose I wish to appoint a trustee to look after my interests and I appoint Smith rather than Wilson to act on my behalf. Smith then

has rights, as my trustee, that Wilson does not, but it would be odd
to explicate that difference as Smith's receiving a 'benefit' which is
withheld from Wilson.[4]

Rights as choices

The main rival to the benefit or interest theory of rights, is the
choice or will theory. Its best known contemporary exponent has
been H.L.A. Hart (1967, 1982; see also Kearns, 1975; Sumner, 1987,
pp. 96–101). Hart, as we have seen, holds that being the beneficiary
of a duty is neither a necessary nor a sufficient condition for
possessing a right. Rather, for Hart, a right is a form of choice.
The essential feature of a duty which yields a right is that the person
to whom the duty is owed is able to control the peformance of that
duty. Thus, for example, a creditor can be said to have a right
correlative to the duty of her debtor because the debtor's duty to
repay is subject to the discretion of the creditor. The creditor may
choose to insist upon repayment, or to relax the terms of repayment, or to release the debtor from the debt entirely. By the same
token, Hart argues that it is inappropriate to speak of a right
correlating with a legal duty where the beneficiary of the duty can
exercise no choice over its performance. For example, in English
and American law, potential victims cannot absolve potential killers
from their duty not to murder; consequently, Hart argues, it is
inappropriate to speak of their having a legal right not to be
murdered. Thus to have a legal right is to have a 'legally respected
choice' (1982, p. 189) and it is the presence of that choice that gives
point to our speaking of rights as well as duties. Hart suggests that
the appropriate image of a right–duty relation is not that of a chain
binding two people together but rather that of a chain which binds
one individual, the bearer of the duty, and whose other end is in the
hands of another individual, the bearer of the right, to use as he sees
fit (1967, p. 58).

   The choice theory implies that it is normally appropriate to speak
of people having rights in respect of civil law but not in respect of
criminal law, for only in civil law do people have the necessary
control over others' performance of their duties. At its fullest, Hart
says, this control would consist of three elements: '(i) the right
holder may waive or extinguish the duty or leave it in existence; (ii)

after breach or threatened breach of a duty he may leave it "unenforced" or may "enforce" it by suing for compensation . . .; and (iii) he may waive or extinguish the obligation to pay compensation to which the breach gives rise' (1982, p. 184). Another area of law in which Hart thinks it proper to speak of rights is that of welfare benefits. Law may not give welfare claimants the full range of choices characteristic of civil law, but typically it still enables them either to claim or not to claim the benefits to which they are entitled and there are often steps that they can take to ensure that the officials concerned perform their duties (1982, pp. 185–6). However, where law does not give persons control over the performance of others' duties, they should not be said to possess rights, no matter how directly and intentionally they benefit from those duties.[5]

For the same reason, Hart originally suggested that rights could be ascribed only to adult human beings capable of choice. We may certainly have duties not to ill-treat animals and infants but to go on to ascribe 'rights' not to be ill-treated to animals and infants is to make an 'idle' use of the term (1967, p. 58). Hart subsequently modified his position in relation to moral rights, but he is still willing to speak of infants possessing legal rights only in cases where an appointed representative may act on their behalf.

Thus, confronted with the question of when it is appropriate to think of duties entailing correlative claim-rights, the choice theorist's answer is: only when an individual can exercise control over the performance of another's duty. Like the benefit theory, the choice theory claims to make sense of other sorts of right too. Thus both liberty-rights and powers can be understood as 'legally respected choices' (Hart, 1982, pp. 188–9). Each involves a bilateral liberty – to do or not to do, to use or not to use. No choice would mean no right. Thus suppose we have been told that Smith had a right (that is, a liberty-right) to join the army. We might reasonably infer from that that Smith was free to join or not to join the army. If we subsequently discovered that Smith had been conscripted and therefore had no option but to join the army, we might reasonably feel that we had been misled. In a sense Smith *was* at liberty to join the army in that he had 'no duty not' to join. But, equally, he had no choice but to join and, in those circumstances, it seems odd to speak of his joining as the exercise of a right rather than as simply the performance of a duty.

Hart concedes that immunities are not analysable as choices (1982, pp. 190–2). For example, freedoms which are constitutionally entrenched so that legistures have no power to remove them, are not alienable by those who possess those immunities. In cases such as these, individuals seem to be merely the beneficiaries of arrangements over which they themselves have no control. Yet Hart perhaps concedes too readily in the case of immunities. Even if individuals are unable to dispose of constitutionally entrenched immunities, they can often divest themselves of more ordinary sorts of immunity, as, for example, when they choose to appoint a trustee to act on their behalf or to join an organisation and place themselves under its authority.

There are a number of things that might be said in favour of the choice theory. Firstly, it, perhaps more than the interest theory, gives a distinct point to rights talk and indicates that there are features of a legal system described by rights which cannot be wholly described in terms of duties. Indeed Thomas Kearns suggests that choice provides the principal rationale for rights (1975, pp. 478–9). A legal system has to be a reasonably stable and predictable system of rules if it is to function properly, but too rigid a set of rules would be less than maximally effective. The institution of rights is a way of introducing a degree of 'limited and informed flexibility' into a legal system, so making it both more reasonable and more effective in operation. Others make the broader claim that the choice theory captures an essential link between rights and the protection of individuals' autonomy, a link which indicates the distinctive normative function performed by the concept of rights in our moral language (Sumner, 1987, pp. 98–9).

Secondly, the choice theory enables us to see our way through the case of contracts and promises involving third party beneficiaries. In the example in which X promises Y that he will look after Z, we can see that it is Y, the promisee, that bears the right and not Z, the beneficiary, because it is Y and not Z who is able to exercise control over the performance of X's duty. If, as part of the agreement, Z *were* given control over the performance of X's duty, then Z too would possess a right (Hart, 1982, p. 187; cf. MacCormick, 1977, pp. 208–9).

Thirdly, much of the language that we use in relation to rights implies something like the choice theory. We speak of people 'possessing' rights which they may 'exercise', 'insist upon', 'waive', and so on, all of which seems to imply that a right is something at our disposal, something which gives us an option.

The main count brought against the choice theory is that it is unduly exclusive. Should we really exclude from the catalogue of rights all of those goods over which we have no choice? Is it crucial to having a right not to be assaulted or a right to a fair trial that one should have the option of being assaulted or the option of being tried unfairly? Is it not odd that the protection afforded to my person and property by civil law gives me rights while that afforded by the criminal law does not? It is clear that choice is a very common characteristic of rights; it is less clear that we should regard it as an indispensable characteristic of rights. MacCormick has suggested that, if the purpose of rights is to secure goods to individuals and if we believe that people should be able to choose what is for their own good, we will hold that rights should be secured to individuals in the form of choices. But that 'liberal' view constitutes an argument about what the *substance* of rights should be; it does not make choice an *analytic* feature of rights. Moreover, even though we might ordinarily prefer to give people the power to choose, choice is not the only good and there may be cases in which we feel justified in depriving people of the ability to dispense with that to which they have a right (MacCormick, 1977, pp. 207–8).

The choice theory also sets close limits on who or what can possess rights. It obviously excludes any notion of animal rights since animals are incapable of choice of the required sort. But the requirement that right-holders must be capable of choice also excludes many categories of human being – not just young children but also the mentally disabled, the comatose, the dead and future generations. Yet it does not seem strange or extravagant to ascribe rights to people falling into those categories.

In fact, in his later writings, Hart has forsaken the choice theory in respect of moral rights. He has allowed that, in moral argument, the concept of a right may be used to focus upon individuals' needs rather than upon their possessing choices. Thus we may legitimately say that the criminal laws against murder and assault secure the moral rights to life and to security of person. But he has remained loyal to the choice theory in his analysis of ordinary legal rights and, while he would accept that criminal law can be said to protect individuals' moral rights, he has remained convinced that there is no reason for lawyers to speak of legal rights corresponding to the duties imposed by criminal law (1982, pp. 192–3).

Rights as titles

The choice and interest theories are not always treated as mutually exclusive. Some writers are sufficiently impressed by both to insist that features of both theories are essential to the analysis of rights (for example, Paton, 1972, pp. 286–90; Flathman, 1976, pp. 75–83; cf. Wellman, 1985). However, as we have seen, both have their inadequacies and it may be that we have to look elsewhere to discover what lies at the heart of 'having a right'.

The concept of a right has not figured in all systems of law, nor has it been a component of all moralities. So what is distinctive about a legal system or a morality which incorporates the concept of a right? Rights necessarily have possessors. There cannot be a right without its being someone's right. That is not uniquely true of rights; it is also true of some other legal and moral concepts. For example, there cannot be a duty or an obligation without its being someone's duty or someone's obligation. But that is not true of normative structures in general. For example, a rule or principle does not have to 'belong' to somebody in the way that a right has to be somebody's right; unlike rights and duties, rules do not have to be 'attached' to specific individuals.

The nearest synonym to 'right' in the English language is 'entitlement' and the possession of a right may be conceived as the possession of a title. What is distinctive about legal or moral systems that incorporate rights is that they invest people with titles. The possession of a title means that the possessor becomes (immediately if not always ultimately) the locus of legal or moral concern. If his title concerns his own actions (as in the case of liberty-rights), it justifies or legitimates those actions. If it concerns the actions of others (as in the case of claim-rights), it provides the ground for others' being required to act in ways that the title requires. The 'possessive' character of rights can also be seen in the way that we think about their 'violation'. When a right is violated, wrong is done, but it is not merely that a rule has been transgressed; it is also that someone has been *wronged*; the wrong is a wrong *to* the right holder. It is failure to do what is *owed to* that right holder.

As I have said, not all legal or moral systems have made room for rights. A system of rules may simply establish a structure of relations and prescribe norms of conduct without vesting titles in anyone. It may set out a structure of right conduct to which everyone is to conform without that right conduct being conceived as 'owed to' any of those whose behaviour it regulates. The Ten Commandments of the Old Testament are often cited as an example of a set of rightless rules (Hart, 1967, pp. 59; cf. Haksar, 1978, p. 196). Those rules are rightless in that they prescribe duties laid down by God, duties which are to be performed because they are laid down by God. Clearly human beings will benefit from injunctions such as 'Thou shalt not kill' or 'Thou shalt not bear false witness against thy neighbour'. But, although the conduct required of human beings by the Commandments may benefit and may have been intended by God to benefit other human beings, that beneficial conduct is not conceived as *owed to* those other human beings, and so human beneficiaries are not conceived as possessing rights to that conduct. The moral demands contained in the Ten Commandments are grounded in the will of God and not in a set of titles which God has given to his human creatures.

This feature of moral or legal systems will often be a matter not of the specific content of rules but of how those rules are conceived. A rule stating 'Thou shalt not kill' *can* be construed as conferring upon individuals a right not to be killed, and a rule stating 'Thou shalt not bear false witness' *can* be construed as bestowing upon individuals a right not to be falsely impugned (cf. Steiner, 1974a, pp. 195–201). But that does not seem to be how those Commandments *were* construed and, for that reason, they are properly understood as 'rightless' rules. The same phenomenon is well known in the history of natural law. Natural law was conceived as a body of rules laid down by God for the governance of his human creation. For centuries it was conceived as simply prescribing a pattern of conduct to be observed by mankind, but, during the later Middle Ages, people began talking of natural rights, and that way of talking became increasingly popular during the sixteenth and seventeenth centuries. That development was symptomatic not of a change in the content of natural law but of a change in the form in which it was conceived. People began to think of God's natural laws as investing

them with titles so that transgressions of those laws wronged not
only God but also the human beings who were harmed by the
transgressors. In that way natural law came to be seen as a source of
natural rights.

That a rule confers a right may be indisputable because the very
term 'right' is included in its formulation. Even if the word 'right'
does not appear, a rule may be so constructed that it is clearly
intended to confer rights. But other rules may be less clear. In those
cases, if we want to discover whether a legal system is right-
conferring, that will depend upon whether, within the legal system
itself, rules are understood to confer rights. That, as Joseph Raz
points out (1984, p. 13), may not be ascertainable by reference to the
law alone; it may be discoverable only by reference to the *intentions*
of the legislators.

Granted all of this, the choice and benefit theories can be
reinterpreted as holding not that a right *is* a choice or a benefit
(or, more particularly, that a legal right *is* a legal choice or a legal
benefit). Rather we might think of those theories as presenting
different views about when it is appropriate to think of a law or a
rule vesting a right or 'title' in an individual. Thus a law designed to
benefit specific individuals may be taken to indicate that those
individuals possess rights to those benefits. The right is not simply
the benefit; rather it is a title to that benefit. But a law which
structures relationships in ways designed to promote the well-being
of particular individuals may be thought of as a law vesting those
individuals with rights. However benefiting is a pointer to the
possession of rights only if the benefits are aimed at specific
individuals; being a merely accidental or incidental beneficiary of
a law does not indicate that that law vests individuals with titles to
those benefits. That is why benefits point to rights only if they are
direct and *intended* benefits. Moreover we may discover cases in
which rights occur which do not obviously benefit the right-holder.
The most obvious reason for investing a person with a right is to
benefit the right-holder himself. But it is not the only reason, as is
evident in the case of powers which are meant to be exercised for the
benefit of others. Equally it is possible for people to be intended
beneficiaries without their being accorded a title to those benefits –
as is illustrated in the case of third party beneficiaries to contracts.

Similarly, if an individual is given control over the performance of
another's duty, that may be taken to indicate that that individual

has a right that that duty shall be performed. It would be unusual to give an individual control over the performance of another's duty if that duty were not also conceived as one owed to that individual. On the other hand, the presence of a choice is only a pointer to the possession of a right; it is not the right itself and it leaves open the possibility that an individual may possess a right even though that individual has no control over its disposition.

Rights and sanctions

There have been a number of other attempts to provide general characterisations of rights – as claims (Stoljar, 1984; Mayo, 1967), as just claims (Ross, 1930, p. 50), as valid claims (Feinberg, 1966; 1980, pp. 148–58), as powers (Green, 1941, p. 110; Plamenatz, 1968, p. 82), as faculties or capacities (Austin, 1911, pp. 286, 398, 687), and so on.[6] It would be tedious to subject all of these to examination. However there is one further attempt to characterise rights which deserves attention, partly because it has had some celebrated exponents and partly because it has figured prominently in attacks upon ideas of natural or human rights. This is what might be called the 'sanction theory' of rights. Typically those who subscribe to this theory do not characterise rights by reference to sanctions alone; rather sanctions are combined with benefits or choices or claims to yield a complete account of rights. For purposes of expounding the theory, I shall combine sanctions with the idea of 'claims'. Clearly not all claims can be considered rights and, according to the sanctions theory, what converts some claims into rights is their being linked to sanctions.

The sanctions theory comes in two forms. As an account of legal or other established rights, it holds that the presence of a sanction upholding and enforcing a claim is essential to that claim's being a right. As an account of moral rights, it holds that a moral claim is a moral right only if that claim ought to be upheld by sanctions.

Bentham incorporated this theory into his conception of legal rights. Thus he wrote, 'when a man is said to have a right . . . the existence of a certain matter of fact is asserted; namely, of a disposition on the part of those by whom the powers of government are exercised, to cause him, to possess and so far as depends upon them to have the faculty of enjoying, the benefit to which he has a right' (1962, III, p. 218). On another occasion he made the role of sanctions in this 'causing' and 'enjoying' more explicit: 'It is by creating duties and by nothing else that the law can create rights. When the law gives you a right, what does it do? it makes me liable to punishment in case of my doing any of those acts which would have the effect of disturbing you in the exercise of that right' (1970b, p. 249). For Bentham, to possess a legal right was to be the beneficiary of another's legal duty and that other was subject to a legal duty only if he was liable to punishment.[7]

This way of viewing rights need not be confined to legal rights. Individuals as members of non-state organisations may be subject to rules and to the imposition of sanctions if they break those rules. If we follow Bentham's logic, being subject to sanctions means having duties and those who benefit from those duties can then be said to have rights. If we are prepared (as Bentham was) to regard social disapproval as a sanction, then social conventions which are upheld by the pressure of social opinion can also be said to confer rights.

Although this way of understanding rights is ultimately unsatisfactory, it is not wholly without point. Suppose that the written law of a society states that its citizens have the right to preach and to practise their religious beliefs. A particular religious minority seeks to avail itself of that right. However every time it attempts to communicate its beliefs to other members of the society, a well-organised gang moves in and, through threatening or actually using physical violence, puts a stop to their efforts. Similarly every time the minority tries to hold an act of worship, the same gang moves in, breaks it up and makes any such act of worship impossible. Meanwhile neither the police nor any other public agency does anything to uphold the minority's freedom of religion. In these circumstances there is some point in denying that the religious minority really has a legal right to freedom of religion. On paper it has that right, but in reality, it might be said, the minority has no such right, for the society does not actually establish conditions in which the minority can preach and practise its religion.

Why, then, should we not make the presence of sanctions a *sine qua non* of the possession of rights? As an interpretation of legal rights, this theory is often part of a larger jurisprudential theory which makes sanctions central to the concept of law. It is particularly associated with the 'command' theory of law which interprets all laws as commands and which understands commands as orders backed by sanctions. That theory is now generally regarded as discredited, for reasons which are too complicated to enter into here. Briefly it fails to appreciate how laws constitute systems of rules rather than bundles of threats (Hart, 1961). More particularly, by reducing having a duty to being threatened with sanctions, it misdescribes the nature of duties, including legal duties. A duty prescribes what we ought to do; it is a reason for action. If we fail to perform our duty, we may suffer sanctions; but our suffering sanctions is consequent upon, and to be explained by, our dereliction of duty. The duty itself does not consist in our being subject to sanctions, any more than the wrong of our dereliction consists in our suffering sanctions. As Hacker observes, 'duty is a guide to action while the threat of a sanction is a "goad", and the former function should be seen as prior to the latter' (1973, pp. 169–70). Thus, even if we accept that to possess a right is to be the beneficiary of another's duty, that is not the same as being merely the beneficiary of another's coerced conduct.

One oddity which would arise if we subscribed to the sanction theory is that we would be unable to speak of individuals having rights which the authorities had failed to uphold. Failing to uphold a right would be equivalent to removing it. Yet we would not ordinarily find it contradictory to observe that someone's right was not being upheld and, if we wished to condemn a government's failure in such a case, we would typically condemn it on the very grounds that what was not being upheld was a right. In the case of the religious minority that I described above, we would ordinarily say (and complain) that its right to religious freedom was not being upheld rather than that it had no such right. Of course legal rights typically are enforced – and with very good reason – but that is not the same as saying that enforcement is intrinsic to the idea of what it is to have a right. Indeed legal systems often contain some legal rights which are in their nature unenforceable in that, when they are violated, no action can be taken for penalty or remedy (Salmond, 1966, pp. 233–4; Raz, 1984, p. 3).

One reason why it is important to appreciate the error of the sanction theory of rights lies in its implication for moral rights. If rights could exist only in the presence of sanctions, that would make a nonsense of the ascription of rights to people as a matter of principle rather than on the basis of established and enforced conventions or rules. Indeed one way in which Bentham sought to make nonsense of natural rights was by pointing to the absence of any sanctions enforcing those rights. But, since the sanctions theory is itself unsatisfactory, moral or natural rights can survive this particular form of assault. However sanctions have sometimes been thought crucial even by those who have embraced the idea of moral rights.

John Stuart Mill did not dismiss talk of moral rights as misguided, but he did believe that sanctions were essential to an understanding of what a moral right was:

'When we call anything a person's right, we mean that he has a valid claim on society to protect him in the possession of it, either by the force of law, or by that of education and opinion. If he has what we consider a sufficient claim, on whatever account, to have something guaranteed to him by society, we say that he has a right to it. If we desire to prove that anything does not belong to him by right, we think this done as soon as it is admitted that society ought not to take measures for securing it to him, but should leave him to chance, or to his own exertions. . . .

To have a right, then, is, I conceive, to have something which society ought to defend me in the possession of.' (1910, pp. 49–50)

In spite of his hostility to the idea of moral rights, Bentham sometimes came close to a similar formulation.

'If I say a man has a natural right . . . all that it can mean, if it mean any thing and mean true, is, that I am of opinion he ought to have a political right to it; that by appropriate services rendered upon occasion to him by the appropriate functionaries of government, he ought to be protected and secured in the use of it.' (1962, III, p. 218)

But this sanctions theory of moral or natural rights is no more satisfactory than the sanctions theory of legal rights. Certainly, if we think the use of coercion is justified at all, we are likely to think that its use to uphold rights is justified. But we are here concerned with what a right *is* and therefore with whether the justifiable use of sanctions should figure in what it *means* to have a right. One reason why it should not is that we would typically invoke rights to justify the use of sanctions. We cannot do that if rights are merely synonyms for 'cases in which resort to sanctions is justified' for the invocation of a right would then be merely another way of asserting 'this is a case in which the use of sanctions is justified' rather than a way of explaining *why* the use of sanctions was justified.

A related way of analysing rights interprets them as entailing a sort of dual claim – a claim against the person on whom the correlative duty falls and a claim upon some third party, usually a government or a community, to ensure that that duty is performed. Stoljar, for example, holds that 'to say that men have rights and especially basic rights, as to life, limb and property, is to say that a person has a claim to be protected by his community or group against certain evils over which he has no control himself, together with a claim for those (mainly legal) institutions which organise this protection, and this not merely against other persons, but also against governments' (1984, p. 37; see also Martin, 1980). This is mistaken in a similar way. If A is B's creditor, A has a right to be repaid by B and B has a correlative duty to repay A. A's right may be a good reason for requiring C (typically a government) to ensure that B performs his duty to A. But that is what it is: a good reason. A's having a right to be repaid does not, of itself, *entail* that some third party is obligated to ensure that he is repaid; rather whether A's right provides adequate reason for some third party's being held duty-bound to intervene to protect that right remains to be argued.

Equally, while we will often appeal to rights to justify the intervention of governments, it is not contradictory to hold that A has a right to x but to deny that sanctions ought to be used to secure x for A. We might take that view because, in that particular case, the use of sanctions would be extremely costly or extremely hazardous. But, in taking that view, we are simply assessing what should or should not be done to uphold A's right to x; we are not denying that A has that right. Consider a more extreme case – the anarchist who holds that the use of sanctions is never justified. In spite of her complete rejection of coercion, an anarchist of this sort can intelligibly ascribe rights to people. Indeed her objection to the use of coercion might itself be grounded upon a claim that coercing people violates their rights and, whatever we might think of that claim, there seems nothing *conceptually* wrong in her appealing to 'rights' to make it.

The idea of sanctions is, then, no more essential to the concept of a moral right than it is to the concept of a legal right. Certainly moral rights will often be associated with sanctions, but the sanctions theory of rights gets that relationship precisely the wrong way round. We do not identify a right as a right because it ought to be enforced; rather we hold that a right ought to be enforced because it is a right.

3   The Morality of Rights

In examining what it is to have a right I have so far given some attention, but not very much, to the distinction between legal rights and moral rights. Of these two sorts of right, it is legal rights that have proved the less controversial. Of course, there can be plenty of argument about what legal rights people ought to have, but that they can and do have legal rights is not generally contested. Similarly there is some scope for argument about what legal rights people actually possess, but that scope is limited by the established legal rules and judicial precedents of a society. Claims about the content of people's moral rights, and the very claim that they possess moral rights, have proved much more controversial. It is time, then, that we attended more closely to the specific idea of moral rights.

Moral rights

We should note, to begin with, that political thought has been more concerned with moral rights than with legal rights. The reason is that rights have been appealed to in political thought for two main purposes: first, in order to establish the function of government – to indicate that individuals have rights which it is the function of government to protect and maintain; second, in order to limit the authority of government – to indicate that individuals have rights which governments themselves must respect. Both of those purposes require rights to be established independently of government, since both instruct government in how it is to act. They cannot therefore be legal rights (in the ordinary sense) since law is itself the offspring of government. We may, of course, want to establish them as legal rights but, if we see this as law 'recognising' or 'acknowledging' rights, rather than 'creating' or 'inventing' them, those rights must have some non-legal foundation. Ordinarily that will entail their being moral rights.

In the past the rights that were most frequently appealed for these purposes were 'natural rights'. Nowadays 'human rights' have moved to the centre of the stage. Just what it is for a right to be a 'natural right' or a 'human right', I shall consider in the next chapter, but both are types of moral right and it is upon the general idea of a moral right that I shall focus in this chapter. What then should we understand by a 'moral right'? To begin with, it is important to clear up an ambiguity concerning the adjective 'moral'. That word might be used to refer to what, as a matter of fact, is the morality of a particular society – to what is sometimes described as a society's 'positive' or 'conventional' morality. To talk about morality in that sense is not oneself to engage in judgements of right and wrong. Rather it is to consider, in a quite matter of fact way, the moral beliefs actually held by the members of a society. Thus identifying people's moral rights in this sense of 'moral' would be no less an empirical matter than identifying their legal rights. It would involve establishing what rights people were accorded by the accepted mores of their society, which rights they could therefore be said to enjoy as a matter of custom or convention in that society. If, according to those mores, people had a right not to be insulted, individuals in that society could be said to have a (positive or conventional) moral right not to be insulted. If, according to those mores, people had no right to practise any but the established religion, individuals in that society could not be said to have a (positive or conventional) moral right of freedom of worship.

However the word 'moral' in the phrase 'moral right' may be used with a quite different import. It may be used not to describe in a detached way what the members of a particular society believe to be right but rather to refer to what is indeed right. This is sometimes spoken of as 'critical' morality in contrast to 'positive' morality. That distinction does not refer to two moralities with different contents, rather it refers to two different sorts of concern with morality. To be concerned 'critically' with morality is to be concerned with what *is* right and wrong; to be concerned 'positively' with morality is to be concerned with the empirical matter of what people believe to be right and wrong. Thus, in this critical sense, my assertion of a moral right can be quite independent of whether other people recognise it as a right. For example, I may assert that people in all societies have a moral right not to be enslaved even though, in a particular society, the institution of slavery is well established and the members of that society do not themselves believe slavery to be wrong. Typically when people assert human rights they are speaking in this critical mode. They mean to say that all humans have these rights. They mean actually to 'ascribe' those rights to humans irrespective of whether, as a matter of fact, those rights are recognised and respected in all societies. Henceforth, when I use the term 'moral' in conjunction with 'rights' I shall use it in this critical sense.

How far can our understanding of moral rights simply parallel that of legal rights? It would be surprising if the two were not closely related and we have already seen that there is much that is common to the idea of rights as that notion is used in morality and law. But the idea of rights has come to serve a somewhat different purpose in morality and has come to acquire nuances which make it something more than a mere replica of its legal uses. Firstly, how far can Hohfeld's typology of rights be employed outside the specifically legal context for which it was intended? The forms of right that Hohfeld distinguished can characterise institutions other than the state and rules other than laws. For example, it is easy to see how individuals as members of organisations such as trade unions, companies, universities, churches, and so on, may possess rights of each of the four sorts that Hohfeld distinguishes.

What about moral rights? Again it is possible to use Hohfeld's typology in relation to moral rights. A moral claim-right would impose correlative moral duties upon others. For example, my moral right not to be ill-treated would entail others' having the moral duty not to ill-treat me. A moral liberty-right would refer to what is morally permitted, to what, morally, one has no duty not to do and is therefore morally free to do. The idea of a moral 'power' begins to get a little more forced but the notion that people have the right to make promises, in that, morally, they are capable of entering into promises, is usually cited as an instance of a 'moral power'. Promises bring into being obligations that otherwise would not exist and people can bring about those obligations only if they are 'morally empowered' so to do. Conversely a moral immunity would consist in being not subject to the moral power of another. Thus we might say that people have a right not to be bound by promises to which they themselves are not parties. That is, morally, I can be bound only by a promise I myself have made; I cannot be bound by promises made by others (unless I have authorised them to act on my behalf) and, to that extent, I enjoy a moral immunity.

Moral rights might also be analysed as clusters of Hohfeldian rights. For example, if morally I have the right to marry whomever I choose, that may be understood as bringing together the moral liberty-right to marry the partner of my choice, the moral claim-right that others should not impede my use of that liberty, the moral power to enter into a marriage of my own choice and a moral immunity against being 'married off' against my will (cf. Wellman, 1978, 1985).

However, although it is possible to find moral equivalents of Hohfeld's four sorts of legal right, that typology is less central to the concept of a moral right. Hohfeld's typology is essentially an analysis of the different institutional forms that legal rights might take. It is designed to distinguish the different forms in which law may give rights to, or 'entitle', individuals. When we move from law to morality (in the critical sense that I distinguished earlier), we shift from an established institution, a social fact, to a network of ideas. I use the loose phrase 'network of ideas' because moral thinking can take different forms. At its most sophisticated and philosophical, it can take the form of a coherent and tightly argued set of ideas of the sort that might be called a 'moral theory'. But not everyone is a philosopher, and people's moral thinking might also consist of a set of beliefs about what is right or good which are not a product of critical reflection, which are only loosely related to one another, and which do not form a rigorously integrated system of thought. But, in either case, the point of thinking in terms of rights is to indicate what people are entitled to do and how they are entitled to be treated. The role of rights in moral reasoning is primarily to *justify* action and restraints upon action rather than to *describe* states of affairs. They figure as elements in an argument rather than as features of an institutional arrangement. Thus the idea that has come to be centrally important to 'rights' in moral argument is simply that of being entitled. How that moral entitlement is appropriately provided for institutionally – whether as a claim, a liberty, a power, an immunity, or some combination of these – is a secondary and subordinate matter.

However this difference in the import of 'rights' in morality is only one of emphasis. People sometimes use the term 'right' in moral contexts in the sense of a mere Hohfeldian liberty. Someone may protest that they have the (moral) right to do x, meaning only that there is nothing morally wrong in their doing x; they mean only that morally they are permitted or 'at liberty' to do x. For example, I might protest in this sense that I have a right to smoke tobacco.

However, for the most part, when people protest that they have a moral right to this or that, they mean to assert something more than the moral innocence of their conduct. They mean to say that they possess a moral title of a sort that others must respect. Dworkin has marked the distinction between these two usages of rights as that between rights in the strong sense and rights in the weak sense (1978, pp. 188–92). A right 'in the weak sense' would be what I have described here as a moral liberty. A right 'in the strong sense' would be a right which has much greater significance and which imposes duties upon others. This has become the primary sense of the term 'right' as it is used in moral and political contexts. Certainly when people assert human rights they mean to assert rights in that strong sense and, henceforth, I shall use the term 'moral right' in that strong sense.

Because moral rights in the strong sense involve duties, they are often said to be claim-rights rather than 'mere' liberty-rights. But there is not a simple equivalence between Dworkin's 'rights in the strong sense' and claim-rights. Consider the assertion of a moral right of free expression, a right which would typically be asserted in the strong sense. The assertion of that right amounts not only to a claim that others are duty-bound not to silence me; it is also an assertion of what I myself am entitled to do. In Hohfeldian terms it is a liberty-right as well as a claim-right. The ingredient of moral rights that the Hohfeldian analysis leaves untouched is the special status that attaches to rights in our moral thinking. It is their possessing that status that distinguishes moral rights as rights in Dworkin's 'strong sense' rather than their being of one or other Hohfeldian type.

That special status is recognised in the language and the emotions that we associate with rights. Rights are things which it is appropriate to 'assert' and to 'demand'. We 'insist upon' or 'stand upon' our rights. Our rights are what, morally, we must be accorded. When we assert that we have a right to something, we do not merely request it, nor do we simply suggest that our having it would be a 'good thing'; nor, again, are we merely putting ourselves forward as deserving cases. We are saying that we are entitled to it, that it is rightfully ours and that, morally, others are obliged to act in ways which respect that entitlement. In claiming our rights, we do not present ourselves to the world as supplicants begging for favours; we inform the world of what we are owed, of what is rightfully ours. To claim a right is to register the strongest kind of claim for which our moral language provides. Correspondingly, when we are denied our rights, we typically respond with indignation or outrage, rather than with mere disappointment; we conceive ourselves as the victims of an injustice rather than as mere unfortunates who have been denied the milk of human kindness.

That is the main reason why rights have been closely associated with ideas of human dignity and of 'personhood'. The clearest way to give moral standing to human beings, to respect them as persons, is to accord them rights. If we wish to stress their equal moral standing, we can do that by according them equal rights (cf. Feinberg, 1980, pp. 151, 156–7; Melden, 1977, pp. 22–6). As I mentioned in the Introduction, the special forcefulness of rights also does much to explain why claims of right have increased, are increasing and show no sign of diminishing. The moral status possessed by rights provides people with an obvious incentive to reach for the language of rights when they seek to safeguard their interests or to promote their favourite causes.

Rights and utility

The special status possessed by rights also explains why, in contemporary moral and political philosophy, theories of rights have come to be juxtaposed to consequentialist theories. The way rights function in our moral thinking is, perhaps, most clearly revealed in arguments about their standing in relation to consequentialist reasoning.

A consequentialist theory is one which identifies some state of affairs as the best state of affairs and then identifies right action as action which promotes the attainment of that best state of affairs.[1] Consequentialism can take any of a number of forms, depending upon which goal or goals it prescribes as the ultimate aim of human conduct. The form of consequentialism that has been most widely espoused and discussed is utilitarianism. Utilitarianism specifies utility as the ultimate good. 'Utility' has been characterised variously as pleasure or happiness or well-being or preference satisfaction.[2] Whatever the precise meaning given to 'utility', utilitarianism recommends that there should be as much of it as possible. It also holds that utility is the *sole* ultimate good, so that all else that is good has value only because, and in so far as, it promotes utility or diminishes disutility. As a social doctrine, utilitarianism holds that social institutions and public policy should aim to maximise social utility or, to use Bentham's famous formula, a society should aim to achieve 'the greatest happiness of the greatest number'. As a doctrine governing individual conduct, utilitarianism holds that individuals should act so as to maximise the well-being of humanity at large, or perhaps even the well-being of all sentient beings. Of course an individual's own utility will be included in the utility of humanity but the good utilitarian individual will be entirely impartial as between her own utility and that of others and, in deciding what to do, she will give no more weight to her own interests than to those of others. Thus, although utilitarianism has sometimes been represented as a rather 'mean-minded' morality, in its unadulterated form it is actually an extremely selfless and demanding morality.

The enduring appeal of utilitarianism has been matched by the controversy that it has attracted. One element of that controversy has focused upon the way utilitarianism appears to conflict with ideas of rights. It does so in two ways. Firstly, utilitarianism recognises only one ultimate source of value: utility. Whatever promotes utility is good and whatever is good is good because it promotes utility. Of course the utilitarian insists that we take the widest possible view when we calculate what will promote social utility. A source of utility for one person may be a source of disutility for another; in working out the best thing to do, we have to weigh utilities against disutilities and take account of the numbers of people that a policy or measure will affect either way, the intensity and duration of their utilities, the long term as well as the short term consequences of the policy, and so on. But utility remains the sole criterion of the good and the right, and the strict utilitarian will allow only quantitative, and not qualitative, discriminations to be made between utilities. As Bentham is supposed to have said, 'quantity of pleasure being equal, push-pin is as good as poetry'. Nowadays utilitarians are more likely to talk in terms of preferences than pleasures but they adopt the same sort of 'neutral' approach to preferences as Bentham advocates for pleasures.[3]

By contrast, rights theorists discriminate between the moral status of different goods or preferences. To say that I have a right to x but no right to y is to give a special status to x which is denied to y. My own desire for x may be no greater than my desire for y; even so, my having a right to x means that x has a moral priority which y does not. Rights theorists do not therefore display the same sort of moral indifference to the content of preferences as utilitarians. Utilitarianism is not properly described as a 'subjective' philosophy: it does not allow that what is good for an individual is simply what that individual chooses to recognise as good; rather it stipulates that utility *is* the good. But it is 'subjective' to the extent that it regards what is good for an individual as merely what proves utile for that individual. In addition it treats the strength of an individual's claim to something either as a function of that individual's strength of preference for that thing or as a function of the utility pay-off he will gain from it. Rights theorists, in discriminating between what people have a right to and what they do not, adopt a more 'objective' moral stance in that the status they accord to goods or preference satisfactions is not geared wholly to individuals' utility gains. For example, rights theorists would typically make a principled and qualitative, rather than merely a contingent and quantitative, distinction between my preferences about how I should live and my preferences about how you should live.

The second, and related, difference between rights theorists and utilitarians concerns how social decisions are to be made 'across' individuals. Utilitarians advocate a simple maximising strategy. The aim should be to maximise social utility and a society is justified in doing whatever enhances its aggregate utility. Of course, as we have already noted, what promotes the utility of one person might frustrate or diminish the utility of another, but we are to handle these conflicts simply by weighing one utility against another and pursuing that strategy which will maximise the net utility of the society as a whole. Rights theorists, by contrast, reject that simple aggregative approach. To attribute rights to individuals is to give them moral claims of special standing. If I have merely a preference for x and others have a competing preference for y, it may be quite appropriate to proceed in the way the utilitarian recommends. But if I have a *right* to x, that makes a difference and it would then be wrong to decide between x and y by way of a mere calculus of preference satisfactions. We have already explained that rights are 'titles' and it would make nonsense of the idea of possessing a title if it could be set aside in a mere calculus of competing preferences.

Rights therefore constitute considerations of a special nature, considerations which stand in the way of a simple utilitarian calculus, and ascribing rights to individuals is one way of preventing their lives being wholly at the mercy of that calculus.

Thus consider the case of freedom of expression. In general that freedom has been favoured by both utilitarians and rights theorists. But suppose a case arises in which a small minority expresses views which are deeply disliked or disapproved of by the great majority of individuals. Once he has done his calculations, the utilitarian may discover that, in this particular instance, social utility would be better served by removing the minority's freedom to propagate its offending views. The rights theorist, by contrast, is likely to take the position that, since the minority has a right to free expression, their freedom of expression must continue to be unimpaired. It may well be that suppressing the minority's freedom would increase aggregate social utility but, even if that is clear, it would not justify violating the minority's right of free expression. That sort of conflict is not unique to utility and rights. Any form of consequentialism 'threatens' rights in so far as it is 'aggregative' in character. And it is not only rights that are threatened by consequentialism, but any moral concern – such as justice or truth or honesty – to which we might give value independently of its propensity to promote the favoured goal of a consequentialist theory.

One well-known account of rights, designed to express the way in which rights constrain consequentialist reasoning, is Dworkin's characterisation of rights as 'trumps' (1978, pp. xi, 90–4, 364–8; 1985, pp. 335–72). Just as a trump card beats cards of other suits, so rights trump ordinary considerations of utility or preference satisfaction. The metaphor is not entirely exact in that Dworkin does not hold that all rights should have an absolute status such that any right must prevail over any consideration of social utility. But rights have a sufficiently special status to make a difference to the way social and political decisions should be reached:

'Someone who claims that citizens have a right against the Government need not go so far as to say that the State is *never* justified in overriding that right. . . . What he cannot do is to say that the Government is justified in overriding a right on the minimal grounds that would be sufficient if no such right existed. He cannot say that the Government is entitled to act on no more

than a judgement that its act is likely to produce, overall, a benefit
to the community. That admission would make his claim of a
right pointless, and would show him to be using some sense of
"right" other than the strong sense necessary to give his claim the
political importance it is normally taken to have.' (Dworkin,
1978, pp. 191–2)

Lyons (1984) expresses the same thought by way of the idea of an
'argumentative threshhold': 'If I have a right to do something, this
provides *an argumentative threshhold* against objections to my doing
it, as well as a presumption against others' interference' (p. 114).
Thus reasons (such as promoting social utility) which might
otherwise be sufficient to justify my being prevented from doing x,
can be rendered insufficient by my having a right to do x.

Another conception of rights designed to bring out their 'limiting'
character is Nozick's description of rights as 'side constraints' (1974,
pp. 28–33). Rights constrain what is morally permissible and they
constitute 'side constraints' in that they set the moral limits within
which goals may be pursued: 'Side constraints upon action reflect
the underlying Kantian principle that individuals are ends and not
merely means; they may not be sacrificed or used for the achieving
of other ends without their consent. Individuals are inviolable'
(ibid., p. 30). As this passage implies, Nozick sees rights as limiting
consequentialist justifications even more severely than do Dworkin
or Lyons, although even he fights shy of insisting that rights must be
treated as absolutely inviolable no matter how horrific the
consequences (ibid., p. 30n).

Yet another way in which this feature of rights can be explicated is
by reference to the idea of exclusionary or pre-emptive reasons (Raz,
1975, pp. 35–48; 1977; 1986, pp. 186–7, 195–6). An 'exclusionary
reason' is one which functions by excluding, rather than by weighing
with or against, other reasons. It is a 'second-order' reason not to
act for other 'first-order' reasons. For example, suppose I promise to
run an errand for you. Had I not promised, I might still have had
reasons for running or for not running the errand. But my having
promised provides me with a (second-order) reason for doing what I
promised which pre-empts other (first-order) reasons which would
otherwise have determined whether I should or should not run the
errand. The promise is not just one more reason to be set alongside
others; it is a different kind of reason. Similarly rights can be

understood as generating exclusionary reasons.[4] If someone has a right, others have reason to act in conformity with the demands of that right. That reason is an exclusionary reason which pre-empts other reasons which might have governed people's conduct in the absence of the right. Understood in this way, the effect of someone Y having a right to x is to displace ordinary utilitarian reasoning about whether Y should have x. A right supplies a second-order reason which excludes rather than merely outweighs first-order utilitarian reasons.[5]

This way of understanding rights helps to explain the special status that they have in our practical reasoning. Indeed it may seem to make that status rather too special. But an exclusionary reason need not be an absolutely overriding reason, all things considered. Certainly, at an ordinary level of reasoning, it functions as a 'second-order' reason which excludes 'first-order' reasons from consideration rather than as just another reason which weighs with or against those other reasons in an 'on balance' calculation of what is the right or the best thing to do. But, at a 'higher' level, the reason for its being an exclusionary reason may be weighed against other reasons and it may be outweighed by those other reasons. That is why, on occasion, all things considered, it may be right to break a promise. Similarly accepting that a right presents us with an exclusionary reason does not exclude the possibility that it may sometimes be right, all things considered, to override that exclusionary reason. Interpreting rights as exclusionary reasons does not therefore entail granting them an absolute status.

Rights, then, place constraints upon consequentialist reasoning. That much is agreed, even though there may be disagreement about the precise nature and the severity of those constraints. However the simple way in which I have juxtaposed rights to utilitarianism up to now is, in fact, too simple. Rights – whether understood as trumps or side constraints or exclusionary reasons – possess a special status, but perhaps that special status can itself be justified in utilitarian terms. Consider the example of freedom of expression again. I suggested earlier that the displeasure caused to the majority by the unpopular views of a minority may convince the utilitarian that the minority's freedom of expression should be curtailed or removed altogether. However, the utilitarian need not reach that conclusion. He may reason that such a move would so imperil the whole institution of free expression that, when all things are considered, the short-term gains in utility secured by suppressing the minority are outweighed by the whole society's long-term interest in maintaining the practice of free expression. In other words, according people rights and respecting those rights may itself be the most utile thing to do. The immediate effect of according people rights will be to place limits on the extent to which their lives can be manipulated for the sake of maximising social utility but, ultimately, those limits may themselves serve to maximise social utility. For example, people may be happier enjoying the security provided by rights than living with the constant fear that their lives will be turned upside down to satisfy the putative demands of utility maximisation.

Does, then, the traditional counterposing of rights and utility rest upon a mistake? Can a consequentialist moral theory like utilitarianism make room for rights – or at least as much room for rights as they ought to have? Before answering these questions, it will be useful to look at the idea that a moral or political theory might not merely incorporate rights but that it might also be rights-*based*.

Rights-based theories

Some years ago, Dworkin suggested that political theories might be classified as rights-based, duty-based or goal-based, according to which of these three moral concepts captured the ultimate concern of the theory (1978, pp. 169–73).[6] Mackie (1984) followed up this suggestion with the broader claim that the same tripartite classification might be applied to moral theories in general. The idea here is not that a morality must consist exclusively of rights or duties or goals. All three concepts might figure in a moral theory; what will distinguish a theory as a member of one of the three groups is which of the three concepts it treats as fundamental in relation to the other two. In some moralities, rights will be the ultimate source of value. In others, the fundamental moral category will be duty; for example, all of the injunctions of a religious morality may ultimately be grounded in our duty to submit to the will of God. In still others, such as consequentialist theories, a goal will provide the ultimate touchstone of right conduct.

Some writers have questioned whether this simple threefold classification is sufficiently comprehensive to encompass all moralities. Dworkin originally proposed the classification in an essay arguing that John Rawls's theory of justice was ultimately rights-based. However, Rawls himself has rejected that description and suggested that his theory is better characterised as 'ideal-based' (1985, p. 236). There is clearly scope for Dworkin's classification to be refined beyond its three basic terms. It may also be that some moralities are based upon a plurality of values. These issues need not detain us, but the idea of a rights-based morality deserves further examination.

What is it for a theory to be X-based? Mackie suggests that the X indicates the fundamental purpose of the morality: 'statements about Xs should be seen as capturing what gives point to the whole moral theory' (1984, p. 180). Thus a rights-based morality is one in which a conception of rights provides the 'point', the motivating rationale, of the morality. If that morality imposes duties and enjoins the promotion of particular goals, those duties and those goals will be justified by reference to logically more basic rights. Notice that that does not mean that a rights-based theory can give value only to things to which individuals can have rights. A rights-based theory may make room for goods which can exist only as collective goods – goods which individuals can enjoy only by sharing in them as members of a group and which are not therefore reducible to a set of individual claims of right. A society might, for example, furnish itself with a public system of law and order which, in so far as it constitutes a collective good, will be enjoyed by the society's members jointly rather than severally. That shared good could still figure in a rights-based morality in that its ultimate value or 'point' might still relate to rights. For example, the ultimate value of the collective good of law and order might reside in its protecting and upholding individuals' rights.

Notice too that, for a moral or political theory to be rights-based, rights do not have to figure in its first premise. Rights-based theories have sometimes taken that form, most obviously when they have been founded upon assertions of 'self-evident' rights. But a rights-based theory might also incorporate a good deal of preliminary argument about what is important in the human condition before eventually coming up with rights. What will distinguish it as a rights-based theory is that, in its order of argument, rights will appear before duties and goals, and rights will provide the foundation for duties and goals.[7] Equally not all rights in a rights-based theory need be basic rights; some may be 'secondary' or 'tertiary' rights stemming from those rights which are 'primary' or basic.

The typology developed by Dworkin and Mackie implies that moral and political theories will be *exclusively* rights-based or duty-based or goal-based. Whether all that is of moral value can ultimately be reduced to only one sort of value in this way is very much open to doubt. Can we not give fundamental importance to more than just one of rights or duties or goals? It may be that a theory which tries to reduce all of morality to just one type of basic concern will be unduly exclusive. Joseph Raz (1986, pp. 193–216) has argued that an exclusively rights-based morality would be impoverished in just that way. It would be unable to take in ideas of virtue, supererogation, 'oughts' that are other than duties, and collective goods which have intrinsic rather than instrumental value. We shall examine the limitations of a morality of rights later on but, for the moment, to cater for Raz's cogent objections, we might understand a 'rights-based' position to be one which gives a fundamental place to rights without that having to entail that nothing but rights can be of fundamental moral value. Alternatively we could think of a rights-based moral theory as a 'partial' theory – as aiming to provide for a part rather than for the whole of moral conduct. For purposes of examining the tension between rights and consequentialism, it is enough that rights might be conceived as 'basic' in the sense that I have described and, more particularly, that rights might be conceived as having a fundamental value which is not reducible to their instrumentality in promoting goals. It is not essential that rights should be thought of as the sole source of value.[8]

Thus we can return to the issue of goals and rights, or more particularly of utility and rights, in this form: can consequentialism provide an adequate home for rights or will rights be provided for adequately only by a rights-based theory?

Rights and goal-based theories

The most basic form of utilitarianism is act utilitarianism, which holds that to act rightly is to do whatever in the given circumstances will promote, or is most likely to promote, the maximum utility of humanity. A number of variants upon this basic form of utilitarianism have been proposed, many of them prompted by a desire to remove or to diminish the conflict between utilitarianism and 'common sense morality'. One of the most popular of these has been rule utilitarianism, which holds that our actions should be guided by rules rather than by attempts to calculate for each individual act what would be the maximally utile thing to do. The rules that should govern our conduct are those which, if they were followed by people generally, would prove maximally utile.[9]

This restricted form of utilitarianism may seem better placed than act utilitarianism to deliver and to uphold rights but, for a number of reasons, it has fallen out of favour. Firstly, since the underlying rationale of the theory remains the promotion of utility, many critics have argued that it is irrational to allow that purpose to be impeded by rules. Secondly, rule utilitarianism is not guaranteed to avoid the consequences of act utilitarianism that are generally found morally unacceptable. Indeed, arguably, by the time all of the relevant considerations and qualifications have been incorporated into the rule governing each situation, rule utilitarianism will turn out to be substantively no different from act utilitarianism (Lyons, 1965).

A third form of utilitarianism, which has been much discussed in recent years and which perhaps holds out the best prospect for reconciling utility and rights, is 'indirect utilitarianism'. Indirect utilitarianism rests upon the idea that we are often more successful in promoting utility by pursuing secondary principles formulated in non-utilitarian terms than by attempting the direct pursuit of utility itself. Thus there is a utilitarian case for endorsing and propagating those secondary, and apparently non-utilitarian, principles rather than persuading people to live according to the dictates of a straightforward act utilitarianism. The term 'indirect utilitarianism' appears to be of recent origin, but the position it describes is not. Hume, J. S. Mill, Spencer and Sidgwick all adopted positions which were versions of, or which were closely akin to, indirect utilitarianism (Gray, 1982, 1983, 1984).

At first sight, indirect utilitarianism may seem very similar to rule utilitarianism, but actually it is significantly different. According to rule utilitarianism, our actions should be prompted by calculations of maximum utility, even though it is maximally utile rules rather than maximally utile acts that should form the subject of that calculation. According to indirect utilitarianism, our conduct should be motivated by rules and principles whose content is conceived other than in terms of utility, even though it is utility that provides the ultimate justification for those rules and principles. Thus the two utilitarianisms present individuals with different (immediate) grounds for action.[10]

The most comprehensive recent statement of indirect utilitarianism, and one which attempts to take rights seriously, has come from the moral philosopher, R.M. Hare (1981). Hare distinguishes between two levels of morality: the critical and the intuitive. At the critical level, choices are made 'under the constraints imposed by the logical properties of the moral concepts and by the non-moral facts, and by nothing else' (p. 40). At this level, Hare argues, moral thinking must be utilitarian. An archangel blessed with perfect knowledge and impartiality could do all of his thinking at the critical level. However ordinary mortals, with their limited powers of thought, their limited knowledge and foresight and their propensity for partiality, cannot. For such beings to live only by calculations of social utility would be disastrous. Hence the need for a subordinate level of moral thinking – the intuitive. Intuitive morality consists of all of those principles, dispositions, attitudes, sentiments and the like that make up the morality of everyday codes of conduct. This morality is 'intuitive' simply in that its ingredients have been typically, and desirably, implanted in us by our moral upbringing and therefore have an instinctive appeal for us. However these intuitions are not self-validating. Ultimately they must be evaluated by the principles of critical morality and they derive what value they have from being endorsed at the critical level. Thus there are good reasons why people should live in accordance with an intuitive morality rather than attempt to live like act utilitarians all the time, but those good reasons are themselves utilitarian.

One complication in Hare's theory is the question of when it is appropriate to operate at what level. A 'prole', who was as weak-witted and ignorant as the archangel was steadfast and omniscient, should always be guided by intuitive morality. But most people are somewhere in between the two and different levels will be appropriate for different individuals and for different occasions. This, Hare points out, is not a matter that can be resolved by philosophy alone, but the weight of his view seems to be that most of us most of the time do best by living in accordance with that intuitive morality that has been evolved to cope with the ordinary business of life. The one major exception arises when we confront a moral dilemma: when two intuitions conflict, we have to engage in critical thinking if we are to resolve that dilemma.

Hare's claim is that most of the values that are supposed to create difficulties for utilitarians, such as justice, truth-telling and promise-keeping, can be dealt with satisfactorily in terms of his two-level view. So too can rights. Hare regards the traditional counterposing of utility and rights as arising from a simple confusion of the two levels of morality. Rights are quite properly given an important place in our moral thinking and taking rights seriously does entail allowing them to 'trump' simple calculations of utility. But that is true only at the intuitive level. Ultimately rights, like all intuitive principles, are justified (or not) by the critical test of utility. One way in which Hare believes that to be evident is that the rights commonly ascribed to people sometimes conflict with one another. That conflict can then be resolved only by reference to some principle other than, and more fundamental than, rights themselves and that, for Hare, must be the critical principle of utility.

This sort of 'split-level' rationale for rights can be offered by consequentialism in general as well as by utilitarianism in particular (for example, Sumner, 1987, pp. 163–98). However not all utilitarians are willing to follow Hare along his indirect route to utility. Some suspect that the two level approach will make calculating right acts more rather than less difficult and worry that the endorsement of intuitive morality will lead to conduct which is, on balance, disutile (Frey, 1985b). In addition we may question whether indirect utilitarianism can deliver the motivation necessary for intuitive morality and whether, in practice, it will be possible to prevent the two levels of morality from seeping into one another (Mackie, 1985; Griffin, 1982, pp. 350–3).

Even if these technical difficulties of indirect utilitarianism can be overcome, two fundamental reservations concerning rights are likely to remain. The first reservation concerns whether utilitarianism, even in an indirect form, would always deliver and respect those rights which we believe ought to be delivered and respected. In any goal-based theory, no matter how sophisticated, values and institutions will be recognised and upheld only to the extent that they promote the favoured goal of the theory. It is hard therefore entirely to eradicate the fear that, at some point, rights will become the sacrificial victims of utility.

A whole collection of stories has been devised to illustrate how utilitarianism might require us to behave wrongly. We might be led to satisfy racists' desires to persecute a racial minority, particularly if the racists are fanatical and many and their victims few; a utilitarian sheriff might be induced knowingly to execute an innocent scapegoat to prevent the injury and damage that might otherwise be caused by a riotous lynch mob; a utilitarian surgeon might kill a healthy individual so that she could give that individual's organs to three diseased individuals, one of whom needs a new heart, another a new liver and a third a new kidney, so saving three lives at the expense of one. There is no end to the horror stories that can be concocted to illustrate the awful possibilities that utilitarianism might endorse. The 'two-level' approach of indirect utilitarianism may be able to avoid many of these horrors, and utilitarians in general may reasonably protest that moralities are devised to deal with the world as it really is and it is against that world that they should be tested and not against all sorts of extraordinary and improbable eventualities (Hare, 1981, pp. 47–9, 130–46). Even so, the indirect utilitarian's inability to find a place for rights at the critical level of morality means that a doubt must always remain about whether that philosophy will deliver and respect rights.

These fears point to a second and deeper doubt about utilitarianism. Even if direct or indirect utilitarianism does yield rights, it does so for the wrong reason. We should think of individuals having rights because they matter and are to be respected as individuals. Rights are what individuals are entitled to in and of themselves. Individuals should not be treated as mere means to be used in the pursuit of a social optimum and they should not be thought of as possessing rights only because and to the extent that their possession of those rights serves some general social purpose. The form in which this complaint has come to be stated is that utilitarianism ignores 'the separateness of persons' (Rawls, 1971, pp. 23–30; Nozick, 1974, pp. 32–3; Mackie, 1985).

An individual making decisions about his own life may weigh one desire against another, sacrifice one of his interests to promote another of his interests, sacrifice immediate pleasures for the sake of his longer-term happiness, and so on. That seems a quite proper way for an individual to reach decisions about the conduct of his life. Utilitarianism deals with a whole society in the same way. It treats a society as though it were one big individual whose diverse preferences and interests can be traded off against one another to reach a conclusion about what is best for that single social entity. But, of course, the crucial difference is that, when an individual sacrifices one of his desires for the sake of another of his desires, the individual who sacrifices is also the individual who gains. When a society sacrifices the good of some individuals for the good of other individuals, the losers are not identical with the gainers. Moreover utilitarianism is ready to sacrifice the interests of some for the interests of others, without limit, provided only that that enhances the overall social good. That is why it stands accused of giving no significance to the separateness of persons. As Nozick protests,

'there is no *social entity* with a good that undergoes some sacrifice for its own good. There are only individual people, different individual people, with their own individual lives. Using one of these people for the benefit of others, uses him and benefits the others. Nothing more. . . . Talk of an overall good covers this up. . . . To use a person in this way does not sufficiently respect and take account of the fact that he is a separate person, that his is the only life he has. *He* does not get some overbalancing good from his sacrifice.' (1974, pp. 32–3)

Thus it is not merely that utilitarianism may not recognise and support all of the rights that we want there to be; the whole aggregative approach of a goal-based theory, like utilitarianism, is at odds with the separateness of persons – with the sort of concern and respect for individuals as individuals that rights theorists typically regard as fundamental.[11]

There remains therefore a gulf between goal-based and rights-based thinking and one which many devotees of rights believe it impossible to bridge. My concern in the last few pages has been not to castigate utilitarianism but to use it as a foil to indicate what is distinctive about thinking in terms of rights and, more particularly, to indicate why a commitment to rights might entail a rights-based theory. However, since I have looked at consequentialism in general through the case of utilitarianism in particular, I must, in fairness, acknowledge one other point about utilitarianism. Utilitarianism is widely regarded as the classic case of a goal-based theory and it is frequently counterposed to rights-based thinking in the way I have indicated. However to represent utilitarianism as goal-*based* may be to misrepresent it. Rather than maximising social utility, the fundamental principle of utilitarianism can be understood as the principle that each individual's utility should count equally (Kymlicka, 1988; Waldron, 1988, pp. 73–4). Giving equal weight to each individual's utility in reaching social decisions will require aggregating individuals' utilities so that, overall, more utility prevails over less: it would be unfair to give more weight to the preferences of some individuals than to the preferences of others, or to give more weight to some types of preference than to other types of preference. Responding to people's preferences in the fair utilitarian way will result in maximising the overall utility of a society; but that maximisation is not the primary purpose of utilitarianism, it is simply a by-product of its giving an equal status to each individual's utility.

Understood in this way, utilitarianism is less clearly a consequentialist (or 'teleological') theory than a non-consequentialist (or 'deontological') theory, and it is less categorically distinct from rights-based thinking. It can claim to respect each distinct individual's claim to have her interests considered equally alongside those of other individuals. Thus Hare argues that the utilitarian can claim to recognise both the separateness of persons and each individual's 'right to equal concern and respect' (1981, p. 154; 1985, pp. 106–12; see also Griffin, 1986, pp. 167–70). It would not be correct to present this more deontological rendering of utilitarianism as what utilitarians have always meant to say. Some statements of utilitarianism are resolutely goal-based in character. For example, the utilitarian D.G. Ritchie, in a book entitled *Natural Rights*, was keen to assert both that 'the good of a community gives us our only criterion for judging what is right for individuals to do' and that 'the person with rights and duties is the product of a society, and the rights of the individual must therefore be judged from the point of view of a society as a whole, and not society from the point of view of the individual' (1895, pp. 99, 101–2). Bentham often formulated utilitarianism in similarly 'collective' terms and evaluated rights solely in terms of what was 'advantageous to society' (for example, 1962, II, pp. 493, 501). But, even in its more deontological form, utilitarianism remains an unsatisfactory haven for rights: ultimately it admits only preferences as its raw material and, in deciding what should be done, it still allows the interests of some individuals to be sacrificed, without limit, to those of other individuals, provided only that that serves to maximise aggregate utility.

Social goals and goal-based rights

Up to now I have stressed the tension between rights and consequentialist reasoning and the need for a theory to be rights-based, at least in part, if it is to meet the aspirations of those who take rights seriously. I now want to make two points whose thrust is in the opposite direction. The first returns to the issue of whether our moral and political thinking should be exclusively rights-based. The second questions whether all important rights must be important for rights-based reasons.

In Dworkin's model of a rights-based theory, all of the goals that a society should pursue would have to be justified, ultimately, by reference to rights. That is, what is good about goals would have to be accounted for by reference to the fundamental rights held by individuals. Is that a plausible or appealing position to adopt? By 'goals' here we are to understand states of affairs which are good for a society at large and which that society therefore has reason to bring about. Examples of such goals might be social stability, the absence of social conflict, a buoyant economy, a vibrant culture, an efficient infrastructure, an educated population, an unpolluted environment, and so on. The value of some of these social conditions might be explained by reference to individuals' rights. Earlier I pointed out that a system for maintaining law and order might take the form (as it usually does) of a public service which benefits the members of a society at large rather than delivering separate benefits to separate individuals. Nevertheless the ultimate reason for having that 'public good' of law and order might reside in its protecting individuals' rights. In other words, its value might be said to lie solely in its instrumentality in protecting rights. In other cases, a collective good might stand in a less directly instrumental relation to rights but might still be thought of as 'complementing' rights. For example, a society might possess a culture of tolerance; that culture would be a general feature of the society and a good which people share in as members of the society. It could not be broken up into separate bits with each individual having a right to a distinct bit of the culture. Nor could any individual *qua* individual plausibly be said to have a right to the entire culture. Nevertheless the culture might still be valued primarily because it complements rights; it might, for example, make individuals less inhibited in their enjoyment of those freedoms to which they do have rights.

However there are still other collective goods whose value is not plausibly reduced to rights. Some collective goods may be of intrinsic value (Raz, 1986, pp. 198–203). For example, if a society possesses a rich and varied artistic tradition, the existence of that tradition is a collective good and one which may be thought to have value in itself and not because it serves some ulterior purpose. Other collective goods may be more instrumental in character but are still more plausibly thought of as enhancing the quality of people's lives as members of a society rather than as delivering goods to which each member of the society has an individual claim of right. Examples of collective goods of this sort are a buoyant economy, an efficient infrastructure, an educated population and an effective system of government. Thus, just as the value of rights does not reside exclusively in their promoting social goals, so too the value of social goals cannot always be explicated in terms of rights.

Even if goals can have value independently of rights, we might still suppose that rights themselves should be valued only for rights-based reasons. In other words, we might suppose that all rights are either basic rights or, if they are non-basic rights, they are still ultimately to be justifed by reference to basic rights. Yet even that is of doubtful plausibility. Some rights are important wholly or primarily as the instruments of social goals. Consider, for example, the right of individuals to criticise their government. That right is most obviously justified by its general utility in promoting good government and in checking the abuse of power – goods which are general to society at large rather than specific to each individual right-holder.

In addition, there may be rights which are important for both instrumental and non-instrumental reasons. Consider the general right of free expression. We may regard that freedom as something to which each individual is entitled simply *qua* individual. However there are also strong instrumental arguments for freedom of expression. Following J. S. Mill (1910, ch. 2) we might hold that the right of free expression is crucial to the general pursuit of truth and to progress in human understanding, or we might value it because it is an essential part of democratic government which, in turn, we might value as a collective good (see Chapters 6 and 8).

Thus our recognition of the moral inadequacies of consequentialism and our reluctance to ground all rights in social goals should not blind us to the possibility that *some* rights may still be important, either wholly or partly, for their instrumentality in promoting social goals.

Who or what has rights?

Having examined the character of moral rights, we can now turn to the vexed question of who or what can have rights. This is often treated as a purely conceptual question – as a question to be settled purely by reference to the concept of what a right is. As we shall see, that view is partly correct and partly incorrect.

Everyone seems agreed that, if rights can be possessed by anyone, they can be possessed by 'persons', that is by adult human beings in full command of their faculties. However 'persons' so defined do not encompass all human beings. What about people who are comatose or insane? What about young children? What about the unborn? Can foetuses have rights? Can future generations, who have yet to be conceived, have rights? And do rights terminate with life or can rights be possessed by the dead?

Rights are also claimed for non-human beings. In recent years it has become common to ascribe rights to animals. If we take that path, how far down the animal chain should we go? And if animals can have rights, why not plants? We worry about the destruction of Amazonian rain forests and the pollution of rivers. Should we therefore suppose that forests and rivers have rights? We also worry about the fate of man-made objects such as works of art and beautiful buildings. Should we therefore suppose that paintings, sculptures and buildings have rights (Tormey, 1973; Goldblatt, 1976)?

Clearly, different understandings of what 'rights' are will yield different answers to these questions. For those who subscribe to the choice theory of rights, it makes sense to ascribe rights only to beings capable of choice. Infants, the dead, the unborn will not therefore bear rights; nor will animals. That is not to say that we cannot have duties in respect of infants or animals. It is simply that, since infants and animals cannot exercise control over the performance of our duties, it is inappropriate to think of their possessing rights.

A similarly restricted view is taken by those like White (1984, pp. 75–92) who focus on the language associated with rights. A right, says White, 'is something which can be exercised, earned, enjoyed, or given, which can be claimed, demanded, asserted, insisted on, secured, waived, or surrendered' (ibid., p. 90). Rights can be possessed only by beings of whom this 'full language' of rights can be used, which means that rights can be possessed only by persons. Rights cannot be 'insisted upon' by dogs or 'waived' by cats. However it seems unsatisfactory to allow the morally significant question of who can possess rights to be determined by conventions of language. In addition, White's language test would seem to exclude the young, the feeble-minded, the comatose, the dead, future generations, none of whom are capable of 'exercising' or 'demanding' or 'waiving' rights. Yet he himself is unwilling to deny rights to these categories of human being and that reluctance seems to owe more to the moral significance of being human than to the implications of linguistic usage.

By contrast, benefit or interest theories of rights are potentially much more generous in their ascriptions of rights. Whoever, or whatever, can be a beneficiary or possess an interest can, potentially, possess a right. Thus the benefit theory can happily ascribe rights not just to 'persons' narrowly defined but to all human beings, present, past or future, young or old, sane or insane, provided only that they are thought capable of benefiting or of possessing interests. It is also easy to see how, within the benefit theory, rights can be extended to non-human beings. Indeed, the benefit approach to rights seems potentially over-generous. We might speak of a flower benefiting from a fertiliser or a lawn benefiting from being watered, but it would be highly unusual to attribute rights to flowers or to lawns. Even if we were to accept that being a beneficiary was a necessary condition of possessing a right, we would be unlikely to accept that it is was a sufficient condition.

It may be that the benefit theorist can occupy a more satisfactory position on this issue by adopting 'interest' rather than 'benefit' as the concept central to his understanding of rights. The class of beings that we think of as 'having interests' is more limited than that which we think of as 'capable of benefiting'. Thus, for example, the reason we do not normally ascribe rights to plants may be that we do not think that plants have interests. The notion of 'having interests' certainly seems more promising as an indicator of who or what can have rights than the simple notion of benefiting. However, since the notion of 'having an interest' is controversial, it yields a conception of right-holders that is similarly controversial. For example, many people hold that animals have interests and that they therefore possess rights; but others deny that animals have rights specifically because they deny that animals have interests.[12]

However all of this conceptual disputation seems to miss what is centrally at issue in the ascription or non-ascription of moral rights to beings. To possess a moral right is to be an object of moral concern, but it is not just that. All of the disputed cases that arise in this area are ones in which, if beings do possess rights, they do so 'passively': their rights are rights that others shall behave in certain ways towards them. In Hohfeldian terms they are claim-rights rather than liberty-rights or powers. Clearly, then, a being will be a candidate for rights only if people have duties in respect of that being; but that being will have a right only if the duty is conceived as *owed to* him or her or it. Or, to put the same point negatively, wrongful treatment of a being can be conceived as a violation of the rights of that being only if that wrongful treatment is conceived as *wronging* that being, or, to use Raz's formulation, only if that duty is *grounded* in the interest of the being. In other words, we think of beings possessing rights only if we think that duties are *owed to* those beings, only if concern or respect for those beings can be the *ground* of our duty. To possess moral rights is to be not merely an *object* of moral concern, it is to be a *source* of moral concern.

Thus consider two sorts of concern about the fate of animals. One worries about the disappearance of species and holds that human beings ought, or 'have a duty', to conserve animals in order to prevent the disappearance of species and the world's becoming a poorer place because of that loss. The other holds that individual animals have interests and that they are owed certain forms of treatment (or abstention from certain forms of mistreatment) out of respect for those interests. The second view is consonant with animals possessing rights but the first view, of itself, is not, for the conservationist's view of what we ought to do in respect of animals is not grounded in a conception of what we owe to individual animals. For example, proponents of animal rights clearly have reason to object to fox-hunting, whereas the conservationist *qua* conservationist need have no such objection as long as foxes remain an unendangered species. If we were to regard species as entities which could be owed duties, we might also hold that species had rights, but it seems odd to think of a biological category as a being which has moral claims upon us. Equally, although there are very good reasons for not cutting down rain forests or polluting rivers or destroying works of art or vandalising buildings, we would not ordinarily explicate the wrongfulness of those actions as derogations of duties owed to, or as acts 'wronging', those entities.

That is why I suggested at the outset that the answer to the question of who or what can bear rights is partly, but only partly, a conceptual one. Conceptually we can think of a being bearing rights only if we can think of others owing duties to, and not merely having duties in respect of, that being. To be capable of having rights, a being must be conceived as a self-contained source of moral obligations. But what sort of being that is remains an issue of moral substance. And that is as it should be. Whether animals, for example, have rights makes a significant difference to the way we should treat them and it would be very odd if the correct treatment of animals could be determined purely by the logical or linguistic peculiarities of the concept of a right.

All of this relates only to who or what can have rights and not to what rights they actually have. If we identify something as a being capable of possessing rights, that still leaves open the question of what rights he or she or it possesses. Clearly there are many rights ascribed to living human persons that cannot intelligibly be ascribed to other sorts of being. It would be nonsensical to ascribe the right to freedom of belief or the right to vote to cats or dogs, or to suggest that those rights are possessed now by human beings who are dead or who have yet to be born. Nevertheless, if we ascribe rights to beings other than living human persons, there is still scope for disagreement over what rights those should be. If animals have rights, are those only rights not to be treated cruelly or are they rights not to be used for any human purpose, however benign? Does every animal have a right that we should not destroy or disrupt its habitat? Might animals even have rights that we should protect them from being preyed upon by other animals? If future generations have rights, what do those rights require of current population policy? If the dead have rights, do those include rights in respect of their reputations – even if they died centuries ago? Thus, while there is some moral significance in recognising a being as one capable of possessing rights, that recognition still leaves a great deal to be settled.

4 Natural Rights and Human Rights

While the idea of moral rights can be extended beyond the human race, historically it is the moral rights possessed by human beings that have preoccupied philosophers. Of those rights, the most celebrated and significant, particularly for political philosophers, have been natural rights and human rights. Those two sorts of right are closely related. Historically the idea of human rights descended from that of natural rights. Indeed some theorists recognise no difference between them; they regard 'natural' and 'human' as merely different labels for the same kind of right. Others are less happy with that simple conflation and, while acknowledging the historical link between the two sorts of right, want to free human rights from some of the features traditionally associated with natural rights. In examining these rights, I will treat them as distinguishable even though they possess some common features.

Natural rights

In the history of political thought, natural rights have been conceived in two different ways. One corresponds to what Dworkin describes as rights in the strong sense. In this tradition, natural rights were conceived as rights of the most fundamental moral importance. They represented the basic entitlements of all human beings and the first obligation of governments was to ensure that the natural rights of its citizens were respected. It was this conception of natural rights that was espoused by the Levellers, John Locke and Thomas Paine and which inspired the declarations of rights that appeared during the American and French revolutions. It was also from this conception of natural rights that the modern idea of human rights evolved.

The other tradition conceived natural rights as rights in Dworkin's weak sense. In effect it reduced natural rights to mere liberties. The most celebrated statement of this conception of natural rights was given by Thomas Hobbes in his portrait of the state of nature, but it was not unique to him. Earlier in the seventeenth century Selden had developed a theory of man's original condition of unfettered liberty, and that theory and its associated conception of natural rights were taken up and developed by other thinkers such as Dudley Digges, Henry Hammond and Jeremy Taylor (Tuck, 1979, pp. 82–118). Spinoza's understanding of natural rights also belongs to this tradition. However for ease of expression I shall refer to this as the Hobbesian conception of natural rights and I shall concentrate on Hobbes in describing it. The other tradition, which historically ultimately proved more important, I shall describe as the Lockean conception of natural rights, since Locke is probably its best known and most influential exponent. I shall begin by describing the Hobbesian conception.

Hobbes thought of natural rights as those rights individuals would enjoy in the state of nature. By a 'state of nature' Hobbes and other political thinkers writing during the sixteenth and seventeenth centuries understood the condition that humanity would be in if there were no government and no organised political community. Some of those who appealed to the idea of a state of nature thought of it as an actual historical condition that had preceded the formation of human society and the establishment of government. Others, such as Hobbes, were more inclined to regard it as an imaginary condition which had not necessarily occurred in human history, but which was still a 'true fiction' in that it described the condition that mankind really would be in if the 'artifices' of government and political society were removed.

Hobbes held that, in such a state of nature, everyone would possess the same right of nature. That right was 'the liberty each man hath, to use his own power, as he will himself, for the preservation of his own nature; that is to say, of his own life; and consequently, of doing any thing, which in his own judgement, and reason, he shall conceive to be the aptest means thereunto' (1957, p. 84). However, as Hobbes himself indicates here, this natural right of self-preservation was merely a 'liberty'; it was not a claim-right imposing duties upon others. Thus each individual's natural right of self-preservation did not impose correlative duties upon everyone else not to endanger his life. On the contrary, since each individual was a threat to every other individual, the right of nature entitled each to attack and destroy anyone else. The state of nature was therefore a state of war in which mutual threat meant that the right of nature gave everyone 'a right to everything; even to one another's body' (ibid., p. 85). Hobbes's natural rights were not therefore a body of mutually compatible claim-rights, respect for which would ensure social harmony and tranquillity. Rather they were a set of clashing liberty-rights which contributed to rather than solved the problem of conflict and disorder amongst mankind. Human beings could achieve the peaceful condition that they all wanted only by contracting to divest themselves of their 'right to all things' and by placing themselves under a common authority. Thus, for Hobbes, the creation of political society required men to renounce their natural rights (with certain limited exceptions[1]) and to subject themselves to a ruler whose authority was unlimited.

In the Hobbesian tradition, then, 'natural rights' were understood as Hohfeldian liberty-rights. They played an important part in explaining the origin or (to put it non-historically) the rationale of political society. But, since they were given up, either wholly or for the most part, with the formation of political society, they ceased to be of any or of much significance in that society. They prescribed neither what governments should do nor what they should not do. All of this was in marked contrast to the Lockean tradition in which natural rights were used not only to explain the origin of political authority but also to define its duties and to limit its extent.[2]

The Lockean tradition of natural rights derived in a much more direct way than the Hobbesian from the centuries-old idea of natural law and it is best understood by way of its origin in that idea.[3] 'Natural law' described a body of rules, governing human conduct, which were conceived as part of a natural order of things. It was most often understood as a law deriving from God and it is most plausible in that theocentric context. God was the creator of the universe and of everything in it. His creation was not a mere chaos of phenomena but an ordered whole in which everything occupied a certain position and was ordained to act in a certain way. Man was as much a part of that created order of things as any other existent and he was equally intended by God to conduct his life according to a particular pattern. Thus man, no less than the planets and the stars, the winds and the seas, the lion and the eagle, was ordained by God to conduct his life according to God's ordinance. That part of His law which God had laid down for man was described as natural law. However, unlike plants and non-human animals, man was subject to God's law in a special way. Through his possession of reason he was able to be fully conscious of the God-ordained natural laws to which he should conform. Through his possession of free will he was able to will to follow those laws, which ẻlso meant that he was capable of defying them. The rest of the material creation followed the design God had ordained for them in an unknowing and unchoosing way. Unlike man, therefore, they were incapable of either good or evil. Natural law was not the only law to which man was subject. There were other injunctions, relating particularly to man's salvation, which man could not know merely through the use of his natural faculties and to which he had access only because they had been 'revealed' to him by God in the Scriptures. However natural law provided the basic rules that man needed to structure his relations with his fellow human beings during his earthly life.

Given this view of things, use of the term 'natural' in natural law is quite readily intelligible. These were laws laid down by God for human beings in general, just as 'positive' or 'civil' laws were laid down by rulers for the governance of particular bodies of citizens. They were 'natural' because they were not 'artificial' laws; that is, they were not man-made. They were as much part of a given natural order of things as what would nowadays be called scientific 'laws of nature'. Thus any particular individual was typically subject to two laws – the laws of nature and the laws of the particular state to which he belonged. Nor were these two bodies of law unrelated. The laws laid down by human rulers should be guided by, and should elaborate upon, the laws of nature laid down by God. A putative man-made law that flouted natural law was, for that reason, not truly a law at all. The laws of nature therefore dictated the basic content of man-made law and also set limits to what rulers could legitimately require of their subjects.

The link between natural law and the Lockean conception of natural rights is very simple. Laws bestow rights and impose duties (subject to the qualifications that we have considered in earlier chapters). Natural law bestows natural rights and imposes natural duties. Locke, for example, gave as the fundamental law of nature that 'no-one ought to harm another in his Life, Health, Liberty, or Possessions' (1960, II, s.6). He then restated that law in terms of the rights it bestowed and the duties it imposed: each individual had a natural right to his life, liberty and property, and each individual had a natural duty not to harm the life, liberty or property of others.

As with the Hobbesian tradition, it is common to find theorists in this tradition investigating natural rights by picturing man in his natural condition – the state of nature. However natural rights theorists in the Lockean tradition understood the moral condition of man in the state of nature quite differently from Hobbes. For Locke, the basic moral rules that man needed to conduct his life were provided by the law of nature and that law was fully available to all men in the state of nature. The state of nature was neither a moral vacuum nor a moral chaos; it was characterised by a structure of moral rights and duties which was supplied by God's natural law. In order to live in peace and harmony and to enjoy their natural rights men had only to abide by that natural law. Thus, for Locke, unlike Hobbes, man's natural condition was not intrinsically one of conflict; on the contrary, morally it was a condition of peace and harmony. Conflicts and difficulties arose in the state of nature not because men lacked a common body of laws to follow but because they failed fully to recognise and to conform to the natural laws that God had provided for them. It was not so much the shortcomings of the state of nature as the failings of fallen mankind that made the state of nature unsatisfactory and that induced men to end it by establishing political authority.

However the establishment of political authority did not mean the disappearance of natural rights. On the contrary, men carried their natural rights forward with them into political society. Locke argued that, in the state of nature, individuals possessed both natural rights to their life, liberty and property and an 'executive right of nature' to do whatever they deemed necessary to protect those rights. When they placed themselves under political authority, men gave up their executive right of nature to that authority so that, henceforth, instead of each and every individual interpreting natural law and judging and punishing offenders, those functions would be performed on behalf of all members of the political community by a single authority. What individuals did not give up was their natural rights to life, liberty and property. The whole point of their establishing political authority was the better to protect their natural rights to life, liberty and property. It would therefore have been nonsensical for individuals to have abandoned those rights on leaving the state of nature. The possession of natural rights was therefore as much a feature of man in political society as it was of man in the state of nature.

In addition the Lockean tradition regarded the upholding of man's natural rights as the primary function of government. For example, the American Declaration of Independence of 1776, having declared that God had endowed all men with rights to life, liberty and the pursuit of happiness, went on to state that 'to secure these rights, Governments are instituted among men, deriving their just powers from the consent of the governed'. Similarly the French Declaration of the Rights of Man and the Citizen of 1789 stated that 'the end of all political associations is the preservation of the natural and imprescriptible rights of man'. But the governments which were set up to safeguard individuals' natural rights might themselves turn into offenders and violate the very rights they were supposed to protect. That they had no authority to do. A government which significantly infringed its citizens' natural rights lost its own right to rule and could legitimately be overthrown. It was in those terms that Locke justified the 'Glorious Rebellion' of 1688. The American and French revolutionaries used the doctrine of natural rights to similar effect. That is one way in which the doctrine of natural rights is said to constitute the 'radical' phase of natural law thinking.

Historically the doctrine of natural rights was also closely associated with social contract thinking. The idea of social contract took various forms (Lessnoff, 1986) but, in general terms it was the theory that, in some more or less literal way, citizens were contracting members of the society to which they belonged and the political authority to which they were subject derived ultimately from, and depended ultimately upon, their own consent. The very conception of man's natural condition – the state of nature – as a condition without human government was itself a part of the social contract tradition, for to suppose that man is naturally not subject to political authority is to suppose that political authority is humanly created. Why this association of natural rights and social contract? It did not have to be so. An Aristotelian conception of the state has been strongly associated with traditional natural law thinking ever since St Thomas Aquinas, during the thirteenth century, integrated Aristotelian philosophy into Christian theology. According to Aquinas man was, by his God-given nature, a social and political animal. He lived as God intended him to, and he was able to achieve the good earthly life that God had ordained for him

only by co-operating with others in an organised political
community. In that sense the state was natural; man's natural
condition was a political one and not the authority-less condition
imagined by seventeenth-century political thinkers. Thus, in so far
as Aquinas might have thought in terms of natural rights, those
rights would have been held by people as members of a natural
political order rather than by isolated individuals in a pre-political
state of nature.[4]

Nor was every exponent of contractarianism a proponent of
natural rights. However the association between natural rights and
social contract was no accident and the shift in emphasis from
natural law to natural rights does much to explain this
transformation in the conception of the political order. Once
individuals were reckoned to possess identical natural rights,
particularly equal natural rights to freedom, they could no longer
be regarded as destined for different pre-ordained roles in a natural
political order. Individuals with equal natural rights stood shoulder
to shoulder as moral equals. That equality meant that none could
claim any natural authority over others. Thus if there was to be
political authority, it had to be established by men themselves and
those who possessed political authority had to be given it by the
'equals' over whom it was wielded. Sir Robert Filmer, the foremost
English proponent of the doctrine of the divine right of kings,
rightly traced the 'error' of contractarianism to the 'new, plausible
and dangerous opinion' of the natural freedom of mankind (1949, p.
53).

Which rights were claimed as natural rights? Life and liberty were
standard. The right to life generally meant the right not to be
murdered. The right to liberty was understood as the right to
conduct one's life as one chose within certain acknowledged limits.
Thus Locke understood by an individual's right to liberty his right
to live as he saw fit provided he remained within the bounds of the
law of nature. Similarly the French Declaration of 1789 stated that
'Political liberty consists in the power of doing whatever does not
injure another. The exercise of the natural rights of every man has
no other limits than those which are necessary to secure every other
man the free exercise of the same rights.' As I have already
indicated, the right to liberty was also sometimes understood to
entail the right of each individual not to be subjected to authority
without his own consent.

Sometimes natural rights were claimed to specific liberties. For example, the French Declaration of 1789 asserted the right to freedom of opinion, including religious opinion, and the right to the 'free communication of thoughts and opinions'. Locke extended the range of natural rights to include ownership of property and that too became a frequently asserted natural right. In addition natural rights theorists were keen to spell out what individuals' natural rights implied for their rights as citizens and for their just treatment by the organs of the state. They also typically claimed that people had the right to resist and to unseat tyrants and oppressors who violated natural rights.

What is generally true of natural rights thinking of the seventeenth and eighteenth centuries is that the fundamental rights attributed to individuals were essentially negative in character. They were 'keep out' notices. They proclaimed that each individual should be left free to worship God in his own way, to express his thoughts, to tend his property, without interference from others, particularly without interference from the state. That generalisation requires some qualification. Conceptions of individuals' natural rights were often associated with conceptions of their rights as citizens, which rights, rather than merely limiting the scope of political life, regulated its conduct. There are also a few instances of eighteenth-century natural rights theorists asserting positive as well as negative claim-rights.[5]

The doctrine of natural rights has attracted a good deal of suspicion and hostility, particularly during the last two centuries, which is due in large part to its claim that rights can be 'natural'. Trees, bees and buttercups are all parts of nature; so, on this view it would seem, are rights. We cannot doubt the existence of trees, bees and buttercups, nor, it would seem, can we doubt the existence of rights. Yet rights clearly do not 'exist' in the same manifest way as these other things; we cannot see rights as we can see trees and bees, nor, unlike gravity or natural radiation, can we infer their existence from our experience of their effects. Not unreasonably, therefore, natural rights theorists have been accused of trying to pass off a highly questionable moral notion as though its presence in the universe were a matter of fact. In truth, it has been objected, there are no rights in nature.

Now if we reconsider the cosmology in which the doctrine of natural rights was originally embedded, the representation of natural rights as natural facts was not at all odd. Clearly rights cannot be thought of as 'existing' in quite the same way as trees and bees, but there is nothing odd about regarding the question of what humanly made legal rights people have as a question of fact. Thus, for example, it is a fact that, currently, people in Britain and the United States have the legal right to smoke tobacco; it is also a fact that, currently, they have no legal right to smoke marijuana. By the same token, if we see the world as created by God and structured according to His laws, then the rights that men possess in virtue of those laws will also appear as matters of fact. Granted the natural law view of things, it is simply 'true' that human beings *qua* human beings possess certain God-given rights, just as it is true that bees live in hives and that oaks grow from acorns. Moreover, given that these are part of a comprehensive design that God has given to his creation, it is quite apposite to think of them as part of the nature of things and therefore to speak of them as 'natural' rights.

Of course, the cosmology that is crucial to this conception of natural rights is very much open to challenge. However, if we take exception to that cosmology, it is important to recognise (although people have frequently not recognised) that what we are faulting is not the use of the concept of a right outside the context of positive law, but simply the claim that there are rights embedded in nature. A rejection of that cosmology would equally entail a rejection of ideas of natural law or natural justice or natural duties.

Is there any justification for continuing to speak of 'natural rights' if we do not accept the theocentric cosmology of which it was originally a part? There are two related grounds on which the phrase might still be defended. First, if we ascribe moral rights to people, rights which we believe they have whether or not those are embodied in codes of positive law, we may call these 'natural' rights simply to distinguish them from the 'artificial' rights which we think of people having only because they have been created by some specific human act. For instance we might say that individuals have a natural right not to be murdered but no natural right to receive a pension. John Rawls (1971), for example, seems somewhat reluctant to speak of natural rights but he does speak of 'natural duties', which duties are 'natural' in precisely this sense. Second, the description 'natural' may be thought appropriate to those rights in so far as human beings are thought to possess them simply in their natural capacity as human beings rather than in their 'artificial' capacity as members of particular organisations such as states. Thus, before we heap ridicule upon the idea that rights can be 'natural', it is important that we should be clear about the precise sense in which they are said to be natural.

Human rights

Even though the description of some rights as 'natural' is defensible in the ways I have indicated, it is perhaps best given up, except by those who share something like a traditional natural law view of the world and for whom natural rights remain 'natural' in a more substantial sense. In this century, the language of natural rights has been largely replaced by that of 'human rights', a term that is less open to misunderstanding. Even so, human rights might still be thought of as natural rights in the limited senses that I have just described. That is, they are rights which all people are thought to possess whether or not they are embodied in systems of positive law. They ought, of course, to be recognised in systems of positive law. But people's possession of human rights does not depend upon such formal recognition, which is why we can speak of governments and laws 'violating' their human rights. Secondly, they remain natural rights in that people are conceived as possessing those rights in their natural capacity as human beings rather than as citizens of particular states. In addition what are called human rights might also be conceived as natural rights in a fuller sense. For many Christian thinkers they are. But the idea of human rights is no longer closely associated with that particular theocentric view of the world.

Human rights are, then, rights possessed by all human beings simply as human beings. They are what Hart describes as 'general' rather than 'special' rights (1967, pp. 60–6) since they are universal to all humanity. By contrast special rights arise only out of some special transaction or special relationship between people, and are therefore confined to those people who are parties to those special transactions or relationships. Examples of special rights are rights arising from promises and contracts, rights attaching to particular offices and social positions, and rights arising from special relationships. Human rights do not presuppose such special transactions or relationships. Merely being human is sufficient to make one a possessor of those rights.

To that extent, the doctrine of human rights is an egalitarian doctrine. It ascribes a number of rights to human beings indifferently and those rights are held equally by all human beings. Just how egalitarian the doctrine turns out to be in effect will depend upon how extensive are the rights which all human beings are reckoned to possess. But at least the doctrine of human rights treats all humanity as its canvas and attributes an equal basic moral significance to all human beings as such. In that way it stands opposed to doctrines which give a fundamentally different moral standing to different categories of people. It is at odds with cultures and ideologies which give fundamentally different moral statuses to people belonging to different races or sexes or religions or classes or castes.

Human rights have also come to acquire a legal or semi-legal status, since they are now embodied in a number of international declarations, conventions and covenants. To that extent, even legal positivists can recognise human rights as 'real' rights. They are legal rights established by members of the international community, although the formal obligations that states acquire in putting their names to the relevant documents are often qualified or unclear. International lawyers do sometimes speak of human rights in this strictly legal sense. Nevertheless the idea of human rights remains fundamentally a non-legal one. That is, human rights are rights which humans are conceived as possessing whether or not they are recognised in positive codes of law. Thus, according to the full-blooded version of the doctrine, declarations and conventions of human rights do not 'create' and 'give' rights to human beings; they simply recognise and announce the rights that human beings have.

The content of human rights

What have been claimed as human rights? The answer is a wide variety of conditions and goods. The most celebrated statement of human rights is the 'Universal Declaration of Human Rights' adopted by the General Assembly of the United Nations in 1948. That document is far from perfect in the way it catalogues and formulates the rights it enunciates and its contents are controversial even amongst those who are committed to the general idea of human rights. Nevertheless it provides a useful starting point for a survey of the sorts of rights that are most commonly claimed as human rights and which regularly appear in declarations of rights.

First, there is the right to life. That might be regarded as the most fundamental of rights since being alive is a prerequisite of enjoying other rights. However, as I indicated in Chapter 1, what more precisely the right to life is a right *to* is open to widely different interpretations. At a minimum, it can be understood as the right not to be murdered. It might also be understood as the right to be safeguarded from murder. Article 3 of the UN Declaration, which states that 'everyone has the right to life' also states that everyone has the right to 'personal security', which implies not only a right not to be murdered but also a right, typically held against a government, to be protected from murder and other forms of personal injury. But life may be threatened by more than just the wilful hostility of human beings. It may also be threatened, for example, by disease or famine. Thus the right to life may become linked to rights to certain material goods and services which figure in later articles of the UN Declaration. The right to life may also be circumscribed in different ways. For example, does a murderer retain his right to life in spite of his taking the life of another, or does he forfeit that right so that he himself can be sentenced to death without his own right to life being violated? Does the right to life permit killing in self-defence? Does it permit killing in wartime? None of these questions is satisfactorily settled merely by asserting a right to life and declarations typically leave these issues unsettled.

Second, rights to liberty or to liberties have always figured prominently in declarations of rights and do so in the UN Declaration. Sometimes what is asserted is a right to liberty as such. However this cannot really mean that people are rightfully free to do whatever they like – for one thing the existence of other people's rights, including their rights to liberty, must set limits to the liberty of any particular individual. The 'right to liberty' therefore is usually either a way of asserting a right not to be enslaved (which right is stated explicitly and separately in article 4 of the UN Declaration) or it is a right to a certain 'area' of personal liberty whose precise boundaries are not spelled out but whose general nature is left to be 'understood' by those to whom the declaration is addressed. It has also become common to assert rights to specific liberties such as rights to freedom of opinion and expression, freedom of religion, freedom of movement, freedom of association and freedom from intrusions into one's privacy.

Third, there is the right to property. For centuries property was regarded as an entirely man-made institution and not something to which there could be a natural right. However Locke's argument that individuals could acquire natural rights to property has proved particularly influential and it has become a common ingredient of declarations of rights, including the UN Declaration (article 17). As with many other rights, just how we are to understand the scope and content of this right as it appears in declarations of human rights is usually left extremely unclear.

Fourth, there are a number of what may be called 'civil' rights – rights which concern the administration of justice and the possible abuse of governmental power. Article 5 provides that no one shall be subject to torture or to 'cruel, inhuman or degrading treatment or punishment'. Article 7 declares that 'All are equal before the law and are entitled without discrimination to equal protection of the law'. Article 11 provides that everyone charged with a criminal offence has the right to be presumed innocent until proved guilty.

Fifth, the UN Declaration includes a number of 'political' rights, rights which relate to the workings of political processes. Article 21 of the UN Declaration, for example, states that 'everyone has the right to take part in the government of his country, directly or through freely chosen representatives'.

Finally, the UN Declaration includes a number of what are usually described as socioeconomic rights. Article 22 states that everyone has the right to social security and to the 'social and cultural rights indispensable for his dignity and the free development of his personality'. Other articles go on to declare that everyone has the right to work, to rest and leisure, to education, to health care and to a certain minimum standard of living. These are sometimes referred to as the 'new' human rights since they are largely, though not wholly, absent from earlier declarations of rights.

These are only loose groupings of rights. The UN Declaration does not itself group rights into 'families' and it includes some articles which do not fit easily into any of the above groupings – for example, article 15, which declares that everyone has the right to a nationality, and article 16, which declares that everyone has the right to marry and to found a family.

Although the UN Declaration is a very important document and an obvious focus for discussions of human rights, it should not be regarded as the definitive statement of human rights. It was produced under difficult circumstances and those who drafted it had to secure the support of governments espousing very different ideologies and of nations with very different cultural traditions. Whatever its defects, it represents a considerable achievement in international co-operation. But it is still a rather ramshackle document and it should not be treated as the touchstone by which the whole doctrine of human rights is to be judged. Some of what are claimed as human rights in the UN Declaration may not be rights at all; others may be rights but not truly human rights. There may also be human rights which go unrecognised in the UN Declaration. Critical discussion of the Declaration must not therefore be confused with critical discussion of the very idea of human rights. As we shall see in the next chapter, there is no single theory which can be spoken of as 'the' theory of human rights. Rather there are a number of theories which share the general idea of humans rights but which advance different reasons for ascribing rights to human beings and which, consequently, differ over what rights human beings have.

With that qualification stated, there are a number of observations to be made about the rights that figure in the UN Declaration. Firstly, the list of rights in the UN Declaration is a good deal longer than the list of rights that appeared in declarations of rights in the seventeenth and eighteenth centuries. Locke, for example, made do with the natural rights to life, liberty and property. The French Declaration of the Rights of Man and the Citizen (1789) stretched to 17 articles, whereas the UN Declaration extends to 30 articles with several rights sometimes figuring in a single article. Further declarations of rights inspired by the UN Declaration, such as the European Convention on Human Rights (1950), and the International Covenant on Civil and Political Rights (1966) and the International Covenant on Economic, Social and Cultural Rights (1966) contain still more detailed lists of rights. Generally speaking, many more rights have been claimed as human rights in the twentieth century than were claimed as natural rights in previous centuries.

In some measure this lengthening list of rights has resulted from a desire to give more precise and detailed statements of the rights that people have. That is, a longer list does not always indicate that the scope of natural or human rights has been enlarged. It is simply that there has been an endeavour to state in greater detail just what people's rights entitle them to. For example, rather than making do merely with the 'right to liberty', the European Convention on Human Rights devotes several articles to spelling out the freedoms to which people have rights, along with details of the circumstances in which those freedoms may be limited or removed and the methods by which that may be done. Similarly the International Covenant on Civil and Political Rights runs to 53 articles, most of them consisting of several paragraphs; roughly half of these are given over to statements of rights, with the remainder devoted to machinery for implementing the Covenant.

However it is also true that, in the twentieth century, rights have been claimed to things that were not generally claimed as natural rights in earlier ages. This is most obviously true of rights associated with the welfare state. As one would expect, changes in moral and political thinking have affected people's thinking about the content of human rights. As people came to think that governments should play a larger role in promoting the well-being of their citizens, so they have been more generous in the rights they have claimed on behalf of individuals. In all of this one might suppose that the idea of natural or human rights has remained constant: all that has changed is people's thinking about what individuals have natural or human rights *to*. However, these changing ideas about the content of rights are also associated with changes in how those rights are conceived so that human rights in contemporary thought are not wholly identical in character with the natural rights of previous centuries.

Human rights and the rights of citizens

Natural rights, as we have seen, were typically thought of as rights that individuals would possess in a 'state of nature'. Since a state of nature was a condition without government and without organised political society, rights which presupposed the existence of government and of organised society could not be natural rights. Thus the socioeconomic rights that figure in the UN Declaration would not have been conceived as natural rights for, by and large, those rights are understood to impose duties specifically upon governments or upon political communities acting through the agency of governments. But neither could political or civil rights be natural rights, nor could rights such as the right to security of person, for those rights also make sense only in the presence of government. They might be claimable as rights of some sort and they might be linked in some way to natural rights, but, within the state of nature cum social contract tradition, they could not themselves be truly 'natural' rights.

These reservations about what can be considered natural rights might also lead us to wonder whether the same should not be said of human rights. Human rights may no longer be (necessarily) associated with the cosmology of natural law but they are still conceived as rights that human beings enjoy simply in virtue of being human. That implies that they are rights which are common to all human beings no matter where they live or when they live, no matter what form of government they live under or whether they live under government at all, no matter what their social or economic circumstances. But, if human rights have to be that general, if they have to be tenable in every possible human condition, can they include rights such as the right to protection by government, the right to 'an effective remedy by the competent national tribunals' when rights are violated, the right to political participation, or the right to social security? The French Declaration of 1789 distinguished between the rights of man and the rights of the citizen. Are some of what are now claimed as human rights not human rights at all but rights which, if they are rights, are possessed by individuals only as citizens of particular states?

That would imply that individuals as members of political communities possess two clearly separate sorts of rights: rights which they hold along with all other human beings and which they possess in all circumstances, including the circumstances of political society, and rights which they hold only as citizens of particular states. There are, indeed, philosophers who interpret the adjective 'human' severely and who argue that rights that individuals can enjoy only as members of states cannot be reckoned truly human rights (for example, Melden, 1977, pp. 179–84).[6] However, before we set about severing the rights of citizens from the rights of humans, we should recognise that they can be joined in a number of ways.

Firstly, there is bound to be a good deal of overlap between the contents of these two sorts of right. For example, freedom of expression and freedom of association can be thought of as rights which individuals have as human beings; but those are also rights which bear importantly upon the way that states conduct their affairs and which citizens can demand should be respected both by those in authority and by their fellow citizens.

Secondly, some rights which are specific to citizenship might be conceived as articulating no more than the constraints that human rights impose upon the way that governments and other agencies of the state exercise their powers. In the case of some of these rights the moral foundation of the rights of citizens in the rights of persons is readily apparent. The right to a fair trial, the right not to be subjected to 'cruel, inhuman or degrading treatment or punishment' and the right to 'recognition everywhere as a person before the law' may all be conceived in that way. In other cases, the link between human rights and citizens rights may be more institutional in character. Thus the right not to be subjected to arbitrary arrest or the right to be presumed innocent until proved guilty can be viewed as requiring institutions and procedures which do not place human rights at risk.

The rights of citizens to fundamental freedoms and their rights to be treated in accordance with the elementary canons of justice can therefore be seen as no more than rights governing the treatment of human beings by the institutions of the modern state. But what about rights that are associated more specifically with political life, such as rights of political participation? These too can be grounded in a conception of human rights. For example, if we hold that human beings possess a basic right of self-determination, we may also hold that, if they find themselves subject to political authority, they are entitled to share in the exercise of that authority (in so far as that is practicable). That is not to say that the case for democracy and its associated rights must be based on a conception of human rights, since democracy can be defended in a variety of ways. But it is at least arguable that political rights such as the right to vote can find a foundation in rights that individuals hold as human beings.

The common thread running through what I have argued so far is that citizens' rights can be seen as the rights that human beings possess under political conditions. Both the use that may be made of political authority and the form that it should take are constrained by the fact that political authority is authority wielded over, and on behalf of, human individuals with rights. But what of those rights which are made *possible* only by the existence of organised political communities? It is one thing to say that the political processes must be of a sort that respect the rights of human beings. It is less obvious that goods and services that are brought into existence by a state can figure in a litany of *human* rights. Given that, for any particular individual, rights such as the right to social security or the right to security of person are claims against a particular government or a particular society, these look more like rights that individuals possess only in virtue of their membership of particular communities. Here, at last, the rights of citizens may seem to leave behind the rights of man.

Even that may be challenged by the determined proponent of human rights. Why should a theory of human rights be constrained by the seventeenth century fiction of a state of nature? Human beings have always lived in communities of one sort or another, so why should their rights as human beings be confined to those that they could reasonably claim in an entirely imaginary asocial condition? Given the ubiquity of the state in the modern world, is it not more plausible and more pertinent to think in terms of rights to which all human beings can lay claim as members of states? If we think in those terms, a catalogue of human rights can include all of those rights which are deemed universal to mankind under present circumstances, including those which, for any particular individual, constitute claims only against his or her state. Of course this extension of the idea of human rights will be plausible only so long as the *same* rights are attributed to the citizens of all states. Once we allow that the citizens of different societies can have different rights, those rights cannot be human rights (unless they are merely different instantiations of the same general entitlements under different local circumstances). As we shall see in Chapter 7, one of the doubts which hangs over the idea of socioeconomic human rights is whether proponents of those rights really mean to attribute identical rights to all human beings. If they do not, then, no matter how generously we interpret the concept of human rights, it is difficult to see how those socioeconomic rights can be *human* rights.

Thus the rights ascribed to individuals as citizens can be grounded in the rights ascribed to them as human beings. Of course that is not to say that *every* right an individual enjoys as a citizen must be traceable to a right that he or she enjoys as a human being. I have sought to show only that the 'rights of man' and the 'rights of citizens' need not be conceived as two unrelated and mutually exclusive categories of right.

Scepticism about human rights

The phrase 'human rights' does not carry the same ontological overtones as 'natural rights'. That is, the adjective 'human', unlike the adjective 'natural', does not carry the suggestion that rights are 'existents' that are part of the given make-up of the world. Nevertheless proponents of human rights are sometimes given to talking about them in terms similar to those used by traditional natural rights theorists. People sometimes say that there 'are' human rights or that these rights 'exist'. They also 'declare' the rights that humans have as though they were merely announcing what is manifestly the case. The very universality of human rights perhaps encourages this way of thinking, for it is tempting to suppose that something that applies to all humanity must be obvious and indisputable. The doctrine of human rights has therefore attracted the same sort of suspicion and hostility as the doctrine of natural rights. Bentham famously dismissed natural rights as 'simple nonsense' and natural and imprescriptible rights as 'rhetorical nonsense, – nonsense upon stilts' (1962, II, p. 501). Some contemporary writers are similarly dismissive of human rights. Alasdair MacIntyre, for example, disposes of human rights with the comment, 'there are no such rights and belief in them is one with belief in witches and in unicorns' (1985, p. 69).

In so far as the critics' objection is that people do not 'have' human rights in the same sense in which they have legal rights, there is some justification for their complaints. Compare the claim 'I have a legal right to x' with the claims 'I have a moral right to x' and 'I have a human right to x'. The last two statements appear to be identical with the first, except that the adjectives 'moral' and 'human' have taken the place of the adjective 'legal'. But these statements are categorically different. The statement 'I have a legal right to x' is an assertion of fact. It is an assertion of institutional fact rather than of brute fact, but it is an assertion of fact nonetheless (Searle, 1969, pp. 50–3; MacCormick, 1974). As such it is either true or false and, if we doubt the claim, we can check its truth against the relevant society's statute books, or its records of customary law, or its case law. Moreover the truth of the claim is quite independent of our opinions about whether it is a good or a bad thing that people should have a legal right to x.

I have already explained why traditional natural law theorists were given to talking about natural rights in the same existential way as we might talk of legal rights. Natural rights were simply rights vested in humans by God's laws, just as legal rights are rights vested in individuals by humanly made laws. There are those – usually described nowadays as 'moral realists' – who would claim the same matter of fact status for human rights. But proponents of human rights do not have to take that view, nor is it a view that most of them take. The claim 'I have a human right to x' may be understood simply as the claim that, in virtue of a moral principle, I, as a human being, am entitled to x. Understood in that way, there is nothing illicit in talk of people 'having' human rights or, more generally, of their 'having' moral rights. Indeed it is somewhat puzzling that so many people should have taken exception to the notion that, morally, people can be entitled to this or that. The belief that humans have rights is no more mysterious than any other moral belief and is utterly unlike a belief in witches or unicorns.

Of course rights which claim a moral foundation are subject to all of the doubts and difficulties that characterise any moral position. When people are in dispute about what is morally right, there is no straightforward equivalent to the statute book to which they can turn in order to resolve their differences. Equally, while the question of what legal rights people have can be resolved independently of whether we think it good or bad that they have those rights, the moral rights that we ascribe to people cannot be similarly independent of our view of what is good or bad. Human rights as moral rights cannot therefore be matters of indisputable truth; they must be controversial in the way that any moral position is controversial. But there is no reason why moral rights should be any *more* morally controversial than any other element of morality. A goodly part of the criticism which pretends to be criticism of the specific idea of human rights in fact relates not to their being 'rights' but to their being 'moral' rights and succeeds as criticism only to the extent that it casts doubt upon *any* moral position (cf. Nielson, 1968; Young, 1978; Frey, 1980, pp. 10–17).

Human rights and ideal rights

One way that some writers have sought to avoid confusion over the character of natural or human rights is by introducing the notion of 'ideal rights'. Real rights are rights which people really have. Ideal rights are rights which they would ideally have. Thus Bentham, on one occasion when he did not dismiss natural rights out of hand, suggested that, if I assert that someone has a natural right to something, 'all that it can mean, if it mean any thing, . . . is that I am of the opinion he ought to have a political right to it' (1962, III, p. 218). Similarly the evolutionary utilitarian, D.G. Ritchie, proposed that when people asserted natural rights they were best understood as referring not to rights which people could be said actually to possess but rather to rights which, in their opinion, 'ought to be recognised' by the law and the public opinion of a society. They were the rights that the would-be reformer would establish in his ideal society (Ritchie, 1895, p. 80). Others have followed Bentham and Ritchie in suggesting that moral rights in general, and human rights in particular, are best interpreted as ideal rights (Campbell, 1974, p. 447; Miller, 1976, pp. 78–82; cf. Campbell, 1983, pp. 18–22).

The attraction of handling natural or human rights in this way is that it emphasises the distinction between 'is' and 'ought' and it makes clear that natural and human rights belong to the realm of 'ought'. However, despite these merits, the representation of moral rights as ideal rights cannot be acceptable to those who take moral rights seriously. On this view, people cannot really be said to have moral rights at all – except in the 'positive' sense that I identified in the previous chapter: rights which are said to be 'moral' only because they are recognised and upheld by the public opinion of a society rather than by its law. But, if we understand the adjective 'moral' in its normal critical sense, proponents of the 'ideal rights' view are really saying that there are no moral rights; there are only moral reasons why rights ought to be brought into existence and, as Bentham remarked, 'a reason for wishing that we possessed a right, does not constitute a right' (1962, III, p. 221). Thus, for example, in the absence of legally or conventionally established rights, we could not say that torturing people or trying them unjustly violated their rights. We could only regret that there was not an established order of rules according to which such actions would be violations of their rights. In other words, reducing moral rights to ideal rights means abandoning the very idea of moral rights and, more particularly, the idea of human rights as these are ordinarily understood.[7]

Of course showing that the idea of human rights is conceptually coherent is not the same as establishing that morally human beings really do have rights. We may find the notion of a centaur intelligible but our being able to imagine a being that is half man and half horse does not establish that there are centaurs. Similarly those who have doubts about human rights may concede that the notion of human rights is intelligible but still insist that it is morally unsound. They may accept that human beings just as human beings are proper objects of moral concern, but reject a morality structured in terms of rights. Or, conversely, they may accept that people have moral rights, but deny that they have any moral rights merely in virtue of being human. Or they may reject both the 'human' and the 'rights' components of the doctrine. So it is time that we turned from the concept to attempts to justify human rights.

5 Justifying Human Rights

There are two fundamental but distinct claims calling for justification in a doctrine of human rights. Firstly, that *human beings* have rights and, secondly, that human beings have *rights*. The first claim centres on the idea that merely being human is itself of moral significance and that is hardly a peculiar notion nowadays. Most contemporary moralities, whether or not they think in terms of rights, recognise that being human makes one a member of the moral community. That is, they share the conviction that there are certain ways in which it is right or wrong to treat *any* human being. Of course, logically, a morality can deny that being human is sufficient to make one an object of moral concern and there have been, and still are, moralities which have drawn the limits of the moral community far more narrowly on grounds such as race or caste or class or nationhood. Even moralities which do give moral significance to being human are likely to give an added moral significance to the specific roles and relationships in which people find themselves, so that we are deemed to have greater moral obligations to our children or parents or friends or fellow-citizens than we have to those who stand before us merely as fellow human beings. So, amongst those moralities which do give moral significance to being human, there can be large variations in the *degree* of moral significance they give to being human.

One further complication is that the range of 'human' in 'human rights' is not always straightforward. Some rights may be extended to the whole of humanity without qualification. For example, the right not to be tortured can be, and ordinarily would be, ascribed to all human beings whatever their condition. But other rights which are spoken of as human rights may not be claimed for all who are biologically human. Consider rights of self-determination. When those are asserted as human rights, there is usually an implicit understanding that those rights are not being attributed to the very young or to adults who are severely mentally incapacitated. There need be nothing sinister in that. It merely betokens that some rights are intelligibly ascribed to human beings only if they possess developed and unimpaired human capacities. That is why some theorists prefer to speak of the rights possessed by 'persons' rather than by human beings. Very often these implicit limits on the range of 'human' in human rights will be uncontroversial, but sometimes they can be hotly disputed, as is well illustrated by arguments about abortion and the right to life.

Conversely some rights which are ascribed to human beings might also be ascribed to non-human beings. Many rights cannot intelligibly be extended beyond the human race, but some can; for example, the right not to be subjected to cruelty might be extended to all sentient beings. Thus not all rights that are human rights need be only human rights. However the main point I wish to make here is that, nowadays, the human rights theorist is unlikely to have to work very hard to persuade us that we owe a certain minimum of concern and respect to human individuals as such. Indeed we are likely to feel that, given the common features of members of the human race, the onus is upon those who wish to deny the moral relevance of humanity to make their case.

That still leaves open a vast range of moral possibilities. Just why being human is morally significant, just how morally significant it is, whether that significance should be expressed in terms of rights and, if so, exactly what rights those should be, are questions which remain to be settled. My purpose in this chapter will be to examine a number of arguments for human rights. Taken together, these arguments illustrate the very different ways in which those questions can be approached and the different sorts of answers that different approaches can yield. Both proponents and antagonists of human rights are often given to arguing as though there must be a single, uniquely plausible, account of the rights that human beings have. That is false. People can and do share the general idea of human rights even though they differ over why it is that human beings have rights, over the specific rights that they have and over the implications of their having those rights. In some ways this diversity of thinking about human rights makes the idea more defensible. The idea that human beings have rights can be more widely shared if it does not presuppose a single highly specific moral theory. On the other hand, when we turn from that general idea to practical questions concerning its implementation, the diversity of thinking associated with human rights obviously poses problems.

Natural law and human rights

As we have seen, historically the idea of human rights derived from the idea of natural rights, which itself derived from the idea of natural law. However we should not simply consign the idea of natural law to history. That idea remains one to which a number of contemporary writers subscribe and which they use to found human rights (for example, Maritain, 1944, 1951; Finnis, 1980).

However the idea of natural law is of limited utility in the task of justification. Although it has been most commonly conceived as God's law, the tradition has been that that law is naturally available to mankind through reason. By using our natural faculty of reason, we can descry the content of natural law. Knowledge of that law does not therefore depend upon its being 'revealed' by a special act of God (even though God may also have revealed some elements of natural law in the Scriptures, for example, in the Ten Commandments). To that extent, the idea of natural law leaves the task of justification still to be performed; human rights may be the rights invested in human beings by natural law, but we still have to establish what it is that natural law requires and why.

Self-evidence

It has sometimes been claimed that it is 'self-evidently' the case that people possess natural or human rights and that the content of those rights is also 'self-evident'. Thus the Declaration of Independence of the United States (1776) asserted famously, 'We hold these truths to be self-evident, that all men are created equal, that they are endowed by their Creator with certain unalienable Rights, that among these are Life, Liberty and the pursuit of Happiness.' The presentation of rights in 'declarations' can itself seem to presume self-evidence. It is as if the rights are just 'there' so that the authors of those documents need do no more than announce or declare what they are. There are also some contemporary writers who use the language of self-evidence in relation to rights (McCloskey, 1985) or who assert rights in a way that implies self-evidence.

Two things may be said in defence of the idea of self-evident rights. First, all moral positions must take a stand on something. Justification typically is of the less fundamental in terms of the more fundamental but it cannot go on indefinitely. At some point we must hit rock-bottom, so that demands for further justification cannot be satisfied and can be met only by the assertion of a basic principle. Thus those who assert 'self-evident' rights may claim to be taking a stand of a sort that, ultimately, must be taken by everyone, whatever their moral view. Second, given that natural and human rights are typically thought of as 'fundamental' rights, they may seem plausible candidates for this logically primitive, unargued and unarguable, status.

However there are also problems in relying upon claims of self-evidence. The most obvious of these is that people often disagree about what is 'self-evidently' the case. Rousseau commented, with 'surprise and disgust', upon how little agreement there was amongst those who claimed to have discerned the content of natural law (1913, pp. 156–7). Were he writing now, he might be similarly struck by the absence of a consensus on the content of human rights. If claims rely upon nothing but self-evidence, all we can do in the face of contradictory claims is appeal to the disputing parties to open their eyes still wider. If, having done that, they continue to disagree about what is supposedly self-evident, they have no way of resolving their disagreement and, unless one party accuses the other of dishonesty, the claim of self-evidence must itself be discredited. Secondly, something's seeming self-evident does not ensure that it is true. For example, at one time it seemed self-evident that the earth was flat and that the sun revolved around the earth. Thirdly, that a person finds a proposition self-evidently true is, in the first instance, a description of that person rather than of the proposition itself.

Self-evidence, then, is not a very promising foundation for rights, and claims of self-evidence have done a good deal to bring ideas of natural or human rights into disrepute. Certainly there may be truths, such as the rules of logic, whose truth seems just obvious and which we accept as self-evident. It may also be that the self-evidence of some truths will be apparent only to those who have reached a certain level of intellectual development (Finnis, 1980, pp. 32, 66–9; Ross, 1930, pp. 12, 29–30). But, given the controversy that surrounds rights, particularly amongst those whom Rousseau described as 'subtle casuists and profound metaphysicians', it is hardly plausible to claim an 'obvious' status for natural or human rights. Theories of rights, like all theories, have ultimately to stand on something, but to take that stand on an unargued catalogue of rights seems unnecessarily peremptory. Surely we can do more than merely assert rights. Surely we can say something to explain and to justify why people have the rights we think they do.

Human rights and human worth

One conviction that underlies most conceptions of human rights is that all human individuals have intrinsic value simply as human individuals. That conviction is articulated in a variety of ways. Sometimes it is expressed through the idea of 'human dignity', sometimes in the formula 'respect for persons', and sometimes by way of Kant's idea that human beings are to be treated as 'ends in themselves' rather than merely as 'means'.

A particularly cogent statement of this sentiment has been developed by Gregory Vlastos (1984). Vlastos distinguishes individuals' 'merit' from their 'worth'. When we assess people in terms of their merit we grade them – as more or less generous, honest, brave, clever, skilful, amusing, and so on. But we do not respond to people only according to their merits and our morality is not wholly of this grading sort. We also regard individuals as having 'worth' simply as individual human beings. For example, we think that all individuals just as human individuals should enjoy the equal protection of the law. Or, to take a rather different example, if we see someone drowning, we believe we should go to his aid simply as a person in need of help and not only if and because he is a particularly meritorious person. Thus by 'worth' Vlastos means to describe that intrinsic value that we do, or should, attribute to human individuals as such.

In addition Vlastos argues that, if we give worth to individuals, we must give worth to what is important to individuals, particularly to their freedom and well-being. Since worth is something that we attribute to individuals equally, it provides the ground for ascribing equal rights to human individuals. Thus all individuals have equal human rights to freedom and well-being. Vlastos goes on to suggest that, if we work through the demands of freedom and well-being, we will arrive at the more specific human rights listed in the UN Declaration.

Vlastos's belief that we can generate a detailed and determinate set of rights from the simple idea of equal human worth may be unduly optimistic, but his claim that the notion of human rights manifests a commitment to something like an idea of equal human worth would be very widely shared. Are those who are sceptical about human rights likely to be won over by this idea? Perhaps not. After all, some of those who reject the notion of human rights may do so just because they regard human individuals as of unequal worth (cf. Feinberg, 1973, p. 90). In that case, the human rights theorist may have run out of arguments – the principle of equal worth may be just the sort of fundamental conviction on which he has to take his stand.

Rights and moral agency

One theorist who thinks that more can be said to convince the sceptic is Alan Gewirth. In an ambitious argument, he attempts to justify human rights by grounding them in the foundations of morality itself. He aims to show that rights are implicit in the very idea of acting 'morally' such that anyone who acknowledges that human individuals are moral agents must accept that they have certain equal rights (Gewirth, 1978, 1982, 1984).

Gewirth describes his approach as a 'dialectically necessary method'. It is *dialectical* because it proceeds by way of what is implied in certain statements that rational agents must be presumed to make. It is dialectically *necessary* because agents, if they are rational, logically *must* be deemed to make these statements and *must* accept what is implicit in them. Gewirth's argument is intricate and abstract but in bare outline it runs as follows. All action has two generic features: (1) voluntariness or freedom – an agent controls his own conduct – and (2) purposiveness or intentionality – an agent acts to attain some end or goal. Thus an agent, in performing an action X, may be described as saying implicitly, 'I do X for end or purpose E'. That entails that he must hold that 'E is good'. But, if he holds that E is good, he must also hold that the conditions necessary for attaining E are good. The most fundamental of these are the conditions of action as such: freedom and well-being. An individual who is prevented from controlling his own behaviour cannot 'act'; and if he lacks the basic ingredients of human well-being, such as life itself, physical integrity, self-esteem and education, he cannot pursue purposes. The agent must therefore hold that he must have the necessary goods of freedom and well-being, which is to hold that he has a *right* to freedom and well-being.

Up to this point, Gewirth's argument functions purely in terms of the claims that an agent must be understood to make about himself. The rights so derived are prudential rather than moral since they are grounded only in what the agent himself needs if he is to act purposively. However, since the agent claims rights only as a prospective purposive agent, rationally he must accept that all other prospective purposive agents equally have those rights. Thus, in claiming rights for himself he must, on pain of self-contradiction, acknowledge that all other agents possess those same rights and that he must respect their rights just as they must respect his. That is what Gewirth calls the principle of generic consistency. It is by way of that principle that he makes the transition from prudential to moral rights. In fact the generic moral rights to freedom and well-being are also human rights, for every human being is an actual, prospective or potential purposive agent. Thus, Gewirth concludes, we can ground human rights in the necessary conditions of human action. Nor does he think we must remain at the level of broad generalities about freedom and well-being. He erects a substantial and detailed hierarchy of human rights upon these foundations and sets out the institutional means necessary for their realisation.

As a justification for human rights, Gewirth's theory has a number of strengths. First, in locating the ground of rights in the conditions of human agency, he provides a basis for rights that relates to human beings as such and which is therefore capable of generating rights which are *universal* to human beings. Second, by arguing from such parsimonious and apparently uncontroversial premises, Gewirth produces a case for human rights that aims to preclude opposition. Rather than being just one possible moral view amongst other competing moral views, the doctrine of human rights becomes one that people *must* accept merely in virtue of recognising human beings as moral agents – or, at least, a doctrine they can reject only at the cost of being 'irrational'. Thus Gewirth's case for human rights aims to provide a justification of a uniquely compelling and uncontentious character.

Gewirth's theory of rights has received a lot of critical attention, much of which has questioned whether the steps by which he moves through his argument have the logically necessary character that he claims for them. Clearly, in a systematic and rigorous justification of the sort that Gewirth offers, a high premium is placed upon the soundness of the links which make up the continuous chain of logic that connects the detailed rights that he attributes to agents to the mere fact of their agency. His critics have attempted to show that those links fail at certain points, particularly when Gewirth makes the transitions from goods to rights and from prudential to moral claims. It is, indeed, difficult not to suspect that Gewirth must be using more than his minimal premises to produce his substantial catalogue of human rights. Nevertheless he has proved a doughty opponent; he has matched his critics point for point and he has remained unconvinced by their attempts to fault his dialectically necessary justification of human rights.[1]

Contract and rights

Traditionally natural rights have been conceived in contrast to contractual rights. Insisting upon the 'naturalness' of rights has been a way of protesting that those rights do not issue from humanly created arrangements. Individuals possessed of natural rights might, of course, enter into contracts, but whatever contractual rights they come to acquire should be regarded as separate from, and additional to, their natural rights.

Clearly human rights, like nat ral rights, cannot be conceived as the contingent products of deals struck between individuals. Nor, for that matter, can the rights of citizens. For centuries the social contract tradition has attempted to ground the rights of citizens in a social cum political contract entered into by the individuals who form a political community, but theorists in that tradition have never succeeded in squaring this alleged contract with the realities of states and societies as we know them. Nevertheless the *model* of contract might still prove a useful tool in an attempt to establish what rights people have.

The most celebrated contemporary attempt to delineate the features of a just society by way of a hypothetical contract is John Rawls's *A Theory of Justice* (1971). Rawls's theory of a just society includes an account of individuals' rights. However in Rawls's theory those rights are conceived as the rights of citizens rather than the rights of human beings since his theory is constructed for a body of people who form a political society rather than for the human race conceived as a single moral community. Even so, Rawls's contractual approach is capable of being adapted to the case of human rights and, even in Rawls's own version of it, the rights he enunciates have a certain universality, in that they represent the rights that should be enjoyed by all citizens in all modern states.

Rawls aims to discover the principles of justice that should structure a society by inferring which principles of distribution would be agreed to by individuals in an imaginary 'original position'. This original position is a condition of uncertainty in that each individual has to agree upon the structure of the future society behind a 'veil of ignorance'. Behind that veil, individuals do not know what sort of individuals they are or what positions they occupy in the society. They do not know whether they are rich or poor, intelligent or stupid, male or female, black or white. Nor are they aware of what Rawls calls their 'conceptions of the good'; that is, they are ignorant of the specific ends to which they wish to devote their lives, and also of matters such as their religious beliefs and philosophical convictions. In other words, individuals in the original position are forced to be impartial about matters such as gender, race, wealth and religious belief because, behind the veil of ignorance, they are unaware of their own sex, race, income group or religious faith. The original position is set up so that the decisions it yields are necessarily 'fair' as between different sorts of individual.

Under these conditions, individuals have to agree upon the way 'primary goods' are to be distributed in their society. Primary goods are goods which all individuals are presumed to want, whatever else they may want. Rawls's thinking here is similar to Gewirth's. Gewirth presents freedom and well-being as the necessary conditions of human action and therefore any human agent must want freedom and well-being. Similarly Rawls's primary goods are the essential means for attaining whatever one wants to attain in life. Any rational person is presumed to want primary goods, whatever else he or she might want. Primary goods include liberties, powers and opportunities, income and wealth, and a sense of self-respect. (Rawls sometimes includes 'rights' in his list of primary goods, but that is misleading since the basic rights that he ascribes to citizens issue from the original position; they are not already parts of it: see Martin, 1985, p. 22. If rights are included in the list of pre-contractual primary goods, they should be thought of as entirely formal categories which have yet to be given content by the contracting parties.) Rawls deliberately uses a 'thin' rather than a 'full' theory of the good to work out the requirements of justice so that, within the principles of justice they establish, individuals are left free to pursue whatever plan of life or conception of the good they think fit. In that way, Rawls's theory of justice is a 'liberal' theory.

The conclusion Rawls reaches is that, under these conditions, individuals would agree to distribute primary goods equally unless an unequal distribution would work to the advantage of the society generally, particularly that of the worst-off group in society. This general conception of justice would, in turn, lead them to adopt two principles of justice. The first of these is that 'each person is to have an equal right to the most extensive total system of equal basic liberties compatible with a similar system of liberty for all' (Rawls, 1971, p. 250). The second principle is that 'social and economic inequalities are to be arranged so that they are both (a) to the greatest benefit of the least advantaged and (b) attached to offices and positions open to all under conditions of fair equality of opportunity' (ibid., p. 83). The first part of the second principle he labels the 'difference' principle, since it specifies the conditions under which inequalities in income and wealth can be considered just.

The two principles are also ranked in 'lexical order' so that the first principle takes priority over the second; that is, liberty can be sacrificed only for the sake of liberty and not for the sake of collective economic gain, although Rawls does allow that this priority may be justifiably relaxed in an economically under-developed society. The second part of the second principle also takes priority over the the first part of that principle so that the requirements of fair equality of opportunity cannot be sacrificed for the sake of collective economic gain.

Rawls goes on to work out the specific structure of institutions that these principles of justice require, although he does this by continuing to use the fiction of contractual agreement. Having agreed upon the two principles, individuals in the original position move to a 'constitutional convention' where they have to decide upon the institutional forms that those principles require. That is followed by a 'legislative stage' where the individuals agree upon the justice of particular laws and policies.

Of the two principles, it is the first which gives rise most straightforwardly to rights. That principle gives each citizen a right to 'the most extensive total system of equal basic liberties compatible with a similar system of liberty for all'. Rawls sees this system of basic liberties as encompassing the rights that are characteristically associated with liberal democracy, such as the right to vote and to run for office, rights of freedom of speech and of assembly, rights of liberty of conscience and freedom of thought, the right to hold property, freedom from arbitrary arrest and the other rights that are normally associated with the rule of law (ibid., p. 61). Justice demands that each citizen is equally entitled to each of these basic rights.

How far we should think of Rawls's second principle of justice as generating rights is less clear. We might think of some of the ingredients of fair equality of opportunity in terms of rights. For example, that principle might be said to entail that each individual has a right to education and a right to free choice of occupation, although Rawls himself does not couch the demands of equality of opportunity in the language of rights (ibid., pp. 87, 275). Rawls's difference principle cannot easily be translated into a set of rights. It establishes a range of inequalities which are tolerable because they work to the general social advantage and which, via the institutions of equality of opportunity, are open to all. The incomes attracted by particular occupations will depend entirely on the workings of the difference principle in a general context of economic freedom and those incomes may well turn out to be different in different circumstances and at different times. So Rawls's theory of economic justice is not of a form that gives a brain surgeon a right to x amount of income and a plumber a right to y amount of income; it does not establish a specific set of 'just rewards'. The closest the difference principle comes to generating something like economic rights is by way of its requirement that inequalities are allowable only if they work to the advantage of the worst-off group, so that provision for a mimimum level of material well-being for all is built into the economic arrangements of the just society; but even that is likely to be a shifting minimum and is therefore not easy to formulate as a right.

The contract from which Rawls derives rights is a hypothetical contract and therefore those rights are not literally contractual rights. Indeed they might be described as 'natural rights'. That is a phrase that, for the most part, Rawls avoids. However he does speak of 'natural duties', by which he means duties which we can be said to have 'naturally' in that we do not have them only if we consent to have them or only if they are created by law (ibid., pp. 114–17). For example, the moral duty not to murder can be thought of as a 'natural duty' in that we do not think of ourselves as having that duty only if we have promised not to murder or only if legislators pass laws prohibiting murder. Rawls thinks of the duties that we have in relation to the principles of justice as 'natural duties'. The hypothetical contractual method enables us to identify what the principles of justice are, but the 'justness' of those principles, and the duties they impose, do not depend upon individuals' literally agreeing to adopt them. By extension, and in the same sense, the rights stemming from the principles of justice may be thought of as 'natural rights'. In fact that is a description to which Rawls himself consents on one occasion (ibid., pp. 505–6n).

Rawls's theory has received a massive amount of critical attention. Here I shall comment only upon his contractual approach as a method for generating rights. How effective is the appeal to a hypothetical contract? The bargaining situation that Rawls constructs, particularly the fiction of individuals' having to reach decisions behind a veil of ignorance, is a graphic and highly evocative way of confronting people with the demands of fairness. But is the contractual apparatus that Rawls constructs any more than a striking moral metaphor? Most of what he has his individuals agree to in the original position derives from the conditions which he builds into the contracting process. For example, the principle that all individuals are of equal moral significance is not a principle which derives from the original position; rather it is a moral assumption that is built into the original position in that all individuals are given an equal status and role in the contracting process. Similarly that justice should obtain between individuals rather than, say, groups is taken for granted in that it is individuals rather than groups that are to negotiate upon the structure of the future society.

Again the principle that the structure of a just society should be uninfluenced by considerations such as race or gender or differences in natural ability or in religious belief is not a conclusion arrived at by the contractors. That is something that Rawls has already determined in placing these matters on the other side of the veil of ignorance. That is not to say that Rawls is 'wrong' to construct the original position in that way; it is merely to point out that most of the moral work that generates the two principles of justice and their associated rights is done by the moral assumptions which structure the contracting process rather than by the contracting process itself. Thus it is only to a very limited and qualified extent that Rawls's rights can be said to be 'grounded' upon a (hypothetical) contract. The same approach used in a context of different moral assumptions would yield different moral conclusions, including a different set of rights.

One such assumption, which relates particularly to the case of human rights, concerns who should contract with whom. How do we determine the boundaries of the community whose members are to be bound by relations of justice? Rawls, in part no doubt for pragmatic reasons, identifies that community with the modern state. But should the scope of justice be so limited? Do not the demands of justice penetrate beyond state boundaries? We might, for example, suppose that the relevant moral community, and therefore the relevant body of contractors, should be the entire human race. In that case, if we leave Rawls's other assumptions unaltered, the contracting parties would come up with the same two principles of justice and the demands of the first principle of justice, concerning the distribution of basic liberties, might remain much the same. But the demands of the difference principle, requiring that the distribution of income and wealth must work to the advantage of the worst-off group, are likely to be radically altered if it is applied to the world as a whole rather than only within the borders of each separate state. We shall return to that issue in Chapter 7.

None of this shows that the contract method is 'wrong'. Appeals to what people would agree to under 'fair' conditions of bargaining can still be a highly effective way of presenting a case for rights in particular or for justice in general. It is simply that most of what we need to generate rights must come not from individuals' making contracts in a moral vacuum but from prior moral judgements about the right conditions under which such a contract should be made. In other words, most of the moral work will be done by the background moral assumptions that provide the context for the hypothetical contract rather than from the contracting process itself. Perhaps that is why, in his more recent writings, Rawls has relied rather less upon the idea of contract and has emphasised rather more a conception of the 'highest order interests' of persons (Rawls, 1980, 1985, 1993).

Self-ownership

John Locke is famous for arguing that individuals possess natural rights to property. But he is also notable for using the term 'property' in a much more extended sense than is normal nowadays. For Locke a man's property included his life and liberty as well as his possessions; in other words, it included all of that to which the individual had a natural right. Thus for Locke the invasion of a person's liberty could be conceived as a form of trespass and the deprivation of his life and liberty (other than as justified punishment) could be regarded as a form of theft. Natural rights marked out what properly 'belonged' to an individual and each individual was, he protested, 'absolute Lord of his own Person and Possessions' (1960, II, s. 123).

In fact Locke's position was a little more complicated than this last statement suggests. He also argued that all individuals were the product of God's workmanship and therefore were ultimately God's property. To take the life of an individual, except as a just punishment, was to take what belonged immediately to that individual but what belonged ultimately to God. That was why an individual could not rightfully take his own life or connive at its being taken by another (ibid., ss. 6, 23); even his own life was not ultimately 'his' to dispose of. However, with this qualification concerning God's ultimate ownership of everything, each individual should be regarded as possessing a property in his own person such that, in their natural condition, individuals were free 'to order their Actions, and dispose of their Possessions, and Persons as they think fit, within the bounds of the Law of Nature, without asking leave, or depending upon the Will of any other Man' (ibid., II, s. 4).

In the seventeenth century it was quite common to use the term 'property' in this extended sense. Nowadays that usage would be unusual. Even so, a similar form of thinking often seems to underpin many contemporary assertions of rights. Thus it would be commonplace to hear someone who resented the interference of another protesting, 'Look, my life is *mine* and therefore I, and I alone, have the right to decide how to live it!' Why should individuals have the right to decide for themselves matters such as which religion (if any) to practise, which career to pursue, and which partner to marry – particularly since others might make better decisions on their behalf? A variety of answers may be given but one of the simplest invokes this idea of self-ownership: because my life is mine, I am the only one entitled to determine its course. The use of the possessive 'my' in these contexts clearly connotes more than a mere phenomenological relation (as in 'my' mother or 'my' fears); the 'my' in 'my life' is strongly proprietorial, it indicates what I 'own' and what therefore I have a right to control.

It has been suggested that it is some such idea of self-ownership that lies at the root of Robert Nozick's theory of rights (Nozick, 1974; Cohen, 1986a, 1986b). Nozick himself does not unambiguously nail his colours to the mast of self-ownership but many of his arguments and, more particularly, many of his objections to the arguments of others imply a commitment to the idea of self-ownership. His commitment to that idea would certainly help to explain why his *Anarchy, State and Utopia* opens with the straightforward assertion that 'Individuals have rights' (1974, p. xi); it is perhaps difficult to be other than dogmatic about self-ownership.

What rights does the idea of self-ownership imply? Most obviously it implies that each individual has a right over the disposition of his physical and mental person. That includes the right of each to determine what use he makes of his talents and abilities. Beyond that, it most readily implies rights to those liberties which are reckoned essential constituents of each individual's right of control over himself. These are likely to include traditional freedoms such as freedom of speech, freedom of religion and freedom of association; to deny an individual those freedoms would be to deny him the right to control his own life. Self-ownership also vetoes the paternalistic treatment of adults or the imposition upon them of patterns of 'virtuous living'. Correspondingly it entails that each individual is duty-bound to respect the 'property' that other individuals have in themselves. However self-ownership implies that those duties will be strictly negative in character: they will demand only that we refrain from trespassing on the lives and liberties of others. Positive duties of assistance are ruled out because those duties would be at variance with the notion that each individual is the sole owner, and therefore the sole rightful controller, of his life, liberty and labour. Thus an unadulterated commitment to self-ownership will normally exclude any claim that individuals have a responsibility to promote one another's well-being.

The idea of self-ownership does leave some scope for differences of view as to where the boundary of each individual's freedom should fall. Obviously each individual's rightful freedom must be limited by each other individual's rightful freedom, but that still leaves scope for different sets of equally compatible freedoms. For example, if some people engage in public conduct which offends or distresses others, does that offensive conduct intrude improperly into the territory of the selves who are offended by it – which implies that it should be prohibited? Or does that conduct, in spite of its unfortunate effect upon others, remain within the rightful territory of those who engage in it? This sort of boundary issue is not readily settled by the idea of self-ownership.

If we move from persons to things, ideas of self-ownership have usually been associated with libertarian economic theories and with strong theories of property rights. That is not true without exception; some proponents of the idea of self-ownership reject claims that this can provide a foundation for natural rights over things (for example, Thomson, 1990, pp. 205–26, 322–47). But the frequent conjoining of ideas of natural self-ownership with claims of natural rights of ownership over things is no accident. Individuals' inviolable rights over themselves include rights over their own labour and therefore rights over the products of their labour; that, in turn, entails that the owners of those products have the right to exchange, bequeath or otherwise dispose of them as they see fit. Any interference with this chain of ownership violates individuals' rights. Thus, for example, Nozick holds that the taxation of earnings in order to redistribute income from some to others is on a par with forced labour (1974, p. 169). It compels some people to work a certain number of hours in order to provide for others' purposes. Nozick protests that principles which endorse this sort of redistribution effectively give some people a partial property right in other people (ibid., p. 172).

On the other hand, the shift from self-ownership to ownership over things is far from uncomplicated. Most 'things' over which people claim ownership are not exclusively the products of their labour, nor are they merely the most recent links in chains of voluntary transfers which reach back to the exclusive products of other people's labour. They usually involve the combination of labour with some natural resource which exists independently of that labour. In other words, the sorts of goods that we normally think of as objects of property – land, shoes, toothbrushes and the like – typically consist of elements which fall outside the 'self' which is the subject of self-ownership and which are not wholly the product of that self. There is no ready way of shifting from ownership of oneself to ownership of something external to oneself. Forging that moral link has always proved highly problematic, particularly under conditions of scarcity where one person's appropriation or ownership of a good is at the expense of another's ownership and use of that good. Thus ideas of self-ownership do not issue unproblematically in the strong conceptions of property rights or in the libertarian economic theories with which they have been most frequently associated (cf. Lloyd Thomas, 1988, pp. 67–91; Waldron, 1988, pp. 398–408; Cohen, 1986a, 1986b; Steiner, 1977b, 1987; Mack, 1990).

Up to now I have treated the idea of self-ownership as a possible foundation for theories of rights. But should it be credited with that fundamental status? If we accept a system of ordinary property rights as legitimate, we need not regard those rights as 'morally basic'. On the contrary, we may accept that system of property only because it seems to be justified by some more fundamental consideration such as its working to the general advantage of a society. Similarly it might be objected that 'self-ownership' should be treated not as morally fundamental but as a way of organising things that stands in need of justification. David Lloyd Thomas (1988) defends the idea that each individual has a right of self-ownership but not because that is a right that individuals can be simply 'perceived' to have. Rather we should 'assign' rights of self-ownership to individuals because the freedoms associated with self-ownership are preconditions of our being able to reach 'more reasonable views about what is worth while in itself' (p. 66). Thus self-ownership is itself justified in terms of what Lloyd Thomas describes as a form of 'experimental consequentialism' – a consequentialism which does not seek to maximise any specific good but which argues for the creation of optimum conditions in which individuals are able to investigate and explore what are good, worthwhile, forms of life.

This sort of argument may win more converts than the mere assertion of self-ownership. But it also threatens to render self-ownership redundant. If there are good reasons, such as the pursuit of truth or of the intrinsically valuable, for individuals' possessing certain freedoms, we can argue simply from those desirable goals to rights to the freedoms that they require and there seems no need to introduce the strongly deontological idea of self-ownership. Thus self-ownership is likely to occupy a significant position in a theory of rights only if it is found intrinsically compelling and morally fundamental. If we are not persuaded that it warrants this fundamental status, we are unlikely to find any place for it at all.

Rights and goods

Many theories of rights centre upon a conception of the 'rightful' treatment of human beings which avoids, or which tries to avoid, any view of what the 'good life' consists in. Individuals are accorded the right to decide for themselves what 'goods' or 'ends' to pursue in their lives. That is true of theories which ground rights in self-ownership and of theories, like those of Rawls, Dworkin and Gewirth, which seek not to impose any conception of the good upon individuals and which regard any such imposition as a violation of individuals' rights. Whether it is either possible or desirable for a theory of rights to abstain completely from substantive judgements about the good is much disputed. Some theorists regard that sort of agnosticism as misplaced and misconceived and, instead, ground rights squarely upon a conception of the goods essential to human well-being.

A clear example of this alternative approach is provided by the work of John Finnis (1980), who locates his account of rights within the natural law tradition. However he believes that the idea of natural law has been much misunderstood and much misrepresented. His own account of natural law is based upon a conception of intrinsic goods and reasonable conduct, rather than upon claims concerning the will of God or the facts of human nature.

Finnis identifies seven basic goods: life, knowledge, play, aesthetic experience, sociability (including friendship), practical reasonableness and religion. That these are indeed goods he holds to be self-evident: their value cannot be demonstrated but neither does it need to be demonstrated. They are 'objective' goods in that their value stems not from individuals happening (subjectively) to desire them but from their being basic aspects of human well-being. Certainly the basic goods are desirable but they are desirable because they are good rather than good because they are desired. There are very many other goods and Finnis concedes that there may be some disagreement over which goods are basic but, for his own part, he suggests that other goods are valuable as ways of pursuing one or more of the seven basic goods he identifies. Each of the basic goods is equally fundamental; none can be subsumed by any of the others and, in particular, the value of the basic goods cannot be reduced to a single allegedly ultimate value such as 'pleasure'.

These goods are not good in any specifically moral sense; they are simply the essential elements of human flourishing. But when we turn to the question of what (morally) we ought to do, the answer is that we should pursue and participate in these goods. That is the essential feature of conduct which is 'reasonable' and reasonable conduct is right conduct. 'Practicable reasonableness' is one of the basic goods but it is a good which should govern our conduct in general since it is the good of 'being able to bring one's own intelligence to bear effectively (in practical reasoning that issues in action) on the problems of choosing one's actions and life-style and shaping one's own character' (Finnis, 1980, p. 88). Finnis sets out a number of principles of practical reasonableness. For example, we are to pursue a coherent plan of life; we are to give due significance to each of the basic goods and rationally to adjust our pursuit of these to our capacities and circumstances; we must not treat other individuals arbitrarily; and so on (ibid., p. 103ff). Practical reasonableness also requires us to act effectively in bringing about good in the world. However that teleological injunction is not to be confused with consequentialism, a form of moral reasoning which Finnis finds 'irrational' (ibid., p. 112), in part because it wrongly supposes that different goods can be reduced to a single commensurable value.

We must also recognise that community is an essential part of the human condition. 'Sociability' is itself a basic good but, in addition, individuals need to co-ordinate their activities and to co-operate with one another in various ways if they are to achieve the other goods. Community takes various forms – family, friendship, economic association, the state, and so on – but in each case individuals form a community in virtue of a shared objective which may be called their 'common good' and their well-being depends upon the promotion of, and their participation in, that common good. Thus we should favour and foster the common good of the communities to which we belong.

For Finnis, these principles of practical reasonableness are the principles of natural law. They are also the source of natural rights. How so? Finnis answers that question by linking rights to justice and duty. Justice he defines broadly as 'an ensemble of requirements of practical reasonableness that hold because the human person must seek to realize and respect human goods not merely in himself and for his own sake but also in common, in community' (ibid., p. 161). Justice is an 'other-directed' aspect of practical reasonableness and concerns those relations and dealings with others which are matters of duty – matters of what is owed or due to others. Rights are the obverse of duties. Individuals have rights to those benefits which others, as a matter of justice, are duty-bound to accord them.

Like natural laws, these rights are 'natural' in virtue of their reasonableness. They are the principles of practical reasonableness understood in terms of the benefits that are owed to individuals as a matter of justice (ibid., pp. 205, 210). Finnis does not produce a comprehensive list of rights but he seems to think that practical reasonableness endorses the sort of rights that have been commonly asserted within the human rights tradition (ibid., p. 214). He acknowledges that rights which are usually described as 'natural' or 'human' (he treats the two as synonymous) are the more fundamental and general rights, but he argues that even the more particular and concrete rights derived from these might be described as 'natural' in that they stem from the same principles of practical reasonableness. In particular, given the central place that Finnis gives to community, and especially to political community, in achieving the basic goods, he would dissent from the tradition which treats natural rights as 'pre-political'. On the contrary, for the most part they would seem to be rights which are to be held and enjoyed in the context of particular communities. In addition, Finnis does not think of rights as individual claims which are to be set against the common good in the way that we counterposed rights to social utility in Chapter 3. Rather the maintenance of rights should be seen as itself a fundamental component of the common good, although other aspects of the common good properly limit the scope that should be given to each right (ibid., pp. 210–21).

Thus rights in Finnis's account are clearly 'good-based'. The relation between the two is not straightforward; he does not say simply that people have basic rights to basic goods. There would, for example, be obvious objections to saying simply that people have (claim-) rights to friendship. Rather what people have rights to depends upon what others owe them as matters of justice, and that itself must be understood in a context of all of the components of the common good of human beings. But ultimately, if not immediately, rights are justified by reference to basic goods. Finnis rejects Dworkin's claim that treating individuals with equal concern and respect requires those in authority to take no view on what is for individuals' good (Finnis, 1980, pp. 221–3). Certainly individuals are equally entitled to respectful consideration by those in authority, but 'the pursuit of any form of human community in which human rights are protected by the imposition of duties will necessarily involve both selection of some and rejection of other conceptions of the common good' (ibid., p. 223).

The persuasiveness of an argument such as Finnis's, which relies upon a 'thick' theory of the good, clearly depends upon how uncontroversial are its 'basic goods'. That some, such as friendship, are goods can hardly be gainsaid; but others, such as religion, are more open to challenge. Something would also seem to depend upon how closely those goods are knitted into human nature and the human condition. Finnis is keen to disavow any attempt to derive 'values' from 'facts' – a standard (and, according to Finnis, unjustified) criticism of natural law thinking (ibid., pp. 17–19, 33–6). Even so his conception of the basic goods is clearly a conception of 'what is good for human beings with the nature they have' (ibid., p. 34) and a theory of the human good that was wholly unconnected to our natures as human beings would, indeed, be a very strange theory. However this still leaves considerable room for manoeuvre and for the fear that people will have certain alleged 'goods' imposed upon them in the name of their rights.

The nature of this liberal fear is perhaps more clearly illustrated by the justification of human rights proposed by Jack Donnelly (1985). Like Finnis, Donnelly rejects attempts to derive an account of human rights from a scientific or quasi-scientific analysis of human nature. Rather, he argues, a theory of rights must be a theory of man's nature as a *moral* being. It must be a theory not of what man is but of what he should become. Human rights are to be understood as those rights which are instrumental to the attainment of that ideal human condition.

Donnelly describes his approach as 'constructivist' since it argues for human rights not by appealing to a nature that man already has but by appealing to an ideal of the human being and the human condition 'constructed' by the theorist. 'Human nature' is itself to be thought of as a 'project' rather than a 'given'; an ideal human nature will be brought into existence by the provision and maintenance of human rights and a government which sustains human rights will 'radically transform' human nature (Donnelly, 1985, p. 31). Indeed Donnelly has high hopes of the efficacy of human rights since he appears to think that a society which protects and implements those rights will thereby establish not merely some of the necessary, but also all of the sufficient, conditions for creating ideally developed moral beings.

Whatever the merits of this 'constructivist' approach, it is easy to see why liberal theorists of rights should be uneasy about it. It opens the way to the construction of an ideal of the human condition which can then be imposed upon people in the name of their rights. If x is good for A such that A is deemed to have a right to x, B may protest that he is duty-bound to ensure that A receives x even though A himself does not want x and even though A has some completely different conception of what is for his good. The doctrine of human rights could then become a vehicle for the imposition of a highly authoritarian, paternalist and dogmatic ideology. If one subscribes to the choice theory of rights, the very concept of what a right is will limit how far rights can be invoked to justify the imposition of (putative) goods upon people against their will (although theories of the good may still severely constrain what individuals are deemed properly to have a choice over). But if one subscribes to the benefit theory of rights, there is nothing in the concept of a right itself to rule out its use in this highly illiberal fashion. A good-based justification, used in conjunction with the benefit theory of rights, will preserve the right of individuals to control their own lives only in so far as that control is itself reckoned to be a fundamental human good.

Consequentialism and rights

A rather different way of relating rights to goods is provided by consequentialism. Despite the antipathy between consequentialism and some sorts of rights thinking, we should not overlook the possibility that rights may be justified consequentially. In Chapter 3, I explained why many people doubt that utilitarianism can provide a satisfactory home for rights. In spite of those misgivings, utilitarianism may still provide a case for rights. Whether, faced with a particular set of circumstances, it does provide that case will always have to be argued. But, in principle, utilitarianism can make room for rights and utilitarians can argue that rights should be given only as much room as their theory permits.

Utilitarianism is but one type of consequentialism. 'Consequentialism' names a set of moral theories which share no more than a common logical structure. In principle, there can be as many different consequentialisms as there can be different conceptions of the ultimately good state of affairs. Rights are likely to have a greater role in promoting some states of affairs than in promoting others, so that the case for rights is unlikely to be spread evenly across all possible forms of consequentialism. Rights may therefore figure more prominently and more significantly in some forms of consequentialism than in others.

On the other hand, worries about the fate of rights within utilitarianism stem not merely from its adopting 'utility' as the goal to be maximised. They stem rather more from its consequentialist structure. In so far as all consequentialisms share that structure, all of them give rise to the same worries about rights. Given that a consequentialist theory will provide a case for rights only if, and in so far as, they promote the favoured consequence of the theory, can we be sure that the theory will provide a secure case for according people all of the rights that we think they ought to have? Even if it does provide that case, does it provide the right sort of case? Should not people's rights be grounded in something more immediate and less contingent and conditional than their instrumentality in promoting social goals?

Since consequentialism as a general type of moral theory leaves the goal of any specific consequentialism still to be defined, it may seem that these worries can be overcome by constructing the ultimate goal of a consequentialist theory in a way that meets them. Why not build rights, or rights-related concerns, into the very goal of a consequentialist theory? Respect for rights would them form part of the state of affairs that ought to be brought about.[2] But the more we move towards that solution, the more we depart from a consequentialist theory *of rights*, since, although the theory as a whole may retain a consequentialist structure, incorporating rights or rights-related concerns in the goal of the theory must entail valuing them independently of their consequences.

If consequentialism can provide a case, if only a contingent case, for some rights, can it provide a case for *human* rights? The answer depends upon our understanding of what it is that distinguishes some rights as 'human'. If by human rights we mean only rights which, at a particular time, may be justifiably assigned to all human beings, then, at least in principle, a consequentialist morality might argue for such rights. But if we think of human rights as rights *grounded* in individuals' humanity – as rights grounded in something about them as individual persons – consequentialism cannot provide a theory of human rights; for a consequentialist theory does not acknowledge that human beings, just as human beings, are bearers of rights (unless, that is, we reduce the catalogue of human rights to the single and simple right to have one's interests taken equally into account in the promotion of whatever consequence is at issue). Rather, whether human beings should be accorded rights will be entirely contingent upon whether the favoured consequence of the theory will be best promoted by those rights. If it will, they should; if it won't, they shouldn't. Thus, on this conception of human rights, even if a consequentialist theory does argue for universal rights, it does not argue for genuinely human rights.

However it bears repeating that consequentialists can remain unmoved by any of these considerations. They can simply stick to their guns and insist that it is not consequentialism that has to justify itself by demonstrating its ability to sustain some independently favoured set of rights, rather it is rights that have to be shown to promote good consequences; if rights are not vindicated by their consequences, so much the worse for rights.

Monist and pluralist justifications

In this chapter we have seen how rights in general and human rights in particular can be argued for in very different ways. In addition we have seen how different justifications can generate different catalogues of rights. Neither of these findings is particularly remarkable, but both are worth stating since, as was noted at the outset of this chapter, people have often presumed that the idea of human rights is one which must be undergirded by a single uncontroversial theory which must, in turn, yield a similarly incontrovertible set of rights. Thus opponents of human rights sometimes suppose that the very idea of human rights is discredited by the mere fact that there is a plurality of views about their foundation and content. Proponents of rights share some of the blame for this state of affairs since they often pronounce on rights in a manner that brooks no opposition. The truth is that rights in general, and human rights in particular, are no less capable of being given different contents and being argued for in different ways than are ideas of duty or justice or virtue.

Another matter we should consider is the form of justification that we should expect rights to have. As some of the theories we have examined illustrate, philosophers have often sought to encompass rights in a single coherent moral theory so that, ultimately, all rights find their basis in the same single moral foundation. That desire for simplicity and coherence, while understandable, may be misplaced. It may be that different rights have different foundations. If we recognise many sorts of value and if we do not accept that those many sorts of value can be reduced to a single value, it may be that different sorts of right stem from different sorts of value. After all, rights to life, to freedom of expression, to a fair trial and to social security are rights to very different things. If people have rights to all of those very different sorts of things, they may have them for very different sorts of reason. We should not therefore take for granted that an investigation into the foundations of rights must be an attempt to unearth a single and all-encompassing 'grand' theory of rights.

Moreover very often we value what we value for many reasons rather than for just one reason. Thus not only may different rights be grounded in different reasons, it may also be that a single right may find a foundation in several reasons. We should not therefore take for granted that a defence of rights must be monist rather than pluralist in form.

In the chapters that follow I shall examine the reasoning that relates to rights to freedom, to socioeconomic rights and to democratic rights. While these chapters are not predicated on the assumption that rights are sustained by a plurality of justifications, some of what I shall say will certainly lend support to that view. I select those three categories of right for closer scrutiny because they are types of right that have figured prominently in thinking and argument about rights. However I do not intend to suggest that these three categories include all of the rights that there might be. On the contrary, some fundamental and widely accepted human rights, such as the right to life and the rights associated with the administration of justice, fall outside those categories. Although I shall examine socioeconomic rights as they appear in the UN Declaration, I shall say relatively little on the complex subject of private property and its associated rights.[3] Moreover rights do not present themselves to us like so many natural objects the identity of which is fixed and given and waiting for explanation. Rights, as we have seen, are theory-dependent, so that they follow upon our arguments rather than exist independently and in advance of them. There are so many possible candidates for rights and they are so diverse in character that we have to be selective about which of them we subject to scrutiny.

6 Freedom, Autonomy and Rights

Despite the diversity of justifications that can underlie rights and despite the diversity of rights that they can deliver, virtually all theories of rights give an important place to freedom. Sometimes the freedom to which individuals are said to have a right is characterised in a general way as a right to 'freedom' or 'liberty' without further qualification. Sometimes rights to freedom are broken down into a set of more specific freedoms such as freedom of speech, freedom of association and freedom of religion.

Institutionally rights to freedom can be provided for in any of the four forms distinguished by Hohfeld. So rights to liberty need not be provided for only as liberty-rights. Certainly, under any legal system, much of people's legal freedom is likely to consist of the residuum left over after a set of prohibitions has been established: people will be legally 'at liberty' to engage in a range of activities merely in that they are placed under no legal obligation not to engage in those activities. As we noticed in Chapter 1, some of the most cherished freedoms – such as freedom of expression or freedom of worship – are provided for in some legal systems merely as liberty-rights: people are legally free to express their views or to practise a particular form of worship merely in that no law prescribes that they should do otherwise.

However freedom may also be provided for by way of claim-rights: individuals may have legal rights that others should not impede their behaving in certain ways. The duties that correspond to such claim-rights may relate very directly to specific freedoms; for example, a legal system may impose upon people duties to refrain specifically from silencing others or from interfering with their religious activities. Alternatively legal duties may stand in a rather less direct and specific relation to particular freedoms. In English law, for example, many freedoms are 'protected' only by a general legal duty to refrain from assault.

In addition the freedom that people enjoy under a legal system is affected significantly by the powers and the immunities that they are accorded by that system. I am legally free to marry or to divorce only to the extent that I am legally empowered to marry or to divorce. I can be confident of my legal freedom to conduct my life according to my own lights only to the extent that I am immune from others' being legally empowered to impose decisions upon me.[1] It may seem more natural to think of powers and immunities as determining people's 'abilities' rather than their 'freedoms'. If a legal system makes no provision for divorce, I am legally unable rather than unfree (duty-bound not) to divorce. If I remain unenfranchised, I am legally unable rather than unfree (duty-bound not) to vote. However, given that the distribution of powers and immunities in a society significantly determines the control that individuals have over their own lives and over the lives of others, it would be pedantic and misguided to ignore what people are legally 'able' or 'unable' to do in assessing what they are 'free' or 'unfree' to do.

Why has the concern for freedom so often been expressed by way of rights? Before turning to rights to particular freedoms, I want to examine the idea that there is a right to liberty *simpliciter*. The right to liberty, unqualified and unadorned, has figured constantly in declarations of rights; it has also been, and still is, the battle-cry of a multitude of causes. But how are we to understand that right? A limited, but nevertheless very important, way in which it might be interpreted is as the right not to be enslaved. Slavery is the most complete antithesis of freedom and universal rights to freedom must stand opposed to slavery. However a society without slavery can still be a society in which people's liberty is severely limited and, most frequently, the right to liberty has been used to claim more than non-enslavement.

So should we interpret the right to freedom literally? Do people have a right to unlimited freedom? That, as Dworkin has argued (1978, pp. 266–78), makes no sense – at least, not if the right to freedom is understood as a right in the 'strong sense'. Laws limit liberty. The law against murder makes me unfree to murder you and you unfree to murder me. The law against libel renders me unfree to libel you and you unfree to libel me. Yet, ordinarily, we would not think of those laws as violating people's rights. On the contrary, we would be more inclined to think of them as upholding rights.

Thus those who insist that there is right to freedom do not usually mean that there is a right to any and every freedom. Just what combination of freedoms and unfreedoms there ought to be is controversial, but the general point here still stands. Unless we think that people should be free to do absolutely anything – to others as well as to themselves – there cannot be a right to freedom without qualification. Typically, then, assertions of the right to freedom come with an implicit qualifying clause enabling us to 'understand' what that right includes and excludes. The 'right to freedom' is to be understood not as an entitlement to unlimited liberty but as an entitlement to engage in a limited sphere of activities.

The right to personal liberty

The right of individuals to decide and to act as each of them chooses within a circumscribed sphere of life may be described as the right to personal liberty. That right may include rights to grand freedoms, such as freedom of expression, but it will also include rights to decide upon and to do all of those small matters that we think are properly under the control of individuals themselves. It is because quite trivial freedoms, like deciding whether to wear a hat or to do a crossword, fall within this sphere of personal liberty that they can be the subject of rights in spite of their triviality.

The securing of an area of moral space within which individuals are free to pursue their own plans and projects is, for many theorists, the chief point of thinking in terms of rights (for example, Lomasky, 1987). Most commonly that idea is associated with a notion that there are certain matters concerning the life of each individual which are properly the business of no-one but that individual. Individuals should be free to live their own lives as they see fit. To that extent, the concern for an area of personal freedom is self-regarding in focus: on matters which concern their own good, individuals should be free to decide for themselves rather than be compelled to conform to others' conceptions of what is for their good. An emphasis upon personal liberty stands opposed to paternalism, although those who insist upon rights of personal liberty are often reluctant to veto every form of paternalism.

The concern for personal liberty can also be other-regarding in focus: it seeks to limit the extent to which individuals may be interfered with for the good of others. Much of the contemporary dissatisfaction with consequentialism derives from the way in which it threatens to ride roughshod over individual liberty. A philosophy which requires everything to be subordinated to the pursuit of its chosen goal recognises no moral space within which individuals are entitled to shape their own lives. Ascribing rights to individuals is conceived as the most effective antidote to that philosophy. When we accord rights to individuals, we 'ring-fence' areas of life within which they are free to act as they see fit. Thus a right to personal liberty provides a defence not only against paternalism but also against the wholesale subordination of individuals to the purposes of others.

This counterposing of individual liberty to consequentialism is most frequently expressed in terms of what 'others' may or may not do to the individual concerned. 'Others' (including governments) must pursue their purposes in ways which respect those liberties to which individuals have rights. That was how we viewed the juxtaposition of rights and utilitarianism in Chapter 3. However it is also worth noticing how the 'ring-fencing' of an area of freedom affects the moral perspective of the individual right-holder. The moral effect of ascribing rights of personal liberty to individuals is to limit the extent to which the conduct of right-holders is governed by duties. If individuals' every action were subject to a duty (for example, 'always act so as maximally to benefit humanity at large') they would be morally at liberty to act only as that duty required; no moral space would remain within which they would be free to act as they chose. Thus, morally, the assertion that there is an area of freedom within which individuals are entitled to act as they choose entails that, within that area, they are without duties to act in specific ways.

That is not to say that an area of freedom must be conceived as an area of total arbitrariness; there may still be reasons why we should use our freedom in some ways rather than in others. But, assuming that people can have no right to do what they have a duty not to do (and no right not to do what they have a duty to do), the claim that individuals have a right to choose amongst a range of actions cannot co-exist with the claim that they are duty-bound to pursue one specific course of action.[2] Quite how we should regard this feature of the morality of rights is open to argument. At best, it might be viewed as preventing individuals from being smothered and

suffocated by moral totalitarianism; at worst, it might be seen as
licensing an element of callousness in human conduct. I shall have
more to say on this question in Chapter 9.

Why should personal liberty be such a favoured candidate for
rights? Several sorts of answer might be given. As we have seen in
the previous chapter, one of these is the idea of self-ownership. If I
am reckoned to own myself, then I am entitled to dispose of my life
as I see fit. An entitlement to personal liberty is conceived, more or
less literally, as a right of owners to do what they choose with their
property. A good deal of ordinary thinking about personal liberty
seems to take that form. How I live my life is often thought to be
'my' business because it is 'my' life and anyone who interferes with
how I choose to live my life is, in effect, trespassing upon a territory
that he has no right to enter. However amongst political
philosophers – particularly recent political philosophers – the
foundation of the right to personal liberty has been most commonly
located not in self-ownership but in the idea of autonomy.

Autonomy

The word 'autonomy' has its origins in two Greek words: 'autos'
meaning self and 'nomos' meaning rule or law. Thus the
fundamental meaning of autonomy is self-rule; an autonomous
person is one who, in some sense, rules himself, one who determines
the course of his own life. Autonomy is a term that has come to be
applied to states and nations as well as to individuals; an
autonomous state or nation is one that is self-governing as opposed
to one which is subject to external control, such as rule by an
imperial power. And just as rights to autonomy or 'self-
determination' are claimed for individuals, so they are claimed for
nations and peoples. I shall examine the idea of collective rights of
self-determination in Chapter 8. In this chapter I shall focus on
autonomy in relation to individuals.[3]

The notion of autonomy is typically given both external and
internal dimensions. Externally it implies that individuals require
some space in which to shape their lives as they choose. My
autonomy is compromised to the extent that others prevent my
acting according to my wishes by subjecting me to physical
impediments, legal restrictions, or psychological and physical

sanctions. Of course at some point it will be quite right that my autonomy should be compromised by such limits, if only to safeguard the autonomy of others. But the condition of people who have no scope to act upon their own decisions cannot be described as autonomous.

The external conditions relevant to an individual's autonomy are not confined to the presence or absence of constraints deliberately imposed by others. If my options in life are seriously limited by my being constantly in pain or by severe physical disability, my autonomy is correspondingly limited. Again, if I live in grinding poverty and have to devote the whole of my life to scratching a subsistence living, my autonomy must be severely impaired since so many options are closed off from me. Some writers regard those sorts of limitations upon individuals' autonomy as constraining their 'freedom' no less than legal prohibitions deliberately imposed by other people. Others prefer to describe them as limits upon what people are 'able' to do rather than upon what they are 'free' to do. But, whichever language we use, it is plain that, even if physical disabilities and material constraints are not reckoned the 'fault' of others, they have a serious bearing upon an individual's autonomy. That is not the same as saying that individuals have a right that any and every constraint upon their autonomy should be removed. Quite what and how much individuals can demand of one another in the name of their autonomy is not settled merely by determining what can count as a limit upon autonomy and we shall consider that more contentious question later on.

It would be possible to use the term autonomy to describe a purely external condition. Individuals' autonomy would then be wholly a function of the extent to which they were unimpeded in acting on their wishes without reference to the origin of those wishes. However the idea of autonomy usually embraces the notion that individuals are capable of making choices and reaching decisions which are, in some sense, authentically their own. In other words, autonomous persons have some active role in determining the course of their lives. Autonomous beings are capable of making choices and of forming purposes so that they themselves are the originators of what they do. A being which was nothing more than a passive respondent to external stimuli would not ordinarily be described as autonomous even though the movements it was caused to make were entirely unimpeded. To be autonomous is to be in some degree the author of one's actions. Of course this supposition may rest upon an illusion. It may be that persons who apparently make choices are really no more than complicated machines that respond to external stimuli. Even if we embrace the possibility of autonomous conduct, there will be limits to the extent to which we can plausibly claim that individuals' lives are self-created. But without some notion that individuals can control their own lives, the idea of autonomy would be drained of its central meaning. Indeed it is most usually *because* autonomy has this 'internal' dimension that autonomy as an external condition is thought to matter. It is because the decisions that they want to act on and the goals that they want to pursue are, in some significant sense, their *own* decisions and goals that individuals should be allowed scope to live according to their own lights.[4]

Respecting people's autonomy therefore entails respecting their ability to arrive at decisions and to make choices. Their autonomy is compromised not only by external barriers to their acting on their own decisions and choices but also by mechanisms which interfere with their ability to make those decisions and choices. If they are subjected to subliminal advertising or to indoctrination, or fed false or misleading information, their autonomy is undermined. That is why subjecting individuals to brainwashing or to other forms of psychological manipulation should be considered just as much violations of their rights as preventing their marrying the partners of their choice or prohibiting the expression of their political views. The internal dimensions of autonomy are also like its external dimensions in being a possible source of positive as well as negative requirements. Autonomy may be thwarted not only by interventions which corrupt people's ability to think for themselves, but also by the absence of facilities necessary for the development of that ability in the first instance. Thus, if we value autonomy, we may be required not only to refrain from interventions which corrupt an individual's autonomy but also to provide what is essential for the development of that autonomy, most obviously education.

Why should we value autonomy? In dealing with that question, I shall distinguish two approaches to the value of autonomy, both of which treat autonomy as of intrinsic value but which conceive its value rather differently and which accordingly provide different foundations for the rights usually associated with autonomy.

Kantian conceptions of autonomy

The first way of understanding and valuing autonomy has its roots in the thought of the eighteenth century philosopher, Immanuel Kant. Kant held that human beings were unique amongst earthly creatures in being capable of autonomous conduct. The behaviour of non-human animals was governed by nature; they did not will to act but acted according to instinct. By contrast, human beings possessed reason which enabled them to deliberate upon the way they should act and to will to act accordingly. In following their rational will, they acted autonomously, for they acted, not under the sway of an external or natural force, but according to their own conception of what they ought to do; they followed a law which they willed to impose upon themselves.

Of course human conduct might not be guided by reason. It might be prompted by appetite or emotion. In that case it was 'heteronomous' because it was caused by features of people's natural make-up rather than governed by rational reflection. So autonomous conduct was something of which human beings were capable rather than something which was necessarily manifested in everything they did. Nevertheless, amongst the animal creation, only humans were able to act autonomously and that was why only they were capable of moral conduct. Only beings that could originate their own conduct were capable of acting morally, and such beings acted morally in following the dictates of reason. Thus, for Kant, there was no tension between acting autonomously and doing one's duty. However this interlinking of autonomy and morality did not entail that individuals could merely 'choose' which morality to adopt. On the contrary, the morality prescribed by reason was a matter of 'practical necessity'. But because moral agents understood that necessity, they themselves willed to act according to its prescriptions. Thus, in following the moral law, an individual acted autonomously in that he acted according to a law that he had prescribed for himself rather than under the tutelage of an external imposition.

Their capacity for autonomous conduct gave human beings a unique status. A being possessed of a will was not be treated as a mere thing. 'Things' had value only in so far as they served human purposes, but autonomous agents, or 'persons', possessed intrinsic value. Persons were not to be used merely as the instruments of others' purposes. Hence Kant's famous formulation of the categorical imperative: 'Act in such a way that you always treat humanity, whether in your own person or in the person of any other, never simply as a means, but always at the same time as an end' (1948, p. 91). All persons were to be regarded as 'ends in themselves' and each person was therefore to be respected and to be equally respected by all other persons.

It is easy to see how this conception of human beings as autonomous agents or 'persons' might underpin a theory of human rights and, more particularly, a theory of rights to liberty. However the link between Kant's conception of autonomy and rights to freedom is not wholly straightforward. Kant's conception of autonomy was narrow in that he held that individuals acted autonomously only in so far as they followed the dictates of reason, which dictates were the same for everyone. If we think about autonomy in this closely circumscribed way, the freedom to which individuals can be said to have a right in virtue of being autonomous might itself be closely circumscribed. If I am autonomous only when I act rationally and if reason speaks with a single voice, a right grounded in autonomy will be a right to act only as that single voice dictates. The freedom that is deemed to issue from our autonomy might therefore be quite nugatory. Indeed Kantian conceptions of autonomy have sometimes been associated with repressive regimes which are completely at odds with what we would normally think of as rights to freedom (Berlin, 1969).

Liberal theorists have taken a much more generous view of what should be regarded as autonomous conduct. They have widened the concept so that it encompasses people's general ability to make choices, to formulate plans and projects and to be the authors of their own aims and aspirations. As such, autonomy remains a distinctively human capacity and something of crucial moral significance. In thinking about how it is proper to treat human individuals and, more particularly, in thinking about what rights they possess, we must take full account of their nature as autonomous beings. Not to allow people the freedom to develop and to act upon their capacity for autonomous conduct is not to accord them the respect to which they are entitled. It is to treat them as less than persons. It is to ignore what is essential to being human and to being able to live a distinctively human life. On this view, then, individuals' rights to personal freedom are grounded in their very natures as human persons.

Thus while liberal theorists of this stripe take a much less parsimonious view than Kant of what can be considered autonomous conduct, their position remains recognisably Kantian in that the critical determinant of individuals' rights remains their status as autonomous beings. Individuals have rights to certain basic freedoms because their nature as autonomous beings must be respected. Very many liberal theorists – including Rawls, Dworkin and Gewirth – can be located within this tradition, even though they otherwise provide significantly different accounts of the rights that people have.

Autonomy and human well-being

Contrasted with conceptions of autonomy in the Kantian tradition are conceptions which value autonomy as an essential constituent of human well-being. In this approach, the normative significance of autonomy resides, not in its being the central feature of personhood, but in its being an essential element of living well. Attending to an individual's autonomy is less a matter of doing what is right than of promoting what is good.

J. S. Mill may be located within this second tradition. Mill himself used the term 'liberty' rather than 'autonomy', but much of his concern for liberty was of a sort that would be articulated nowadays in the language of autonomy. He placed a high value upon individuals' being able to develop their own distinct identities and modes of life and his *On Liberty* is the most celebrated defence of individual freedom in the English language. At the beginning of that essay, Mill disavowed any claim to rest his case on 'the idea of abstract right' and protested his continuing belief that utility was 'the ultimate appeal on all ethical questions' (1910, p. 74). That, of course, implied that every argument he mobilised in defence of freedom found its ultimate justification in the promotion of utility. Many of the arguments he deployed were indeed of a consequenti-alist nature, particularly his celebrated defence of liberty of thought and discussion. But the strength of Mill's commitment to individual liberty has led many of his interpreters to question his loyalty to utilitarianism. Rather, they have suggested, Mill was, consciously or unconsciously, committed to some non-utilitarian ideal or principle which provided a less contingent and more immediate foundation for individual freedom, though just what that non-utilitarian commitment might have been has itself been much disputed.

Mill possessed a far from simple understanding of of 'utility'. He held that our understanding of utility should be 'grounded on the permanent interests of a man as a progressive being' (1910, p. 74). In an imaginative and highly persuasive reinterpretation of Mill's thought, John Gray (1983) has argued that foremost amongst those permanent interests were security and autonomy. Those Mill regarded as 'vital interests' which should therefore be protected as rights. While his theory remained utilitarian in a broad sense, Mill pursued an 'indirect' route towards his goal since he believed that utility would be best promoted if society were constrained in the pursuit of its other interests by rights safeguarding the security and autonomy of its members. This does not mean that, for Mill, autonomy functioned only as a conduit for the attainment of utility. Being able to make choices about one's life was, for Mill, partly constitutive of, rather than merely a means for attaining, the happy life. What Mill described as the 'higher pleasures' were available only to human beings who had developed a capacity for autonomous thought and action. Human happiness must be understood in relation to the distinctive nature of human beings. Given their capacity for deliberative thought, human well-being could not be understood without reference to that capacity. Moreover autonomy was essential to human happiness, not only in relation to the natures that individuals shared as human beings, but also in relation to those differences that marked them off as individuals. Mill believed that 'each man has a unique range of potentialities, expressible in a relatively small range of possible lives, and that the actualisation of these potentialities is indispensable for any man's greatest well-being' (Gray, 1983, p. 80).

On Gray's reading, therefore Mill's eloquent argument for rights to individual liberty was grounded in part upon an ideal of autonomy. But the normative thrust of that conception of autonomy derived, not from a deontological assertion of the respect that was owed to autonomous agents merely as such, but from a belief in the centrality and indispensability of autonomy to human well-being. Individuals had rights to liberty because those rights were essential to the enjoyment of autonomy, and autonomy itself was to be cherished because it was an essential constituent of happiness – in the fullest and distinctively human sense of that term.

A more recent account of autonomy and its value, which also departs from the Kantian tradition, has come from Joseph Raz (1986). For Raz, what should command our attention is not merely individuals' possession of those abilities that make up the capacity for autonomous conduct but rather the desirability of the autonomous life that those abilities make possible (p. 372). The ideal of personal autonomy is 'the vision of people controlling, to some degree, their own destiny, fashioning it through successive decisions throughout their lives' (p. 369). No life can be wholly self-created but, even so, the ability to choose one's goals and relationships is an important part of individual well-being, particularly in the circumstances of modern developed societies. Personal autonomy is available to individuals only to the extent that they possess the appropriate mental abilities, have an adequate range of options to choose amongst, and are free from coercion and manipulation. But the good of autonomy lies not in the presence of those conditions but in the autonomous life that they promote. Nor does the good of autonomy reside merely in the act of choosing. An evil life is no better, and perhaps rather worse, for being chosen: 'Autonomy is valuable only if exercised in the pursuit of the good' (p. 381). However, for Raz, unlike Kant, this view does not issue in a narrowly constrained conception of autonomy. There is a multiplicity of good forms of life and it is choice amongst those many good forms that makes autonomy both meaningful and valuable.

Raz locates the value of freedom in this ideal of personal autonomy. Freedom, understood both as the absence of coercion and manipulation and as the presence of worthwhile options, has value because it promotes autonomous lives. Consequently rights to freedom also find their ultimate justification in their contribution to that ideal. However Raz does not forge a simple direct link between autonomy and individual rights of a sort that is commonly found in liberal thinking. His liberalism is distinguised by a rejection of 'moral individualism' and an insistence upon the importance of the general structure and culture of a society for the possibility and viability of personal autonomy. An autonomous life can be lived only in a context of shared institutions, values and opportunities. For example, the conditions for autonomy that characterise modern societies include collective goods such as a culture of tolerance, a range of career options and certain forms of marriage. Since these can exist only as collective goods, they cannot be the objects of individual claims of right and, since they are essential for an autonomous mode of life, there cannot be a right to personal autonomy as such. Raz still finds an important place for rights in his vision of a liberal society and he accepts that there are good reasons for giving some of those rights a constitutionally entrenched status. But those liberal rights occupy that important place, not as individualistic moral principles which provide the foundations upon which the whole society is constructed, but as institutional devices which contribute significantly to the arrangements and the public culture of a society designed to sustain and promote the ideal of personal autonomy.

Raz's account and evaluation of autonomy differs markedly from that found in many earlier statements of liberalism, including that of J. S. Mill. Nevertheless I have bracketed Raz with Mill here because both give ultimate moral significance to autonomy as an essential element of the good life rather than as a capacity which confers a special moral status upon individual persons. Both therefore take routes to rights which are different from, and rather less direct than, those followed by liberals in the Kantian tradition.

Neutralism and perfectionism

These two ways of valuing autonomy may seem at no great distance from one another and in some respects they are not. Theories which value autonomy as a constituent of human well-being necessarily presuppose that human beings are capable of autonomous conduct. Likewise theories which value autonomy as the central constituent of personhood do not deny that autonomy is essential to living well. What I have identified as two approaches to the value of autonomy may in some writers appear as different emphases or perspectives, rather than mutually exclusive appraisals of autonomy. Nevertheless there remains a significant difference in these two approaches and one which manifests itself in different conceptions of the role of the state in relation to rights.

Kantian conceptions of autonomy have come to be associated with 'neutralist' liberalism, that is, with a view that the state should remain neutral on the question of the ends to which its citizens should devote their lives (Jones, 1989). Liberals who take that view do not, of course, hold that the state can or should remain neutral on every matter of value. A state cannot remain neutral on the question of what sorts of rules should provide the framework within which individuals are at liberty to pursue their ends. However neutralists attempt to keep the question of what that framework should be separate from the question of the ends to which individuals should devote their lives. They attempt to maintain a distinction between the 'right' and the 'good'. A conception of 'right' provides the framework within which individuals are to pursue their own conceptions of the 'good'. What constitutes the 'right' or 'just' framework is a question on which neutralists differ, but they remain united as neutralists by a shared belief that that framework should not be based upon any particular conception of the good. What conceptions of the good individuals should pursue is a matter which should be left to individuals themselves. To deprive them of the right to decide that matter for themselves would be to deprive them of the respect which they are owed as autonomous agents.

Of course whatever system of rights is established by a society is likely to make the pursuit of some conceptions of the good easier than others. For example, a society which accords equal rights of religious freedom to all of its members will make life more difficult for those who believe they are religiously obligated to compel everyone to conform to their own uniquely true faith than for those whose beliefs impose no such coercive obligations. A society which apportions resources to its citizens more or less equally will make the satisfaction of cheap tastes easier than the satisfaction of expensive tastes. But the different impacts of these rules upon different conceptions of the good would be purely incidental consequences of establishing just arrangements for a society, including granting equal rights to its citizens. They would not stem from judgements that some religions should be discriminated against because they are false or that some tastes should be discouraged because they are bad.

As these examples indicate, the phrase 'conception of the good' is something of a grab-bag with very diverse contents. On the one hand, it contains mundane matters such as what food I eat, what music I listen to and whether I spend my spare time bicycling or playing chess. On the other hand, it contains more exalted matters such as commitments to particular forms of life which stem from religious beliefs or philosophical reflection. But what places all of these things in the same bag is that they are all matters about which individuals should be free to decide for themselves. For the neutralist, a state which seeks to impose or to favour any particular conception of the good, exalted or mundane, violates the rights of its citizens as autonomous agents.

Neutralist liberalism stands in contrast to 'perfectionist' liberalism for which Joseph Raz (1986) is the leading contemporary spokesman. The term 'perfectionist' is potentially misleading. In this context it is used simply to describe theories which incorporate a standard of human excellence. Whereas neutralist theories hold that the state should remain agnostic on the question of the good life, perfectionist political theories stand four-square upon a conception of the good person and the good life. Perfectionist liberalism typically rests upon a conception of the good life as the autonomous life (although there are also other ideals on which a perfectionist liberalism might be based). Thus, whereas neutralist liberals hold that the character of individuals as autonomous agents requires the state to abstain from a commitment to any particular conception of the good, perfectionist liberals hold that the state should commit itself to a particular conception of the good, the good of the autonomous life, and its institutions, laws and policies should seek to promote that good. That may well go along with a notion that, in promoting that good, the state is promoting that to which individuals have rights – although, as Raz argues, many of the essential features of a society which promotes autonomy may be collective goods which cannot be factored into individual rights. But, on the perfectionist view, individuals' rights are geared towards the attainment of a particular good – autonomy – and are both justified and satisfied by the promotion of that specific good rather than by the promotion of no particular good.

Autonomy as an instrumental value

In the theories of autonomy that we have examined so far, autonomy has been accorded an intrinsic value and has provided an ultimate foundation for the rights to liberty associated with it. However autonomy might also be valued instrumentally. If it is valued instrumentally, the ultimate good for which it is valued might still be conceived as a good of the autonomous individual. For example, the good served by an individual's autonomy might be seen as that individual's own happiness (identified separately from his autonomy) or his self-development or his self-realisation. Each of those goods might still serve as a foundation for an individual's rights to liberty, even though the substance and the justification of those rights will then be less immediately related to one another.

Autonomy might also be valued as an instrument for the attainment of goods other than those enjoyed by each autonomous individual. Mill, for example, suggested that one of the benefits of individual liberty was that people were free to engage in 'experiments in living' from which everyone might learn (1910, p. 122). To that extent, the rights associated with autonomy might figure in a goal-based justification of freedom. However, the pre-eminent focus amongst theorists who have stressed the rightness or desirability of a significant sphere of personal freedom has been upon the individuals who bear that freedom. That is, the justification for an individual's having a right to a sphere of personal freedom has been found most frequently in what is right, or what is good, for that individual. Even in Raz's communitarian liberalism, the guiding ideal remains one of *personal* autonomy.

Rights to specific freedoms

As well as asserting or implying a right to a sphere of personal freedom, declarations of rights typically assert rights to specific freedoms such as freedom of expression, freedom of association and freedom of religion. If individuals have rights to personal liberty, it may seem unnecessary to ask why they should have rights to those specific freedoms, since those freedoms may be encompassed by the personal liberty to which each individual has a right. In that case, the justification for rights to specific freedoms will be provided by the justification for the right to personal liberty.

However very often other sorts of concern have underpinned the assertion of rights to specific freedoms, which is why declarations of rights have singled out those freedoms for special mention. Consider the case of freedom of expression. That might be seen as merely one part of the sphere of freedom to which each individual has a right *qua* individual. But that is not the only or even the most obvious reason for upholding it as a right. We might instead focus upon freedom of expression as a prerequisite of democracy. In that case, the right of free expression will find its foundation in the grounds of democracy and democracy, as we shall see in Chapter 8, is something that can be justified in very diverse ways. More generally we might stress the importance of freedom of expression as a mechanism for checking the abuse of political power, whatever form that political power takes.

Alternatively we might, like Mill (1910, ch. 2), argue for freedom of expression as essential for the pursuit of truth. If people are denied the freedom to propagate and dispute opinions, they are deprived of the most effective instrument for sifting truth from error. Even if the beliefs we hold are true, we can be confident of their truth only so long as they can withstand challenge. In addition we should remember that, if opinions are to be censored, that censoring will be done by those who wield political power and there is ample reason to doubt the competence and impartiality of governments as arbiters of truth. In these simple but highly compelling arguments, the emphasis is not upon what is due to each person as an autonomous individual but upon what is essential for a state of affairs in which individuals share a common interest. The right of free expression is located, not in the interest that each has in the propagation of his own views, but in the shared interest each has in the propagation of everyone's views.

Or consider the case of freedom of religion. It is almost inevitable that someone who holds that individuals have a fundamental right to autonomy will hold that that right includes the right to freedom of religion. Given the potentially enormous significance that religious faith can have for the whole character of an individual's life, it is difficult to see how individuals could be reckoned autonomous if they were unable to control the religious, or irreligious, character of their lives. But consider the position of devout Christians or devout Muslims. They cannot believe that, at the level of fundamental principle, individuals have rights to pursue any faith they choose. For the committed Christian all individuals ought to believe in and worship the God of Christianity and all should endeavour to live truly Christian lives; at the most fundamental level, no individual has the right to do otherwise. Similarly the devout Muslim would hold that all individuals should be governed by the Koran and he could not accept that, at the most fundamental level, individuals were entitled to be Buddhists or Hindus or Zoroastrians or atheists.

Does it therefore follow that Christians and Muslims cannot acknowledge a right of religious freedom? It might. History is replete with examples of people who have denied, in practice as well as in theory, that anyone has a right to practice any but the one true faith. Even when ideas of religious toleration began to emerge, those often did not entail any notion that people had a 'right' to indulge in heresy or infidelity. On the contrary, what was being 'tolerated' was beliefs that people had no right to hold and practices in which they had no right to engage. The idea of a 'right' of religious freedom was a relatively late development in the history of humanity.

It is not the case, however, that Christians, Muslims, or the adherents of any other sort of religious faith, can find no justification for a society's according rights of religious freedom to its members. Even if everyone ought to believe in and to practise the one true faith, it does not follow that any human being is divinely authorised to compel those who fail so to do. Indeed, as Locke claimed of Christianity (1968, pp. 59–65) a religion may itself enjoin its adherents to tolerate rather than to persecute those who fall into error. It might also be, as very many advocates of religious liberty have argued, that religious practices are of no value unless they are accompanied by sincere belief and sincere belief is not something that can be achieved through coercion.

More pragmatically, those who possess a religious faith are as capable as anyone of recognising the hazards involved in giving governments authority over matters of religious belief. They can also recognise that allowing each body of believers to follow its own path may be the only practicable basis upon which people of different faiths can live together in spite of their different faiths. The diversity of beliefs present in the world might even induce the faithful to entertain doubts about the unique truth of their own beliefs and the comprehensive error of the beliefs of others. In other words, a certain amount of humility about their own beliefs might induce people to allow that others should be entitled to live according to their own conscientiously held beliefs.

Historically these sorts of considerations have been extremely important in persuading people that individuals should enjoy rights to liberties such as freedom of expression and freedom of religion.

They have been much less conspicuous in more recent political philosophy. In part that stems from the reluctance of many contemporary philosophers to make the possession of rights, particularly rights to liberties, contingent upon claims about their consequences. But the unsatisfactory nature of unqualified consequentialism should not prevent our recognising that some of the strongest arguments for upholding rights to specific freedoms *are* instrumental in character. Present-day political philosophers are also noticeably more reluctant than their predecessors to place much weight upon purely pragmatic considerations, such as the risks involved in granting governments power over matters of belief. Again that has seemed too contingent a foundation for freedom. What if governments were wholly trustworthy? What if politicans were entirely competent, incorruptible and uniquely informed about the truth? But there is no reason why we should be discomfited by these questions. Political philosophy should provide for the world in which we live. It need not pretend to be utterly naive and it will be sadly ineffectual if it can never learn from the experience of mankind.

How much freedom?

So much for reasons people have had for wanting to propound rights to freedom. But what precisely is the freedom to which people have rights? As was said at the outset, there can be no right to unlimited freedom. Even the specific freedoms to which people are said to have rights are not usually unbounded. The right to freedom of expression is not normally understood to include the right to libel, nor is the right to freedom of religion usually thought to encompass the right to practise child sacrifice.

Sometimes the very concept of freedom is moralised, particularly when it is used as a slogan, so that its range is confined to the liberty to which people have a right. People might then be said to have an unqualified right to freedom because the necessary limits are built into the concept of freedom itself. In that case, rightful constraints upon my actions, just because they are rightful, will not be conceived as constraints upon my freedom; but little is achieved by that linguistic move and it is better to confront openly and directly questions of which actions we should or should not be entitled to perform rather than to pretend that answers to those questions are contained within the very idea of freedom.

The precise content of rights to freedom is an immensely complex and contentious matter and, perversely, I shall say relatively little about it. The remarks that follow are intended to indicate what is at issue in establishing the specific content of rights to freedom rather than to settle just what that content is. In examining that issue, MacCallum's simple triadic analysis of statements concerning freedom is of considerable help. MacCallum (1967) points out that the structure of any complete statement about freedom must be of the following form: X is free from Y to do or to be Z. In other words, in describing someone's freedom, we must specify who it is that is free (X), what it is that they are free from (Y), and what it is that they are free to do or to be (Z). Different people may enjoy different freedoms; they may find themselves impeded by one sort of obstacle but not by another; and they may find themselves prevented from performing one sort of action but not another. MacCallum's analysis applies equally to claims about what people are *unfree* to do and to claims about the freedom that they *ought* or *ought not* to enjoy.

If we take the first element of MacCallum's triad, it is perfectly possible that one person may be rightfully free to do what another is not. For example, the owner of a car may permit me to drive it but not you. However rights to the sorts of general freedoms with which we have been concerned in this chapter are typically ascribed to all members of a society or, still more widely, to all humanity. Yet even those rights may not be completely universal. As was pointed out in Chapter 5, the 'human' in human rights is not always unqualified. Who we think is or is not entitled to a particular freedom must be linked to why we think that freedom should be a right. If, for example, we found rights to freedom upon the capacity for autonomous conduct, that provides reason for extending those rights to all who possess that capacity, but not to those, like young children, whose autonomy is undeveloped or to those, like the severely insane, whose autonomy is seriously impaired.

Consider now the third element of MacCallum's triad – what people should have the right to do or not to do, or the right to be or not to be. That is the most complex and controversial component of rights to freedom, but, since the general rights to freedom with which we are concerned here are thought of as possessed by all persons equally, that itself may seem to determine the content of those rights. If freedom is a good, we might suppose that each person should have as much of it as possible, consistent with every other person having the same freedom. Hence we should aim for the greatest possible equal freedom. That is not the same as saying that there should be unlimited liberty, since each person's liberty is limited by each other person's liberty. Rather each person should be deemed to have a right to as much liberty as is consistent with every other person's having a right to the same liberty.

Attractive as that idea might be, it harbours two difficulties. The first is that the principle of maximum equal liberty implies that we can decide what rights people have by engaging in purely quantitative judgements about freedom. But discriminating between the value of different possible combinations of equal freedom involves qualitative judgements. For example, most of us would prefer a state of affairs in which we were equally free to conduct our lives without the threat of being assaulted to a Hobbesian state of nature in which we were equally free to assault one another. But that cannot be explained as merely a preference for more freedom over less. Rather it represents a preference for some types of freedom over others. Optimising freedom therefore requires us to differentiate between the relative values or significances of freedoms rather than merely to calculate the largest quantity of freedom.

The second difficulty is that freedom is not the only good (unless, that is, we so stretch its meaning that 'freedom' comes to include everything that we value). It might therefore come into competition with other goods. For example, freedom to sell or carry weapons might increase risks to personal security; freedom to build without restriction might make for an uglier environment; and freedom to roam the world in a diseased condition might endanger public health. It is not clear that we should allow freedom to override everything else that we value.

In spite of these difficulties, the idea of equal liberty remains a powerful constraint upon the content of people's rights to freedom. It rules out, for example, a society in which some are masters and others slaves, or a society in which the practice of some people's religious beliefs is allowed to take precedence over the practice of other people's religious beliefs. However the two difficulties contained in the idea of 'maximising' equal liberty are pointers to the way we are to go about giving further substance to rights to freedom. Firstly, arguments for freedom do not argue for indiscriminate freedom. Ideas of self-ownership or ideals of autonomy, for example, imply that it is more apposite that we should have the freedom to control our own lives than the freedom to control one another's lives. Those ideas will also lead us to rank some freedoms above others: for example, freedom of religious belief or freedom to choose one's spouse above freedom to decide where to park one's car. Even if we take arguments for specific freedoms, those will often imply a degree of discrimination in the freedom that they justify. For example, arguments for free expression that appeal to the pursuit of truth or the needs of democracy will provide little defence for obscenity. In addition different arguments for the same specific freedom may argue for differences in the detail of that freedom. Obscenity may figure nowhere in the prerequisites of democracy or the search for truth but it may be less easily dismissed in arguments for free expression that plead the case for artistic freedom. We must, then, look to arguments for freedom to indicate not only why there should be freedom but also what sorts of freedom there should be, both in general and in detail.

We must consider more than the value of different sorts of freedom in calculating the scope of rights to freedom. We must also consider how other goods rank in relation to various sorts of freedom. It would be convenient if we could find a single simple formula for making that calculation but, given the diversity of things that we value, no such formula is likely to do the job adequately. Mill's famous harm principle – 'the only purpose for which power can be rightfully exercised over any member of a civilised community, against his will, is to prevent harm to others' (1910, p. 73) – aims to provide us with such a formula, but it suffers from well-known limitations. Mill's principle indicates which actions are eligible for restriction rather than which, all things considered, ought to be restricted; what should be reckoned 'harmful' is often open to dispute; and, arguably, the promotion of benefits as well as the prevention of harms should figure in our calculations. Clearly weighty arguments for freedom are designed to weigh heavily against considerations which compete with freedom, but undifferentiated freedom will not always be the overriding good.

It is because different sorts of arguments for freedom argue for
different quantities and qualities of freedom and because those
must, in turn, interplay with a variety of legitimate concerns other
than freedom that the *precise* scope of individuals' equal rights to
freedom is both complex and controversial. However we should not
make too much of those complications. Doubt and discord are not
spread evenly across all of the freedoms to which people claim
rights. Even when rights are fuzzy at the edges, they can be firm at
the centre. For example, we may be unsure whether, or how far,
people should be free to pry into the private lives of politicians, but
absolutely sure that they should be free to investigate and to
publicise the use that politicians make of their public offices. We
may be unsure whether people should be entitled to (paid or unpaid)
leave from work to attend acts of worship or religious festivals, but
absolutely sure that they should be free to attend religious
ceremonies during their own uncontracted time (Jones, 1994).

Rights and obstacles to freedom

Finally consider how the second element of MacCallum's triad,
concerning what people can be free or unfree from, bears upon
rights. We care not only about what people should be free or unfree
to do. When they are properly rendered unfree, we also care about
how that freedom is removed from them. A goodly portion of rights
thinking has been concerned with that matter. Rights theorists have
commonly insisted that, if human conduct is to be constrained, that
should be done by the rule of law rather than by arbitrary dictat,
that law itself should be administered in a fashion that tries to
ensure that people are treated justly, and that the punishments
which a judicial system imposes should not be of an unnecessarily
cruel or degrading kind.

Thus, even when people have no right to a freedom, we can still
discriminate between acceptable and unacceptable ways of depriving
them of that freedom. But consider now how MacCallum's second
element relates to freedom rather than to unfreedom: if people have
rights to be free, what is it that they are entitled to be free *from*? The
answer to that question is complicated by arguments about what can
count as 'obstacles' to freedom and what, therefore, can count as
'freedom' (Gray, 1991). For example, some theorists hold that only

physical restraints remove freedom. Rather more hold that laws remove freedom, some because they think that being under an obligation of any sort removes freedom, others only because and in so far as law-breakers are threatened with sanctions. Some hold that psychological conditions can limit freedom; others do not. Most hold that people can be said to be unfree only in so far as their actions are constrained by other human beings, but some hold that both human and non-human obstacles should count as obstacles to freedom.

Not all of these arguments about what can count as an obstacle to freedom (and therefore what can count as 'freedom') are closely relevant to arguments about rights. For example, the school of thought that holds that only physical impediments can be said to cause unfreedom holds that laws do not make us unfree because we can act in defiance of laws and that it is nonsensical to hold that someone can be simultaneously unfree to act illegally and yet able to act illegally (for example, Steiner, 1974b; Parent, 1974). However those who take this unusual view of the relation between laws and freedom are unlikely to argue that laws are utterly without significance for human beings and the rights they possess.

That portion of the argument about obstacles to freedom that is perhaps most significant for arguments about rights concerns material resources. Simply stated, the issue is this: should we hold that possessing more or fewer resources is equivalent to possessing more or less freedom? Clearly people's wealth usually has a considerable bearing upon their options in life; does my wealth therefore affect what I am 'free' to do, or merely what I am 'able' to do? If I cannot go to Australia because I cannot afford the air fare, am I unfree, or merely unable, to fly to Australia? How we answer those questions would appear to have a crucial significance for rights. If lack of material resources amounts to lack of freedom, rights to the freedom to do x or y will include rights to the resources necessary for the accomplishing of x or y. If lack of resources is not lack of freedom, rights to freedoms will be much more modest in what they demand.

Presented in this way, it may seem that the question of what people have a right to be free from is to be settled by reference to the semantic issue of what can count as an obstacle to freedom. For example, if poverty should not be described as 'unfreedom', the right to freedom will not include the right not to be impoverished.

Debates about freedom have often been conducted in this way, as though substantive questions about people's rights could be settled by reference to the proprieties of linguistic usage. Linguistically it is, of course, true that a right to freedom can include a right to some particular thing only if that particular thing falls within the range of what we mean by 'freedom'. But that does not legitimate our turning substantive questions into linguistic squabbles.

For one thing, we might allow that economic resources fall outside the realm of freedom, so that resources relate to what people are 'able' rather than 'free' to do, yet still hold that people have rights to resources for the very same reasons that they have rights to freedom. For example, if our commitment to freedom (interpreted narrowly) derives from a commitment to an ideal of personal autonomy, that same ideal may lead us to argue that people are entitled to those resources essential to their leading autonomous lives. Conversely we may take a more generous view of freedom and include within its meaning the opportunities opened up by the possession of resources, yet deny that people therefore have rights to those resources. For example, we may hold it reasonable that others should have the negative obligation of not placing obstacles in the way of my flying to Australia – such as not withholding my passport or not making it illegal for me to visit Australia – but unreasonable that they should have a positive obligation to stump up my air fare. That would be to say (quite intelligibly) that my right to fly to Australia included a right to be free from some obstacles but not free from others.

Just as people sometimes confine 'freedom' to what they believe individuals are rightfully free to do, so they are often inclined to use the term 'freedom' to describe only what they believe people are rightfully free *from*. If you believe that others are morally responsible for my lack of economic resources, you are more likely to describe that constraint as a limit upon my 'freedom' than if you believe that no-one (except perhaps I myself) can be held responsible for the imposition or non-removal of that constraint (Miller, 1983; Jones, 1982). But then it is our moral thought that guides our usage and not usage that determines our moral thought.

Thus, although economic resources have a tremendous impact upon our options, we cannot hope to settle whether people have rights to resources merely by reference to the idea of freedom. Providing an answer to that question would require us to go deeper and wider and to address the whole range of issues that bear upon the ownership and distribution of resources. In the next chapter I shall examine just one of those issues: whether human beings have rights because they have needs. However, in shifting our focus from the idea of freedom to the idea of needs, we should not lose sight of the fact that the concerns of this chapter may relate closely to those of the next (cf. Sen, 1985).

7 Socioeconomic Rights

The final clauses of the UN's Declaration of Human Rights list several rights which are usually categorised as 'socioeconomic'. Those rights are further elaborated and provided for in the UN's International Covenant on Economic, Social and Cultural Rights. They include rights to social security, including security in the event of unemployment, sickness, disability, widowhood or old age, rights to food, housing and clothing, rights to medical care and rights to education of various sorts. They also include rights to work, to just and favourable conditions of employment, to protection against unemployment, to just and favourable remuneration, and to rest and leisure, including periodic holidays with pay. Everyone is also said to have the right 'freely to participate in the cultural life of the community, to enjoy the arts and to share in scientific advancement and its benefits'.

These are sometimes described as the 'new' human rights, since their inclusion in statements of human rights, though not without precedent, is historically recent. Their presence in the UN Declaration reflects shifts in thinking during this century about the proper role of the state and the responsibility it should assume for the well-being of its citizens. In particular, many of them are associated with the 'welfare state'. In examining the arguments that surround socioeconomic rights, I shall focus particularly upon the notion of 'welfare rights' since, if there are human rights to socioeconomic goods, welfare rights seem the strongest candidates.

The representation of welfare rights as human rights has proved controversial. Many who are sympathetic to the idea of welfare rights regard them not as human rights but as citizens' rights: individuals hold those rights only as members of particular societies and, as the circumstances of those societies vary, so, inevitably and legitimately, will the content of welfare rights. The very formulation of the UN's socioeconomic rights has led some to question their universality; they seem skewed towards the circumstances of individuals living in western industrialised societies rather than to the condition of mankind at large (Milne, 1986, pp. 2–3). Moreover, when set against the economic realities of the contemporary world,

146

the generous way in which some of those rights are formulated has provoked complaints that the drafters of the Declaration failed to recognise the difference between fundamental human rights and desirable but distant objectives.

If we shift our focus to the idea of 'rights' (of whatever sort) to welfare goods, that idea has also failed to find a consensus. Nor does the current dissensus map neatly onto a right–left political spectrum. Libertarians challenge the legitimacy of the welfare state and some do so on the very ground that state welfare measures violate individuals' rights. Socialists, on the whole, are more sympathetic to welfare rights, but some deride the welfare state as no more than an emollient designed to make capitalism more acceptable, while others shun talk of rights as unacceptably individualist. Even liberals and social democrats have sometimes doubted whether rights provide the appropriate moral apparatus for dealing with questions of distributive justice.

Why, in spite of these various misgivings, have so many people wanted to associate welfare goods with rights? There are at least three reasons. One is that welfare goods are generally regarded as absolutely fundamental to the quality of people's lives. Indeed, up to a certain point, they are essential for human survival. If fundamental rights are geared to what is fundamentally important for human well-being, we cannot exclude material resources from their domain. More particularly it is often remarked that, without a minimum of material well-being, civil and political rights are of little relevance or value for human beings. The concept most frequently used to express the special significance of socioeconomic goods is 'need' and I shall spend much of this chapter considering whether need can provide a foundation for rights.

A second reason for the invocation of rights has to do with the nature of each society's obligation to provide for the welfare of its members. Welfare goods will usually benefit their recipients but that need not be why they are provided. Education is often justified as investment in human capital, social security may be conceived as a way of sustaining consumer demand, and health care may be provided to secure an efficiently functioning workforce. Asserting rights to welfare goods is a way of insisting that governments or societies are obligated to provide those goods for the well-being of their individual members. It is to insist that welfare policy should be driven by more than the pursuit of general social goals whose attainment incidentally may or may not benefit individuals and minorities.

Thirdly, welfare provision, particularly in western societies, has often been associated with ideas of charity and with a consequent stigmatising of welfare recipients. Convincing people that there are rights to welfare may be a way of overcoming that stigma. If people think of themselves as entitled to welfare goods, rather than as supplicants in receipt of other people's charity, that may help to dispel the sense that there is something demeaning about being a welfare recipient (Jones, 1980).

All three of these reasons imply that welfare rights must be conceived as more than merely legal rights. If we appeal to the idea of welfare rights in order to establish the proper content and motivation of government policy, those rights cannot themselves be mere creatures of government. If welfare rights are to eradicate stigma and to persuade people that they have just entitlements, they must be more than legal rights, otherwise welfare provision may be regarded as no more than legally enforced charity.

The material goods that enable human beings to satisfy their wants are diverse in character and indefinite in quantity. So how can people be said to have rights to specific types and specific amounts of those goods? As I have already indicated, the driving force behind the socioeconomic rights listed in the UN Declaration, and behind the general idea of welfare rights, is the notion that human beings have needs. People may crave all sorts of things, but there are some things which they need and, because the satisfaction of those needs is crucial to their well-being, they may be said to have rights to what they need. Our first task, then, is to consider whether needs do indeed give rise to rights.

Needs and rights

Needs are commonly contrasted with wants and two of those contrasts are particularly significant for the relation between needs and rights. The first is that needs have an objective quality that wants do not. It is hard to see how we could discover what a person wants without either asking her or inferring her wants from her behaviour. By contrast, we can identify at least some of what a person needs without consulting the person who has those needs.

For example, we know that all human beings need food, water and air. A doctor may know what course of treatment a patient needs even though the patient herself remains ignorant of those needs. Thus needs, unlike wants, seem to constitute objectively identifiable ingredients of human well-being of a sort appropriate for a theory of rights. In addition, whereas wants seem irreducibly subjective and various, the objectivity of needs holds out the prospect of there being needs which are universal to human beings and which can therefore provide a foundation for universal rights.

The second feature of needs that is particularly relevant for rights is that claims of need seem to have greater normative force than expressions of desire. If I say 'I need x' that statement carries a greater note of urgency than if I say 'I want x'; there seems more reason for my having x if I need it than if I merely want it. Thus needs would seem to have a priority over wants, a priority of the sort that we would ordinarily associate with rights. Of course needs and wants do not have mutually exclusive territories. Someone may want what she needs or need what she wants. Moreover, in so far as the satisfaction of needs is crucial to a person's well-being, her needs may coincide with her 'strongest' wants. Nevertheless neither notion can be subsumed by the other: needing is not the same as wanting and wanting is not the same as needing.

Needs relate more closely to interests than to wants. The distinction between interests and wants in some ways parallels that between needs and wants. Just as people may not want what they need or need what they want, so their wants may not coincide with what is actually in their interest (unless, that is, we claim that what a person 'really wants' is what is really for her good rather than what she herself experiences as wants). One reason for this parallel is that, ordinarily, people have an interest in having what they need. But, once again, the domain of needs is not identical with that of interests. Even if I have an interest in receiving all that I need, we would not ordinarily say that I need all that I have an interest in receiving. If I have an interest in what I need, that would seem to indicate an interest of a special sort – the sort of interest that we would regard as a 'vital' or a 'fundamental' interest.

Thus a need appears to be something crucial to a person's well-being, something of a different order from her wants or her preferences and something in which she has not merely an interest but a vital interest. Can we therefore say simply that people have a *right* to what they need? There are a number of reasons why we cannot. The most significant of these is that 'need' is a less discriminating notion than its use in political argument would suggest. Several writers have argued that claims of need are, on their own, incomplete (for example, Minogue, 1963, pp. 103–12; Barry, 1965, pp. 47–9; White, 1975, pp. 105–7). If I claim, 'I need x', you can ask, 'what for?', and my claim remains incomplete until I have specified the end for which I need x. Thus a full need statement must be of the form 'A needs x for y'.

This analysis has two significances. Firstly, the statement that A needs x can be fully intelligible only by reference to some y, the purpose, for which x is needed. For example, if I assert my need for a specific sum of money, that will remain puzzling until I add an explanation, such as 'to buy a car'. Sometimes the purpose for which something is needed will be sufficiently obvious not to require articulation. For example, if I say 'I need a new car battery', it is hardly necessary for me to add 'to make my car function' (although even car batteries can be used for other purposes). But, even when we can take a purpose for granted, the logical form of the need statement remains A needs x for y. The second significance concerns justification. If needs are merely the instruments of purposes, the justification for satisfying a need will turn, not upon its being a need, but upon the purpose for which it is a need. Thus, if A needs x for y, our assessment of whether A should receive x will depend, not upon our estimate of x alone, but upon our estimate of x in relation to y. For example, our response to A's claim that he needs a baseball bat is likely to differ according to whether he adds 'to play baseball' or 'to beat you over the head'.

Thus, so far from needs forming the foundation of rights, it may seem that they are not independently capable of justifying anything at all. The moral force of claims of need may seem entirely dependent upon, and subordinate to, the moral status of the ends to which they are directed. In addition, given their instrumental character, claims of need would seem ubiquitous and indiscriminate. Some needs may be serious and pressing but others can be quite trivial (for example, 'I need a new coat to look my best', 'I need a cup of coffee to wake me up'). This feature of need threatens to remove all practical significance from the distinction between wants and needs. Wants and needs may remain distinct concepts but, if my needs can be merely for whatever will enable me to satisfy my wants, those needs can have no moral or political significance other than, or greater than, my wants. (The instrumental analysis of needs does not, of course, have to regard want satisfaction as the only end for which something may be needed.) That is another reason why needs may begin to look unpromising as foundations for rights.

However all of this may seem to dismiss needs too readily. Is the notion of need really so trivial? Can all of those who have invoked needs in political argument, often with great passion, have been guilty of so elementary an error? Does nothing but misunderstanding explain the sense of moral urgency that typically accompanies our talk of needs? If we are to sustain the common belief that there is something special about needs claims, it would seem that we can do so only by identifying a class of needs which are in some way different from run-of-the-mill instrumental needs. That is, we must find some way of identifying a set of needs which are 'basic' or 'fundamental' and which therefore enjoy a status different from that of more incidental needs. Philosophers who have undertaken this task have generally adopted one of two strategies.

The first retains the notion that needs are instrumental but seeks to identify a set of needs that are general to human beings whatever the ends they wish to pursue. Rawls's (1971) primary goods may be understood as providing for basic needs in this sense. Primary goods are goods which it is rational to want, whatever else one wants, because they are essential instruments for the pursuit of one's ends, whatever those ends happen to be.[1] In that way, goods such as basic freedoms and opportunities, income and wealth, can be conceived as providing for fundamental needs. On some occasions Rawls himself identifies primary goods with needs (1982, pp. 172–3; 1993, pp. 178–90; cf. Goodin, 1985, pp. 621–5). Others have added more specific goods, such as health care and education, to his list of goods which minister to generalised needs (for example, Weale, 1978, pp. 45–69). Gewirth's insistence that autonomy and well-being are fundamental to the attainment of any human purpose might also be interpreted as a conception of basic human needs (cf. Plant, 1991, pp. 203–13).

The merit of conceiving basic needs as 'universal means' is that it enables a set of needs to be identified which are common to everyone because they are essential instruments for pursuit of any purpose. Those needs are not therefore contingent upon the particular wants of particular individuals. But, in the present context, the main failing of this approach is that it is insufficiently discriminating to enable us to identify needs with rights. For example, if *all* income and wealth falls within the category of fundamental need (understood as universal means), an appeal to need can do nothing to prioritise claims to income and wealth. 'Need', so understood, can contribute nothing to the determination of who ought to have what. Rather we have to resort to quite separate notions, such as equality of resource holdings or equality of welfare levels or Rawls's difference principle or maximum average utility, to determine whose claims of fundamental need should be satisfied and in what measure.

The second way in which fundamental humans needs may be identified is by focusing upon what human beings must have if they are to function properly as human beings (for example, Wiggins, 1985; Griffin, 1986, pp. 40–55; Thomson, 1987; Doyal and Gough, 1991). In this sense, human beings need air and a certain minimum of food and water. If these basic needs remain unsatisfied, they will be debilitated and eventually die. Interpreted in this way, basic needs do not have to be confined to what is necessary for mere survival. For example, physical and mental health and a measure of autonomy might also be identified as essential to living a characteristically human life (Doyal and Gough, 1991, pp. 49–75). Understood in this way, the notion of 'basic need' retains an element of instrumentality – having what we need to function adequately as human beings is a prerequisite for our being able to pursue whatever purposes we have. But instrumentality is not central to this understanding of basic need. The touchstone here is a notion of human flourishing or well-being and well-being is not a 'goal' to be pursued by way of air, food and water; rather it is a condition constituted, at least in part, by having sufficient air, food and water and whatever else is deemed a basic human need.

Ordinarily this conception of basic need relies upon the notion that human beings have a given nature, the maintenance and development of which indicates what are basic human needs. Those needs are also typically identified by a negative test: if the basic needs of human beings are not satisfied, they will 'ail' or be harmed. However, within this approach, basic needs can be defined more or less generously depending upon the generosity with which human well-being is itself characterised: the larger our conception of human well-being, the broader will be our conception of basic needs. In addition, the more we move away from a solid core of need tied to human survival to a more generous conception of basic need tied to a larger and potentially more disputable conception of human well-being, the more controversial 'basic needs' will become. For example, 'spiritual needs' or 'needs of the soul' (Weil, 1987, pp. 3–38) can be presented quite plausibly as basic needs but the precise content of those needs is clearly more controversial than is the content of elementary physical needs.

This conception of basic need offers a more promising template for rights. It is more discriminating than an interpretation of basic needs as primary goods or 'universal means' and it focuses upon needs of especial urgency. As I have indicated, the content of basic needs, so understood, may be controversial but there is no reason why we should suppose that the content of rights must be uncontroversial. However there remain reasons why the transition from even these sorts of basic needs to rights will not be wholly straightforward.

One problem lies in the relative indeterminacy of basic needs (Griffin, 1986, pp. 43–5). Although the non-instrumental notion of basic need aims to be less open-ended than the notion of primary goods, it still leaves us with the question, how basic is 'basic'? If shelter is a basic need, just how good does housing have to be before it satisfies that need? If education is a basic need, what quantity and quality of education does that need encompass? This indeterminacy does not mean that the notion of 'basic need' is entirely without value but it does mean that any set of rights founded upon basic needs will be infected with a similar indeterminacy. This is a serious limitation, since the crucial question that arises in relation to rights to goods such as education, housing and health care is 'a right to how much?' Without some way of fastening upon an answer to that question, assertions of rights to these goods will be little more than rhetoric.

In addition we are likely to discover that the limits of basic needs do not coincide with the limits of rights. There are two elements to this disjunction. Firstly, the basic needs of human beings as such may fall short of the minimum quantity and quality of goods to which all individuals are said to have rights, particularly in developed societies. For instance, when individuals are said to have a right to 'an adequate standard of living', that standard may well be set above the minimum that human beings require merely to function as human beings. Secondly, and conversely, basic needs may exceed what can reasonably be claimed as a right. It is commonly remarked that the potential demands of health care and medical research have become so great that societies could devote almost all of their resources to those purposes. If we identify physical and mental health as basic needs, all of that expenditure could be said to be devoted to the meeting of those basic needs. Yet, given the other purposes for which a society may reasonably use its resources, it would be unreasonable to hold that individuals' rights require that so large a proportion of a society's resources should be devoted exclusively to medicine. In addition, people can have needs which it is impossible rather than merely unreasonable to satisfy. Someone who has a virulent disease may intelligibly be said to have a need, and a basic need at that, for a cure, even though no cure is currently available. But it would be nonsense to claim a right to a good which does not exist or which cannot possibly be supplied. In these cases, then, rights fall short of, rather than exceed, the bounds of need.

These remarks are not intended to be wholly dismissive of the notion that needs can provide a foundation for rights. Some recent work on the notion of need has done much to rehabilitate what was beginning to look like a very damaged concept (for example, Thomson, 1987; Doyal and Gough, 1991). For all its limitations, the notion of basic need may be quite plausibly invoked in arguments about what ought to be considered a right. However these reservations do suggest that we may not be able to use basic needs in any simple way to 'fix' what people have a right to; the minimum level of resources to which people are said to have a right in a given society at a given time may owe more to an idea of a minimum quality of life that everyone ought to enjoy in those given circumstances than to a fixed set of human needs.

One feature of the modern world which indicates this is the phenomenon of the 'rising minimum'. Because people's expectations have risen along with rising standards of living, the notion of need is itself sometimes said to be wholly relative to a given standard of living (for example, Benn and Peters, 1959, pp. 144–6). Many needs theorists reject that sort of relativising of the notion of need. Certainly needs may change in character and even become more demanding of resources, without that necessarily signalling a shift in our underlying notion of basic need. For example, to live I need to eat; to eat I need money and to gain money I need to work; to work in a developed society, I may need a car; but, in this case, the shift to needing a car is simply a shift in a 'derivative' need which ultimately connects back to a constant and universal human need – the need to eat (Thomson, 1987, p. 101). Changes in needs may therefore be circumstantial rather than fundamental. Even so, if the minimum standard of living to which all members of a society have a right is reckoned to rise as the wealth of the society grows, the content of that right cannot coincide with a conception of 'absolute' human need.

Before moving on from the subject of needs and rights, it is worth noting two other ways in which rights may fall short of needs. First, we may hesitate to translate some needs into rights, not because those needs are not basic or because they cannot be met, but because we are reluctant to impose upon people the duties that meeting those needs would entail. However, before examining that reason for not translating needs into rights, a note of caution must be sounded about whether we should always think of needs-based rights as primarily 'duty-imposing'.

Rights stemming from needs are often represented as consisting essentially of demands upon others, as though their primary moral effect were to impose positive duties upon others. That emphasis on the duty-imposing character of needs can be misleading. In so far as needs are used to determine the rightful distribution of resources amongst a population, they are not a matter of some 'giving' to others or some acquiring duties to perform tasks for others. Rather they simply determine, partly if not wholly, the proper distribution of resources amongst a group of people. Needs-based rights can therefore be rights to and over a set of resources rather than rights 'against' others. Of course, where there has been an initial allocation of resources without reference to needs – for example, via market processes – distributing according to need will ordinarily involve *re*distributing resources. That redistribution will then have the appearance of some 'donating' to others. But the institutional structures used to achieve a distribution according to need should not be mistaken for the moral structure of claims of need themselves. In so far as people have a right to a set of resources which are essential for meeting their needs, needs-based redistribution should be seen as a means by which people are allocated the resources to which they are entitled and not as a process in which some perform duties of (legally coerced) giving out of deference to the needs of others.

With that qualification stated, we can now concede that sometimes meeting needs will entail imposing duties upon others. Where that is so, we can ask whether it is acceptable that others should have to bear those duties. For example, people are often said, quite plausibly, to need love and affection. Let us set aside the special case of parents and children. Even adults can be said to need love and affection. Do they therefore have a right to love and affection? If we are reluctant to answer 'yes', that may stem, in part, from our doubts about whether it is possible to deliver love and affection on demand. Genuine love and affection must be genuinely felt and we may doubt whether it is possible to drum up those feelings as a matter of duty. But, even if we overlook those doubts, we may still be reluctant to concede a right to love and affection because that right would demand from others more than it is reasonable to require of them. However great the need for love and affection and however desirable it is that it should be satisfied, we may still be unwilling to sanction the intrusion into people's lives that a right to its satisfaction would entail. We may feel that same reluctance even in relation to more modest needs such as the need for friendship. In particular, giving significant value to individual autonomy will entail setting limits upon the extent to which one person can be made the servant of another's needs.

A second and rather different consideration which might affect our moral response to people in need is the reason for their being in need. Suppose that people's life-chances have been scrupulously equalised but that, even so, some individuals have ended up in a state of penury because they have squandered their resources in a self-indulgent and dissolute life-style. Do those reckless individuals then have a right that their self-induced condition of need should be relieved by their more provident fellows? This question indicates that the transition from needs to rights might depend not only upon the urgency of the needs at issue but also upon how those needs came about. We are likely to feel more generously towards those whose needs are a consequence of natural misfortune or of social forces beyond their control than towards those whose needs are a consequence of their own folly. Even if we are unhappy about leaving people to suffer the full consequences of their irresponsible actions, we may still bridle at the suggestion that the wilfully profligate have a *right* that the consequences of their irresponsible actions should be borne by others.

Human needs and human rights

The relationship between needs and rights is therefore a complicated one, but we should not allow those complications to obscure the fundamental truth that a certain quantum of material and non-material goods is essential to human well-being. In so far as thinking about rights is stimulated by a concern for what is crucial to the well-being of human individuals, a certain minimum of socioeconomic goods remains a strong candidate for rights.

But should we think of those rights as *human* rights? Not everyone is satisfied that the socioeconomic rights listed in the latter part of the UN Declaration are properly included in a declaration of 'human' rights. The best known critique of the idea of socioeconomic human rights is that of Maurice Cranston (1967a, 1967b, 1973). Cranston proposes three tests that an alleged right has to pass before it can qualify as a genuine human right. His claim is that the traditional civil and political rights, such as the rights to life, to liberty and to a fair trial, pass these tests, while the newly claimed socioeconomic rights do not. The first test that Cranston proposes is 'practicability'. Rights entail duties but people can have duties to do only what it is possible for them to do. Given the economic conditions that prevail in many countries in Asia, Africa and South America, it is impossible for their governments to provide all of their inhabitants with goods such as 'a standard of living adequate for their health and well-being' and therefore idle to assert that all of those inhabitants have a right to that standard of living. Thus socioeconomic rights fail this first test. By contrast, traditional civil rights, such as rights to freedom of speech or freedom of association, require little more than restraint from governments and are therefore 'practicable' in all societies.

Cranston's second test is 'universality'. A right must be genuinely universal if it is to qualify as a human right. However Cranston requires that human rights be universal in two different ways. Firstly, a genuinely human right has to be a right *of* all. But, Cranston argues, a right such as the right to periodic holidays with pay is a right claimed on behalf of some rather than all human beings – a right claimed only for those individuals who are employees. Secondly, he holds that a truly universal right is one which imposes a universal duty so that a genuinely human right has to be a right *against* all. A traditional civil right, such as freedom of expression, which demands only non-interference can intelligibly be asserted against the world at large. It can be said to impose a universal duty. But socioeconomic rights are asserted as claims upon particular governments or particular societies rather than the world at large. Hence, if they are rights, they must be 'local' rights that individuals hold only as citizens of particular states rather than universal rights which they hold as members of the human race.

Cranston's third test is 'paramount importance'. Again he reckons that the traditional civil rights represent fundamental demands of justice, whereas desirable facilities such as holidays with pay are of a different moral order. Unlike some critics of the UN Declaration, Cranston does not wholly reject the aspirations of those who assert socioeconomic rights. These may certainly represent desirable objectives and, even if they are not human rights, the citizens of some societies may defensibly claim them as moral rights of another sort. But, for mankind as a whole, they constitute ideals to be striven for rather than entitlements that can be demanded here and now. Cranston's claim is that those who drafted the UN Declaration confused rights and ideals and his worry is that this confusion might imperil the status of genuine human rights. If some alleged rights are really ideals which are desirable but distant objectives rather than entitlements which must be honoured here and now, genuine human rights may also come to be treated as distant ideals and so be pushed 'out of the clear realm of the morally compelling into the twilight world of utopian aspiration' (Cranston, 1967a, p. 52).

If we accept Cranston's three tests, that which is urged least convincingly against the idea of socioeconomic human rights is the test of 'paramount importance'. The material essentials of life seem plausible candidates for rights just because they are of 'paramount importance'. Indeed, given the circumstances in which much of the world's population lives, access to those material essentials will often be of much greater importance than civil rights such as freedom of expression or freedom of movement. The test of paramount importance therefore does nothing to discredit the status of the 'new' human rights as rights. However Cranston's other tests – practicability and universality – pose greater difficulties for the idea of socioeconomic human rights.

Something can be, and has been, said in reply to Cranston on these two scores (Raphael, 1967b, 1967c; Watson, 1977; Plant *et al.*,

1980, pp. 73–82; Donnelly, 1985, pp. 90–6; Gewirth, 1982, pp. 64–6). To claim that a right such as a right to social security is not a universal right (a right *of* all) because not everyone will need to resort to a welfare facility such as social security is rather like claiming that the right to a fair trial is not a universal right because it will be operative only for those who find themselves accused of a crime. Everyone can be said to enjoy a right even though the right is one that they will need to take advantage of only in certain circumstances. In addition there are some socioeconomic rights, such as the right to education or the right to health care, which, logically, are obviously assertable on behalf of all human beings.

Cranston also requires that human rights be rights claimed *against* all whereas, for any particular individual, a socioeconomic right is normally claimed against a particular government or a particular community rather than against the world at large. Socioeconomic rights are rights *in personam* rather than rights *in rem*. But this may be said equally of some traditional civil rights. The right to personal security, for example, is a right that an individual normally holds against his or her government rather than against all human beings indifferently.[2]

We might also question whether Cranston is right to hold that a universal right has to entail a universal duty. For example, all children might be said to have the right to be cared for such that that right to care is universal to all children even though, for any particular child, the corresponding duty of care falls upon his or her parents or guardian. Similarly the right to education or to health care might be asserted on behalf of all human beings even though, for any particular right-holder, the duty to provide those goods falls upon his or her government or society. Alternatively, we might allow that universal rights do entail universal duties but still hold that the particularity of socioeconomic duties in the contemporary world can be reconciled with the universality of socioeconomic human rights. Even if universal rights give rise to universal duties, those universal duties might be more conveniently and more effectively performed if humanity is divided up into groups, with each group being assigned responsibility for honouring the rights of its own members (Goodin, 1988). Thus the world of states might be conceived as one in which the universal duties of mankind have been transformed into a number of special duties of states so that those duties can be discharged more effectively. At the level of ultimate principle, the duties which we owe our compatriots are neither more nor less than those we owe foreigners but, at a subordinate and practical level, there is reason to accept that individuals owe special duties to their fellow-citizens as part of a division of universal moral labour.

As for the test of practicability, it cannot be denied that not all societies have the wherewithal to satisfy fully all of the socio-economic rights listed in the UN Declaration, but, we might still say, like Raphael (1967b, pp. 63–4), that each government has a duty to meet them in so far as it can. Moreover some civil rights, such as the right to personal security, are similarly dependent upon resources, so that the honouring of some civil rights might also be more practicable in some societies than in others.

Although there is force in each of these replies to Cranston, the central point remains that whether and how far a society can provide economic goods for its members depends upon the resources available to that society. A rich nation can provide more and better welfare rights for its citizens than can a poor nation. If people living in the United States or Sweden are deemed to have more and better welfare rights than people living in India or Mali, it is hard to see how all of those welfare rights can be considered human rights. Of course, one might respond to this by holding that each individual has a human right only to so much welfare as can be provided by each and every state in the modern world. Anything beyond that lowest common denominator exceeds what people are owed as a matter of right or, at least, what they are owed as a matter of human right. However the proponents of socioeconomic human rights are unlikely to find acceptable such an impoverished conception of human welfare rights.

Alternatively one might respond to Cranston's complaints by objecting that national boundaries are morally irrelevant and that all individuals should be entitled to draw equally upon the world's resources to satisfy those socioeconomic rights. However the fact is that the world remains one of independent states, each with rights over its own territory, and it was in those terms that the UN Declaration was conceived. Article 22 of the Declaration, for example, asserts that everyone has 'the economic, social and cultural rights indispensable for his dignity and the free development of his personality' but adds that the realisation of those rights is to be 'in accordance with the organization and resources of each State'.[3]

Thus it would seem that Cranston's central point – that the socioeconomic rights included in the UN Declaration are, at best, rights that people have as citizens of particular societies rather than as human beings – is hard to gainsay.

However, before accepting that conclusion, we must consider whether the general idea of human welfare rights might be reconciled with differences in the quantities and qualities of welfare goods available in different societies. Might there be good reasons why the same human welfare rights need to be provided for in different ways in different societies?[4] One such reason is that human beings live in different natural and cultural circumstances. People living in different climatic conditions require different sorts of shelter and housing. Different diseases prevail in different parts of the world and make for different medical priorities. Education has to be adapted to the different cultures of different societies. Thus universal rights can quite properly find expression in different forms of provision in different parts of the world. However this does not take us very far in accounting for the variations in welfare provision that characterise the current world, for most of those variations are matters not merely of some receiving different from others but rather of some receiving more and better than others.

A second and more persuasive consideration is this. The nature of individuals' needs cannot be divorced from the society in which they live (Weale, 1983, pp. 35–8, 76–91). People conduct their lives in significantly different social contexts and what they need in order to achieve a given level of well-being cannot be divorced from the context in which they live. Thus 'minimum needs are not simply satisfied by providing the physical necessities of life, for example adequate food, clothing and shelter, but require also for their satisfaction a level of provision for persons that is suitable for social agents, interacting with others in a specific society' (Weale, 1983, p. 35). Recognition that needs are 'socially relative' in this way is potentially of much greater significance than recognising that individuals' needs are relative to their natural and cultural environments, for, if needs are 'socially relative', there is much greater scope for allowing that some people simply need *more* than others, that the same needs can demand a different quantitative as well as a different qualitative response. Thus it might be argued that, if an individual is to function as a member of a society like the USA or Germany, he needs a higher minimum income than he would require if he were a citizen of Kenya or the Philippines. Likewise people living in the developed West might be said to need an education that is not merely different from that required by members of the less developed world; they also need education that is more extensive and recognisably 'better'.

The notion of 'socially relative' need that is being invoked here is quite consistent with the idea of universal rights. It is not being claimed that Americans should receive more than Kenyans simply because Americans have a more extravagant conception of need. Rather the claim is that the welfare recipient in America has to have more than the welfare recipient in Kenya if each is to function in the same way and at the same level in their respective societies. Minimum incomes, for example, will have to be set at different absolute levels if they are to achieve effectively equal levels of welfare in the two societies. Thus individuals are conceived as possessing fundamentally (if not immediately) identical needs and therefore fundamentally identical welfare rights; it is simply that unequal amounts of resources have to be disbursed in order to secure equivalent levels of social well-being in different societies.

There is clearly much to be said for this socially relative conception of individuals' needs. But again we have to ask how far it can take us in reconciling universal claims of right with the disparities in welfare provision to be found in the modern world. In the first place, it seems a more compelling consideration for some welfare matters than for others. Social security measures certainly have to be adjusted to the society for which they provide. But it is not at all obvious that the 'relative' health care needs of people in poorer societies should be reckoned any less demanding, or capable of being 'equally' satisfied by a lower standard of medical treatment, than those of people in affluent societies. Secondly, if all of these differences were no more than adjustments to secure equal outcomes in different societies, we would have to conclude that welfare recipients in affluent societies were (absolutely) no better off than those in poor societies and that, given a choice, people would be wholly indifferent between the two. That too seems unsustainable.

A third reason for holding that equal rights constitute claims to unequal resources is, in some ways, a more specific version of the appeal to socially relative needs. As we have seen, there is a high degree of agreement that, if people have rights at all, those rights include civil rights to fundamental freedoms, such as freedom of expression and freedom of association, and political rights, such as the right to participate in some way in the political processes of their society. But if those civil and political rights are to be of genuinely equal value, they must be underwritten by a guaranteed minimum of material well-being for, without that, the rights of citizens will be formally equal but effectively unequal. Citizens who are supposed to be equal in status will, in reality, be unequal in their ability to participate in the civil and political processes of their society. Thus the level of material well-being, education and the like that a person will need in order to operate on terms equal with others in civil and political matters will depend upon the general standard of living of the society in question. Once again we have a reason why people's equal entitlements should lead to different levels of provision in different societies.[5]

As a justification for welfare rights this argument claims both too little and too much. It claims too little because, if we were really serious about ironing out inequalities in political influence or 'effective' freedom, we would have to go far beyond the measures normally associated with basic rights to material goods. It claims too much because this is not why welfare goods and services really matter to people, or why they should matter. If I live in slum housing, or am in chronic pain, or cannot provide an adequate diet for my children, or live constantly on the edge of hypothermia, probably the last thing on my mind is that these conditions impede my freedom to publish or my right to run for political office. For most people welfare goods matter for the immediate impact they have upon the quality of their lives and not because of their instrumental importance for their civil and political rights. That is not to say that civil and political rights do not matter or to deny that political and civil rights may be important to people in attempting to improve their lot in life (but notice that that puts the order of importance the other way round). It is to say simply that, for the most part, worries about civil and political rights are more convincing as subsidiary than as primary reasons for being concerned about welfare rights.

Thus, although there are some reasons for holding that universal welfare rights should give rise to different detailed entitlements in different societies, none of those reasons taken singly, nor all of them taken together, is really sufficient to reconcile the idea of universal welfare rights with the sorts of disparities in welfare provision that characterise the modern world. The critical factor here is not – as it is often supposed to be – that each individual's welfare rights are held against only some rather than against all individuals. Rather it is that each individual's welfare rights are regarded as a claim only upon a specific pool of resources, that of his own society. As long as we continue to think in those terms, the representation of welfare rights as human rights seems unsustainable.

We may, of course, continue to hold that identical distributive principles should apply in all societies but that is not enough to give us universal rights, for the same distributive principles applied to societies of different aggregate wealth will yield rights to resources which are pitched at different levels for different societies. Nor can we square the circle by appealing to the idea of 'conditional' rights. All human beings might be said to have identical socioeconomic rights subject only to the condition that the economic circumstances of their respective societies permit those rights to be fulfilled (Meyers, 1981). But that is really to say no more than that people possess the same rights under the same conditions and different rights under different conditions and that, since the relevant conditions are currently different in different societies, all humans do not possess the same rights.

Nor, again, can we resolve the incongruity by resort to what Joel Feinberg has identified as a 'manifesto sense' of rights (1973, p. 67). Feinberg's use of this notion lends substance to Cranston's complaint that rights have become confused with ideals. People allegedly have 'manifesto rights' when they have needs which ideally would be met but which, because of conditions of scarcity, no-one is under a duty actually to meet. For Feinberg, these needs always constitute claims worthy of serious consideration and, as such, are 'permanent possibilities of rights', but, if we do not believe that people really have claim-rights to the goods in question, it is at best confusing and at worst dishonest to pretend otherwise. This is particularly so if the 'scarcity' which allegedly prevents the relevant needs from being met exists only if we take for granted that each individual's need constitutes a claim only upon the resources of his own society. If each society's 'property right' in its 'own' resources is allowed to trump 'outside' individuals' claims of need, the claim that those needs 'cannot be met' is really masking a claim that they 'ought not to be met'.

Human rights or citizens' rights?

Where, then, do we go from here? For those who are strongly committed to the idea of welfare rights, there would seem to be two major alternatives. One is to forsake the idea of human welfare rights and to stress instead that welfare rights are rights that individuals have as citizens of particular societies. The other is to hold fast to the idea of human welfare rights and to challenge the commonly accepted notion that societies have exclusive 'property rights' in the resources that fall within their territories.

There are a number of things that might be said in favour of the first alternative. To begin with, it is perfectly possible to combine a 'thin' theory of human rights with a 'thick' theory of citizens' rights. So the notion of human welfare rights can be jettisoned without jeopardising welfare rights as such. Many socialists and social democrats, who are amongst the keenest to assert welfare rights, would conceive these as rights that individuals hold as members of particular communities rather than as members of the human race. There is also a strong tradition in social policy thinking of grounding welfare rights in ideals of citizenship and community (Marshall, 1950, 1981; Harris, 1987; Freeden, 1990).

What can justify our limiting our horizons in that way? One possible answer is that people have identities and loyalties as members of particular communities and that cannot and should not be ignored. Individuals as citizens are already enmeshed in particular normative relations which must be taken as moral 'givens' and it is wrong to abstract individuals from those particular contexts and treat all individuals as if they were only contingently related to one another. On this view, it is quite proper that people should possess rights and duties which are special to them as members of particular societies rather than common to humanity as a whole. Those who stress nationhood or ideals of community are likely to take this view (Walzer, 1983; Miller, 1988; Harris, 1987) – although emphasising the particularity of nations and communities may result not only in a rejection of ideas of universal rights but also in an unwillingness to generalise about citizens' rights.

Alternatively we may resort to more general forms of argument. One such is that the goods produced by a society belong to that society, so that only the members of that society have a claim upon them. Thus Rawls (1971) regards societies as 'schemes of cooperation' in which individuals combine their labours and arrange their lives for their mutual advantage. The goods generated by that social co-operation belong to the members of the co-operating community and that is why the boundaries of that community provide the limits within which those goods are to be distributed justly. If we think of Rawls's difference principle generating rights to a minimum of material well-being, the level of that minimum will vary from society to society but, given Rawls's assumptions, that outcome is quite acceptable.

There is, indeed, something a bit odd about individuals, merely in virtue of their humanity, being entitled to demand of others, 'feed me', 'clothe me', 'house me', as opposed to simply 'leave me alone'. Food has to be cultivated and gathered, clothes have to be made and houses have to be built. If no-one expended the effort required to produce these goods, there would be no food, clothing or housing to which people could have entitlements. To that extent, people may be more intelligibly thought to have rights to socioeconomic goods as members of productive communities rather than as isolated and unattached individuals. We have also seen how the needs of individuals must, in some measure, be related to the specific social and cultural contexts in which they find themselves.

Similar conclusions may be reached by focusing upon collective rights of self-determination. If each political community claims the right to be self-determining, that may seem to entail that it, and it alone, bears the responsibility for providing for the well-being of its citizens. Can we reasonably hold 'outsiders' responsible for coping with conditions in a society if those outsiders can have no voice in the affairs in that society? In the case of individuals we would ordinarily hold that, if they want the freedom to make decisions for themselves, they must also accept responsibility for coping with the consequences of those decisions. It would seem intolerable and inequitable if individual A had persistently to save individual B from the consequences of his own actions, if at the same time A could exercise no control over how B acted (cf. Jones, 1985). In the same way, it might be said that, if political communities wish to be autonomous, they must bear the full responsibilities that go with that autonomy. Welfare goods and services do not simply spring out of the ground. They have to be produced and provided. If a people claims an exclusive right of control over the sorts of policy matters relevant to the provision of welfare goods and services, it cannot expect others to make good the failings of those policies.

There are, then, a number of imposing reasons for containing socioeconomic rights within political boundaries rather than viewing them as genuinely universal rights. However there are also reasons why proponents of socioeconomic rights should find themselves pulled in the direction of human rights. For many theorists the impetus behind socioeconomic rights is provided by the needs of individuals as *human beings*. Thus, if those needs generate rights at all, it would seem that, in the absence of any further qualifying argument, those rights must be rights that individuals have *as* human beings. This would seem particularly so for theorists, like Gewirth, whose arguments are rights-based and who ground rights in the prerequisites of moral agency (Gewirth, 1978, 1982; Plant *et al.*, 1980, pp. 37–51, 93–6). If rights are grounded in moral agency such that all moral agents have those rights and have them equally and if, further, those rights include rights to a certain level of material well-being, it is hard to see how we can avoid the conclusion that there must be full-blooded human rights to material goods. It is a curious feature of much political argument that it starts out with premises that relate to human beings as such, but ends up with conclusions which apply only within national boundaries. But if an argument is grounded in individuals' *humanity* and if it is rights-*based*, such that all of the relevant duties stem from those rights, it is hard to see how it can generate fundamentally different entitlements for different human beings.

In a rather different vein, some have argued that the distribution of resources across the world is entirely fortuitous and that it is morally unacceptable that people's lot in life should be determined by this accidental feature of the world (Beitz, 1979, pp. 136–43; Barry, 1982; Richards, 1982). In Rawlsian language, the international distribution of natural and human resources is 'arbitrary from the moral point of view' and we should do our best to mitigate the consequences of that arbitrariness. In addition Charles Beitz has argued that the world is now so interdependent economically that, instead of conceiving each nation-state as an independent scheme of co-operation, we should think of the entire world as a single scheme of co-operation (1979, pp. 143–76). Both of these observations imply that principles of distributive justice should no longer be hemmed in by the boundaries of nation-states but should be applied to the entire globe as a single community.

Of course we do not have to think of socioeconomic rights either as exclusively human rights or as exclusively citizens' rights. All individuals as human beings may be deemed to have rights to a certain minimum of material well-being but, as citizens of particular societies, they may also be reckoned to have further welfare rights which extend beyond that universal minimum. As long as the world remains divided into more or less independent political communities, it seems unlikely that individuals' welfare rights can be thought of wholly without reference to the particular societies to which they belong. Rather than give no significance to political boundaries, a proponent of socioeconomic human rights might do better to accept that those boundaries have some significance but to insist that there is still a minimum of material well-being to which all humans are entitled without reference to those boundaries (cf. Shue, 1980; Vincent, 1986).

In fact the idea that all individuals have a right to at least subsistence is by no means new. Even Locke (unlike some of his modern disciples) held that property rights should be overridden in cases of extreme need. God, he argued, 'hath not left one Man so to the Mercy of another that he may starve him if he please'. While God allowed a man to acquire property, he had also given

> 'his needy Brother a Right to the Surplusage of his Goods; so that it cannot be justly denied him, when his pressing Wants call for it. . . . 'twould always be a Sin in any Man of Estate, to let his Brother perish for want of affording him Relief out of his Plenty. As *Justice* gives every Man a title to the product of his honest Industry, and the fair Acquisitions of his Ancestors descended to him; so *Charity* gives every Man a Title to so much out of another's Plenty, as will keep him from extream want, where he has no means to subsist otherwise.' (Locke, 1960, I, s. 42)

Locke spoke of the obligation to provide relief as an obligation of 'charity', a term which in our age has come to denote acts of grace and favour. But Locke clearly understood 'charity' to mean something stronger than that: those in 'extream want', he said, have a right, a 'Title', to the goods they need to survive (cf. O'Neill, 1989; Tierney 1989, pp. 639–44). In Locke's day it would not have been practicable to have thought of this right in transnational terms but, in the circumstances of the modern world, it is hard to see why the implications of an argument like Locke's should stop at national boundaries. If individual property rights should not be allowed to stand in the way of people's survival, why should 'societal' property rights?

Rights and distributive justice

In arguments about transnational economic obligations a distinction is discernible between those who approach these questions by way of principles of distributive justice and those who focus upon basic needs and basic rights. That points to a final question about the 'rights approach' to economic matters which arises whether we think of those rights internationally or intranationally.

There are two sorts of approach to the distribution of economic goods which give primacy to rights. One is the sort of libertarian position associated with Robert Nozick (1974) in which people have rights over themselves, including their labour, and in which (somehow) they acquire rights over natural resources. Starting out from these rights, people both give up rights over some goods and acquire rights to other goods by entering into voluntary transactions. Provided people have acquired goods either by rightful acts of 'original' acquisition or by transactions freely entered into, they have a right to those goods. Any attempt, either by individuals or by governments, to deprive people of goods so acquired violates their rights. The other approach which gives primacy to rights is the one we have concentrated upon in this chapter. A basic minimum is identified to which people are said to have a right such that, however a society, or the world at large, distributes its goods, that minimum must be secured for everyone.

In their unqualified forms, these two approaches are clearly opposed to one another. Part of the thrust of rights-based libertarianism has been to challenge claims that people, merely as citizens or as human beings, have right to the goods and services associated with the welfare state. However the two approaches can be combined. We might provide for a guaranteed minimum but, above that minimum, allow resources to be distributed according to market mechanisms. That, with a certain amount of qualification, describes the position in most western societies.

There are, however, approaches to the distribution of goods which question the utility of 'rights' in this area. Rather than establishing guaranteed minima or leaving everything to the free play of market forces, we might think of the entirety of a society's resources as a good to be distributed fairly amongst the members of that society. In that case we require a principle of fairness or justice to instruct us in how we should distribute available resources amongst people. A fixed catalogue of rights detailing entitlements to specific goods seems the wrong instrument for that purpose. Thus Brian Barry objects to declarations which enumerate rights to socioeconomic goods because such declarations 'use the language of absolute distributive principles', which principles are 'the wrong conceptual apparatus' for this sort of matter (1965, pp. 149–51). For example, article 25 of the UN Declaration announces that people have a right to an 'adequate' standard of living. But is it really appropriate to think in terms of rights to such more or less fixed minima? 'Surely, other things being equal, the object should be the highest possible average income, properly distributed' (Barry, 1965, p. 149). In other words, rather than trying to stipulate fixed quantities of cake to which everyone can be said to have a right, we should think in terms of distributive principles which can determine how the whole cake, big or small, should be sliced.

Barry's immediate objection would seem to relate more to the setting of arbitrary minima than to the language of rights. His reservations question not so much the *right* to an adequate standard of living as the right to an *adequate* standard of living. However the language of rights in this area does perhaps predispose people to think in terms of fixed quantities. People are inclined to assert rights to health care or to education or to a basic income as if those rights, like rights to freedom of expression or equality before the law, could be laid down in a simple determinate fashion without reference to the resources available at a particular moment. That tendency is reinforced when those rights are thought of as entitlements that people have 'just as' individual human beings or 'just as' individual citizens.

Equally, if we shift from conceptions of absolute minima to more fully distributive standards, the language of rights can begin to look superfluous. It is, of course, quite intelligible to say that people have a right to their fair share or to their just portion of a community's resources, but, in judgements such as these, the real moral work is done by principles of fairness or justice and little is contributed by adding the language of rights to those principles. If we know what a just distribution is, we can settle what people should have without calling upon ideas of rights; but, in the absence of any independent criterion of distributive justice, the notion that people have rights will not tell us how to divide the cake.

That is not to say that the language of rights is necessarily 'wrong' in this area. There is a case for establishing minima and there are strong arguments against simple 'patterned' principles of justice which would have us distribute a society's resources as though we were dividing up a cake that had appeared from nowhere (Nozick, 1974, pp. 153–74), but, we should be aware that, if we begin by thinking about these issues in terms of rights, that conceptual apparatus might, of itself, steer us towards some sorts of distributive arrangements and away from others.

8   Democracy, Groups and Rights

Democracy and rights seem two closely related subjects. That is especially true in liberal democratic thinking which unites a concern for democracy and individual rights. Yet there is also a longstanding worry about the way in which democracy bears upon rights, as if one were a threat to the other. So what is the truth about that relation?

The first task we encounter in examining this question is the identity of democracy itself. That, of course, is a much disputed matter and there is a great deal of ideological competition in the modern world for proprietorship of the term 'democracy'. Here I shall simply stipulate a meaning of the term to serve as basis for the analysis of this chapter. By democracy I shall understand a form of decision making in which all of those who are bound by the decisions have the right to participate equally in their making. The fundamental idea of democracy is that of a people, a 'demos', ruling itself and it is that idea that I have sought to capture in this definition. In spite of the controversy that surrounds the meaning of 'democracy', it is unlikely that anyone would deny the adjective 'democratic' to the sort of decision procedure I have just described. The complaint that my definition is more likely to evoke is that it is hopelessly idealistic. It sets the standard for democracy so high that no modern political system does or could meet it. However my definition is intended to characterise democracy in its ideal or pure form. Actual political systems which claim to be democratic should be understood as more or less close approximations to that ideal and, of course, there will come a point at which a regime will be so far removed from the ideal that it becomes plainly 'undemocratic' rather than merely less democratic (cf. Lively, 1975, pp. 29–51).

My other defence of this idealised definition is that, in what follows, I shall be concerned mainly with the way democracy and rights are related in principle. That relation is best pursued by way of an unadulterated notion of democracy. The modifications required by the messy world of practice can be built in at a later stage.

Democratic and non-democratic rights

How far does a commitment to democracy entail a commitment to rights? In the first place, it is useful to distinguish between two sorts of right: 'democratic' and 'non-democratic'. Democratic rights are rights which are essential constituents of the democratic process; non-democratic rights are rights which are not.

The most obvious democratic right is the right to vote. A political system which does not extend that right to its adult population, even though it requires them to comply with its decisions, cannot be described as democratic. We would also normally require that a democratic right to vote must be a right to a vote which counts equally with other votes. Ideally conceived, a democratic system is not only one in which all citizens may participate but also one in which each citizen may participate on terms equal with others. But a right to participate equally in decision making goes beyond mere voting. It also entails a right to take part in other aspects of the decision-making process that preface the ultimate act of decision taking, such as discussion and debate. That is why the right to speak, the right to hear and the right to publish are also properly characterised as 'democratic' rights. To these we may add 'secondary' democratic rights which are rights in virtue of their being essential to participating in a particular form of democracy. Political parties, as they exist in the modern world, were unknown to the democracy of ancient Athens largely because its direct form of democracy and its filling of government posts by lot made them unnecessary. But political parties have become crucial to the functioning of indirect democracy in modern states so that, in those states, the right to form and to belong to political parties is properly included in the list of democratic rights.

Thus there are certain rights which are intrinsic to the democratic process and whose respect is demanded by democracy itself. We may even say that those rights set limits to what a majority may do in the name of democracy. Such a majority would act undemocratically, in spite of its being a democratic majority, if it used its powers to deprive any section of the 'demos' of these democratic rights. There is, then, at least one way in which a limit on the power of the majority is consistent with democracy itself. A constitution which divested its democratic legislature of the power to remove democratic rights would be no less a democratic constitution for limiting the power of the 'demos' in that way. Such a constitution would be at odds with the doctrines of popular sovereignty and the sovereignty of the majority but, as we shall see, those doctrines are neither identical with, nor entailed by, a commitment to democracy.

But what of rights such as the right to a fair trial or the right to freedom of worship or the right not to be tortured? Those too are rights treasured by liberal democrats and they are sometimes spoken of as 'democratic rights'. However, in the case of those rights, the addition of the adjective 'democratic' is no more than misleading rhetoric. In truth, those are non-democratic rights. They do not form part of the democratic process and they rest upon concerns other than democracy. That does not imperil their status as rights. It means simply that they are directed at concerns other than democracy and must be justified independently of democracy. Thus, while it would ordinarily be wrong and undemocratic for a minority to be deprived of its right to vote, it would be wrong but not undemocratic for that minority to be deprived of its right of freedom of worship. There should be nothing surprising in that. It betokens merely that democracy is not the only thing that matters to us and that very often rights are grounded in concerns other than democracy.

The same may also be said, in part, of rights such as the right of freedom of expression and the right of freedom of association. I have already explained how and why these may be considered democratic rights. But not every 'expression' nor every 'association' constitutes a form of participation in the democratic process. Nor do those freedoms matter only as constituents of a democratic process. A defence of someone's freedom to preach the doctrine of transubstantiation, or to marry the partner of his or her choice, is unlikely to find a convincing foundation in the prerequisites of democracy. Thus, in principle and in part, even rights such as these may be non-democratic rights. In practice, of course, it is extremely difficult to divide these rights into democratic and non-democratic portions, partly because almost any matter *may* find its way onto the democratic agenda, and partly because people's freedom to do or to say a particular thing may be important for both democratic and non-democratic reasons.

I have already given some examples of rights which are, fairly straightforwardly, non-democratic rights. Some other examples of rights, which, if they are rights, are non-democratic rights, are the right to strike, the right to privacy, the right to health care, the right to an abortion, the right of a foetus not to be aborted, the right to marry, the right to divorce, the right to own property, the right not to be subjected to cruel and unusual punishment, and the right to be treated as an equal before the law. Indeed most of the rights that people assert fall into the category 'non-democratic', even though people are fond of attaching the adjective 'democratic' to them merely for its rhetorical effect. I describe these as 'non-democratic' rather than 'undemocratic' rights because they do not challenge the legitimacy of democracy as a form of government; they are simply concerned with matters other than the process of political decision making and are therefore concerned with matters other than democracy. If someone asserted the right of a king to rule a society, that would properly be described as an 'undemocratic' right and, of course, for a monarchist, it would be no less a 'right' for being 'undemocratic'.

Although 'non-democratic' rights are not 'undemocratic' rights, they can still come into conflict with democracy. That is one way in which the distinction between 'democratic' and 'non-democratic' rights has significance. What the majority of a 'demos' wants may be at odds with that to which we think individuals have a right. Hence the traditional counterposing of the 'will' of the majority to the 'rights' of the minority. There is a real issue here, but it should be kept in perspective. There is no reason why the will of the majority *must* come into conflict with the rights of the minority; people, through the democratic process, may very well choose to endorse those rights. In a society in which respect for rights is heavily ingrained in the public culture, the will of the 'demos' may press only rarely against the limits set by non-democratic rights. In addition the possibility of conflict between public decisions and individual rights is not special to democracy; it arises only because government in *any* form may seek to do things which are at odds with individuals' rights. Even so, rights asserted *against* government will, in a democratic context, be rights asserted against democracy. If we seek to constrain government action, either in theory or in practice, by enumerating non-democratic rights, those rights represent constraints upon democracy. Indeed the actual effect of entrenching rights in the constitutions of democratic societies is just that. Bills of rights of that sort institute rights in the form of immunities; they deprive the 'demos' of the power to do things which would infringe those rights.

Three other links

However, there are three other ways in which rights may be linked
to democracy even when they are not 'democratic rights' in the strict
sense that I have described. Firstly, democracy may be the political
system which is most likely to respect and to maintain non-
democratic as well as democratic rights. Democracy has often been
represented as a threat to rights, particularly to the rights of
minorities, but, as I have pointed out, that is primarily because *any*
form of government is potentially a threat to rights. Democratic
majorities are certainly capable of violating the rights of individuals
and of minorities and have often done so, but, a priori, there is no
reason to suppose that democratic forms of government will violate
rights more frequently and more seriously than undemocratic forms
of government. Indeed the track record of different forms of
government suggests that, although it does not come with built-in
guarantees, democracy may be the best option if our concern is to
have a form of government that is least likely to violate non-
democratic rights.

Secondly, some rights may be linked to democracy in that, while
they do not form part of the democratic process, they are still
important to the functioning of that process. A good example is the
right to education. Receiving an education is not, in itself,
participating in the democratic process and education is important
for non-political as well as political reasons. Nevertheless a
population that is unable to understand the issues which it
confronts cannot perform the role that democracy requires of it.
Similarly, if a particular section of a population is wholly
uneducated or only poorly educated, it will not be able to
participate in the democratic process on terms equal with others
even though it enjoys the same formal democratic rights as the rest
of the population. The same may be said of certain welfare rights
which ensure that people do not sink below the level of material
welfare they need if they are to function as citizens of a democratic
society. Thus, although these may not be 'democratic rights' in the
strict sense that I have stipulated, the case for their being rights may
be made by reference to the prerequisites of democracy, even though
that case is likely to be made in other terms as well.

Thirdly, and perhaps most importantly, our reason for being
committed to democracy may be a reason for being committed to

more than democracy. Suppose, for example, that I am fundamentally committed to a principle of fairness and I am committed to democracy as the fairest way of making collective decisions. I shall also be anxious to see that principle of fairness embodied in other of a society's arrangements, such as its conduct of trials. Thus my reason for being committed to democracy may also be a reason for my being committed to certain non-democratic rights, such as the right to a fair trial, and for seeking to deprive the democratic process of the power to set aside those rights. Or consider the argument from self-determination. I may be committed to the principle that, as far as possible, individuals should be able to determine the character of their own lives and I may embrace democracy as the form of collective decision making most consistent with that principle. But, given my concern for self-determination, I may also be anxious that individuals' lives should not be wholly at the mercy of public decisions and so accord individuals' rights to freedoms which limit the jurisdiction of the democratic process. Thus, once again, my reason for being committed to democracy would also be a reason for being committed to non-democratic rights which, implicitly if not explicitly, set limits to the scope of the democratic process.

Is there a right to democracy?

This last issue raises the question of the foundation of democracy. I have shown that some rights are integral to democracy and that some other rights can be linked to democracy even though they are not intrinsic to the idea of democracy. But is democracy itself the object of a right? Do people have a right to be governed democratically or, to put the question in other terms, is democracy itself rights-*based*?

Historically demands for democracy have frequently been phrased in terms of rights. The Levellers, in the seventeenth century, asserted people's right to be governed democratically; so did the authors of the American Revolution in the eighteenth century. The French Declaration of 1789 stated that 'Legislation is the expression of the general will. All citizens have a right to participate in shaping it either in person, or through their representatives.' In our own day, article 21 of the UN Declaration states that 'Everyone has the right to take part in the government of his country, directly or through freely chosen representatives.' Statements such as these, together with the unique aura of legitimacy that surrounds democracy in the modern world, may suggest that democratic ideals are indeed rights-based. However democracy may be justified in a great many ways. All of these justifications, in so far as they argue for democracy, must also argue for those rights essential to democracy. But an argument in favour of democratic rights need not be a rights-based argument.

Some of the most celebrated arguments for democracy are instrumental in character. That is, they seek to justify democracy as instrumental to the attainment of some good which is, in principle, separate from democracy itself. Purely instrumental arguments imply that there is nothing intrinsically good or right about democracy; rather democracy is to be valued only because and in so far as it brings about good results. Of those instrumental arguments, the simplest and most obvious turns on the quality of decision that issues from democratic decision procedures. It goes like this. The purpose of a decision procedure is to make decisions; the best decision procedure is that which yields the best decisions; therefore democracy is the best decision procedure if and because it produces the best decisions. We may call this the 'decision-centred' argument.

In its general form, the decision-centred argument leaves open the question of what are the 'good' or the 'best' decisions according to which democracy and other decision procedures are to be evaluated. A number of possibilities are on offer: maximum social utility, various ideas of justice, a godly society, different ideals for humanity, and so on. Potentially there are as many decision-centred arguments for democracy as there are ideas about what constitutes goodness in public decisions. This diversity of view about what constitutes 'good decisions' has done little to dampen the enthusiasm or the confidence with which democratic theorists have claimed that democracy delivers the best decisions.

In terms of Dworkin's classification, this sort of argument for democracy must rank as goal-based rather than rights-based. In so far as it yields a case for democracy, it yields a case for democratic rights, but that does not entail that individuals can then demand democracy 'as of right'. On the contrary, a decision-centred argument would hold that individuals ought to have democratic rights only if there ought to be democracy, and that there ought to be democracy only if democratic decision making is likely to yield the best decisions. Good decisions will be good for the members of a democratic community but those decisions constitute a collective good in which all citizens share rather than the sort of good to which each citizen could plausibly have an individual claim of right.

The decision-centred argument is not the only form of instrumental argument for democracy. Appeals are sometimes made to other sorts of benefit that are alleged to flow from democracy. It is sometimes claimed that democratic decision making is more efficient because people are more willing to abide by decisions that they have had a hand in making. Democracy is sometimes said to have an integrative effect upon a community, although there is plenty of contemporary evidence to the contrary. Mill famously argued that democracy was good because political participation had an improving effect upon the intellectual and moral quality of a population (Mill, 1910, pp. 202–18). However none of these claims is readily translatable into an argument for democracy of a rights-based character.

On what grounds, then, might individuals claim a right to be governed democratically? As I have already pointed out, it is quite implausible to suppose that an individual, all on his own, could have a right that an entire community should organise its public life in a democratic fashion. If a right is to figure in the foundations of democracy, it must be phrased more modestly. A more plausible way of conceiving that right is as follows: if an individual is to be subject to political authority, he is entitled to play a part in the exercise of that authority. Why should individuals be thought to have that right? Some commentators on democracy argue that, in the modern world, political equality has come to symbolise a basic equality amongst human beings such that anyone who is excluded from, or who is treated unequally in, the political realm will suffer a loss of self-respect (Rawls, 1971, pp. 234, 544–5; Miller, 1978, pp. 92, 95–6). In this argument, equal voting rights and the other equalities associated with democracy are important, not for what they contribute to the process of decision making, but as public acknowledgements of the equal status accorded to individuals. The wrong that would be done to individuals or groups who were excluded from the political process would be the failure to recognise them as people whose worth and standing were no less than those of others. People have a right not to be treated in that publicly humiliating fashion.

Under modern conditions this argument has considerable force, but as a general argument for democracy it also has obvious limitations. In a society with a democratic, or a near-democratic, political system and public culture, it is clearly humiliating and stigmatising for a section of the population to find itself excluded from the public rights and roles enjoyed by others. But in a society with quite different institutions and values, such as a traditional monarchy, people's inability to participate in government may in no way adversely affect their self-respect or their standing in the eyes of others. Thus this appeal to the psychological consequences of political rights provides a less than fundamental case for democratic government.

Rather more imposing rights-based arguments for democracy are provided by the two justifications that I touched upon in the previous section: fairness and self-determination. The argument from fairness runs as follows. The interests of individuals who form a political community are equally affected by the decisions of that community. Any particular decision may, of course, affect the interests of some individuals more than those of others, but if we take the entire set of decisions, we can say that all members' interests are equally at stake in the political process. If we accept that the well-being of one individual should matter neither more nor less than the well-being of another, and if, like Mill, we suppose that each individual is the best guardian of his own interests, we arrive at democracy as the right form of decision making. If individuals' interests are equally at stake in a political process, those individuals, as a matter of fairness, have a right to play an equal part in that process to ensure that their interests are taken equally into account (cf. Cohen, 1971, ch. 15; Jones, 1983).

In principle, of course, people's interests can be taken equally into account by a political process in which they have no part. In addition individuals may not always be the best judges of their own interests. However those who best judge my interest need not be those who will do most to promote it. Mill wisely characterised each individual as the best 'guardian' of his own interest and, if we want to ensure that a political process does indeed take equal account of the interests of all who are subject to it, the evidence of history is that the best strategy is to invest all of them with equal political rights.

The argument from self-determination draws upon values that we examined in Chapter 6. Let us suppose that we place a fundamental value upon autonomy of a sort that yields a right of self-determination. We may then hold that, if individuals' lives are to be subject to collective decisions, their rights of self-determination require that they should be entitled to play an equal part in the making of those decisions. If an individual had no right to take part in the making of decisions to which she was subject, that would be inconsistent with her right of self-determination. If she had a right to a greater part than others in the making of decisions to which those others were equally subject, that would be inconsistent with their rights of self-determination. Hence we arrive at the equal rights of participation associated with democracy. The argument here is close to the previous argument, but it remains distinct in that it pivots on the right of each individual to be self-determining rather than on the right of each individual to have his interests taken fairly into account in public decision making. The implementation of either of those rights-based principles would, of course, have to take full account of the practical constraints placed upon the achievement of democracy by modern political circumstances.

The right of self-determination, or something like it, is the right which has been asserted most frequently in demands for democracy. But it also poses a problem. If a 'demos' is not entirely of one mind, a decision will be reached – typically by majority vote – which is not unanimously approved. Some individuals will then have to conform to a decision which is not the decision that they wish to impose upon themselves. To that extent, they will not be self-determining. In those circumstances, as Mill observed, so-called 'self-government' may turn out to be 'not the government of each by himself, but of each by all the rest' (1910, p. 67).

Two points may be pleaded in mitigation. Firstly, there remains a significant difference between, on the one hand, being entirely excluded from a decision-making process and, on the other, having a right to contribute equally to that process even though one might be outvoted. Secondly, granted that collective decisions have to be made, decision making by majority vote secures a greater measure of full-blooded self-determination than any alternative way of making decisions (cf. Graham, 1986, pp. 86–91). On these grounds democracy may claim to be the form of collective decision making that comes closest to respecting individuals' rights of self-determination even though it does not ensure that everyone will be self-determining all of the time.

Must we accept that individuals' rights of self-determination have to be compromised in this way? Rousseau (1968) famously thought not. He held that a body of people that formed a genuine community shared a common good for which they possessed a 'general will'. Under the right circumstances, a democratic majority could be relied upon to discern whether a proposal conformed to that general will. Voters who found themselves in a minority would have simply misjudged the general will. That minority would then have to conform to the majority's judgement but their autonomy would remain unimpaired because the majority was simply promoting a good common to all citizens, a good which all citzens must want, and a good which therefore the minority must 'really' want in spite of its own misjudgement. Thus both the majority and the minority of individuals would be self-determining because they would be conforming to a general will which was the will of each and everyone of them.[1] Rousseau's ambitious attempt to reconcile autonomy with authority via democracy runs into a number of well-known objections. The most obvious of these question whether there is reason to suppose that majorities will be right and minorities wrong in their judgements of the general will and whether there will always be a good common to a body of individuals to provide the foundation for a general will.

Could it be that we encounter difficulties in fully reconciling democracy with self-determination only because we are working with the wrong right of self-determination? Might it be that the rights of self-determination relevant to democracy are not the rights of individuals but the collective rights of peoples? Before turning to that question, we must investigate the idea of 'group rights'.

Group rights

A group right properly so called is a right possessed by a group *qua* group. It is not to be confused with a right which is common to a group of individuals but which each individual possesses as an individual. For example, a group of Protestant individuals, who are distinguished as a group by their Protestantism, may each possess the right to practise their religion. But that right may be conceptualised as a right held by each Protestant as an individual rather than one held by the group of all Protestants *qua* group. If Protestant forms of worship were prohibited, that would violate the rights of individual Protestants rather than a single right possessed by a collective entity encompassing all Protestants.

By contrast, consider the right of a country to have a seat at the United Nations. That right cannot be factored into a set of separate rights each of which is held by the individuals who make up the members of that country. If it is a right, it is a right held by a country *qua* country. In a sense a group right is still an individual right in that a group can be conceived as possessing rights *qua* group only if it is conceived as a single unified entity. Group rights may therefore be said to be held by 'group individuals'. Thus we can think of a nation or a cultural group or a religious community as having group rights only in so far as we conceive of those rights as held, in each case, by a single integral entity.

Assertions of 'the rights of minorities' are often ambiguous as between these two sorts of right. Often when people use the phrase 'minority rights' they refer merely to rights held by individuals. Those rights come to be spoken of as 'minority rights' only because they are threatened, actually or potentially, by a majority. For example, when people speak of a minority's rights to express its views, they often mean no more than that all individuals have the right to express their views, even though their views may be held only by a minority of their fellows and even though those views are disliked by the majority. In other words, the phrase 'minority rights' may be no more than a short hand expression for rights which are actually held by *all* individuals and which each individual continues to hold even when that individual finds himself or herself in a numerical minority.

However minority rights may also refer to rights held by a minority *qua* group. For example, when someone speaks of the right of a nation to have its language preserved and respected, the right must be a right held by the nation as a collectivity. The conception is not that each individual member of the nation has, as a separate individual, a right that the language shall be preserved and promoted in public life. The claim is rather that that nation as a whole has a right to have its language recognised and maintained. The relevant nation may even be conceived as an entity which reaches both backwards and forwards beyond the current generation of individual nationals.

Since the ascription of rights turns not only upon the way the world is but also upon the way we see the world, a right may sometimes be interpretable in either of these forms. For example, governments have sometimes made it illegal for an ethnic minority to speak its own language; they have also sometimes attempted to suppress entire cultures. If those acts violate rights, whose rights do they violate? The answer might be the group rights of the persecuted minority. But the violated rights might also be construed as the rights of individuals to speak their native tongue or the rights of individuals not to be deprived of the fundamental good of cultural membership (cf. Kymlicka, 1989, pp. 162–81, 1992; Kukathas, 1992).

If we accept that groups can have rights, that, of itself, does not tell us which groups have rights or what rights they have, but the sort of rights most commonly ascribed to groups in political contexts are rights of self-determination or autonomy and, to that extent, the most prominent candidates for group rights will be groups which are appropriate units of self-determination and for which self-determination is thought to have significant value. That is one reason why nations and ethnic groups are more likely candidates for group rights than red-haired people or car drivers.

The thinking that underlies the assertion of group rights of self-determination often resembles that associated with individual rights of self-determination. In Chapter 6 I identified two sorts of reasoning that are used to underpin the value of individual autonomy. One focuses upon the respect owed to persons merely as persons while the other focuses upon autonomy as an ingredient of human well-being. Parallels to those two forms of argument can be found at the level of groups. Assertions of group rights of self-determination are often based upon a conception of a group as an entity with a distinct identity and life of its own which others must recognise and respect. In other words, they often rely upon a notion of respect for groups which is akin to that of respect for persons. However a group's right of self-determination may also be upheld because that self-determination is reckoned essential to the well-being of its members, just as a measure of individual autonomy may be thought essential to the well-being of an individual person (for example, Margalit and Raz, 1990).

In spite of these parallels, the nuances of self-determination may be rather different for groups than for individuals. In relation to individuals, self-determination connotes choice and there are indeed some sorts of groups for which choice will also be an important component of self-determination. But what is of crucial value for many groups, such as groups distinguished by shared traditions and cultures, is the continuation and preservation of an inherited form of life. For those groups, self-determination will be less a matter of exercising choices than of being able to continue with an inherited form of life and being safeguarded from policies and external influences which threaten to undermine that form of life.

Many of the issues raised by group rights merely replicate those raised by individual rights, but there are two worries that are special to group rights. The first concerns the identity of the group which is alleged to possess rights. Human beings – and even the 'higher' of the non-human beings – are easily individuated. We do not agonise over whether you and I are separate individuals. But the identity of groups as distinct entities is often problematic. In law these problems are easily obviated in that law itself defines what counts as a legal corporation and determines what rights that corporation has. But very often people want to ascribe rights to non-legal or pre-legal entities whose identity is far from clear.

Once again, 'nations' provide the most obvious example. In so far as nationhood is used to indicate which units of population should be self-governing, it is nations which determine where political boundaries should fall and not political boundaries that determine the identity of nations.[2] But the identity of nations is notoriously problematic. A group which claims to be a nation will often find itself included within a larger group which also claims to be a nation. It may also find its claim challenged by smaller groups within its population which themselves claim to be nations. Even if there is agreement about the 'level' at which nationhood occurs, there is often sharp disagreement over precisely what population a nation includes and over the territory which 'belongs' to each nation. That is why very widespread agreement in this century that each nation has a right of self-determination has frequently done more to promote bloody conflict than international harmony.

The other anxiety attracted by group rights concerns the rights ascribed to the group. Group rights are often directed 'outwards' as claims upon or against other groups or individuals external to the group. For example, a nation's right of self-determination is asserted principally to inform the rest of the international community that they must not interfere with the conduct of that nation's affairs. But group rights might also be directed 'inwards' to those who make up the group. They may be conceived as rights held by the group collectively against its members severally. There is no analogue to that in the case of individual rights. An individual cannot have rights against parts of himself such as his ears or eyes or legs. However it is at least intelligible that a group might have rights against its individual members. Nor need there be anything sinister in that. For example, a group of individuals who form a club might be said to have the right, as a group, to require each of its members to pay the club subscription and to expel members who fail to pay that subscription. Or a yachting crew might be said to have a right as a group that each of its members should play his full part in their common endeavour. There seems nothing menacing in either of those group rights.

The worries start to arise when the rights claimed for a group demand more of its members than is consistent with their rights as individuals. Does a group have the right to deprive its members of basic liberties if their use of those liberties might erode the pattern of life characteristic of the group? Should a group have a right to require some of its members to sacrifice their lives to secure the aims of the group? The stress upon the identity of a group as a bearer of rights may become so great that its individual members are effectively denied any separate identity or purpose. They may become like the 'members' of a human body which can exist and function only as parts of a single organism; they may cease to have any claim to exist or to function independently of the group. In other words, they may cease to have any rights as individuals.

Individuals and their rights may be threatened not only by this sort of over-inclusiveness, but also by the exclusiveness of group identities. An overriding concern for the identity and integrity of a group may sanction the purging from its 'body' of individuals who are deemed 'alien' elements, a practice that has recently manifested itself in 'ethnic cleansing'. Thus enthusiasts for the rights of groups and enthusiasts for the rights of individuals may find themselves seriously at odds with one another.

There are very good reasons for these worries about group rights, but they are only 'worries' and they should not be allowed to discredit the very idea of group rights. Sometimes what matters most to people are traditions, practices and institutions that they enjoy, and can enjoy, only as members of collective entities. Given the special moral significance that rights possess, it is difficult to see what could justify our confining that significance to things which matter only to individuals as separate individuals and our refusing to allow that the same sort of moral significance might attach to things of fundamental value which people can experience and enjoy only in association with others.

Popular sovereignty and democratic rights

Let us now return to the question of whether there can be a right to democracy. Could that right be the group right of a people or 'demos'? The first question we need to consider is what gives a people a collective identity as a 'people'. The idea of democracy does not itself tell us who should form a 'demos'; all it tells us is how decisions ought to be made within any given decision-making unit. Other doctrines do purport to answer that question, most notably nationalism, but many modern states do not constitute nations in the traditional European sense and, even in Europe, nationalism has caused more problems than it has solved in delineating state boundaries. In truth, little may distinguish a people as a people other than their being subject to a common jurisdiction. However we may still hold that a body of people that is subject to a common authority has, merely in virtue of that shared condition, a group identity and a collective right to determine its own destiny.

The doctrine that a people is entitled to be the ultimate arbiter of how it is governed is the doctrine of popular sovereignty. According to that doctrine, whatever form of government a people endorses is the rightful form of government for that people. There are obvious difficulties in that doctrine. 'The people' may not be unanimous, in which case what counts as the voice of the people will have to be the voice of some of the people rather than all of the people. In practice, there will also be some indeterminacy about how much choice a people must have and how much enthusiasm it must manifest, before a political system can claim popular endorsement. I shall not pursue those difficulties here. Clearly, they have not prevented the doctrine of popular sovereignty achieving wide appeal in the modern era.

The doctrine of popular sovereignty is often elided with democracy but a simple conflation of those ideas is mistaken. To be committed to popular sovereignty is to accept the rightfulness of whatever form of government a people endorses; to be committed to democracy is to be committed to the rightfulness of one particular form of government. Neither commitment entails the other. Popular sovereignty rules out the exclusive rightfulness of democracy and an unconditional commitment to the rightfulness of democracy rules out popular sovereignty. Of course one might combine the doctrine of popular sovereignty with a belief that democracy is the best form of government and therefore the form of government that a people ought, or is best advised, to adopt. But that would be still to accept that a people has the right to choose an undemocratic form of government and that a form of government so chosen is no less rightful for being badly or unwisely chosen.

So, if we are in search of the right of a people to be governed *only* democratically, we shall not find it in the doctrine of popular sovereignty. But does that right make sense anyway? A collective right of self-determination vetoes external impositions and entitles a people to determine how it shall be governed. But a collective right exclusively to democracy would be the right of a people to be governed in one specific way only. In relation to whom would a people hold that right? Itself? In an age, such as the sixteenth century, when peoples and governments were conceived as separate existents and when governments (usually monarchs) were thought of as 'set over' peoples, it made sense to think of peoples having rights in respect of governments. But when government is conceived as something generated by the people itself, the right of a people to be governed only democratically would be a right constraining what the people itself might do, and the right of a people against itself would be a very odd right. Of course, once a constitution has been established and specific governmental offices and political roles are in place, it may well be possible to speak of constitutional rights that a people has in relation to those who wield authority over it. But we are concerned here with pre-constitutional rights and, as I have tried to show, the right of people to be required to rule itself in one specific way only is a very strange right.

Hence, if there is a right to be governed democratically that must be a right held separately by those who make up the people rather than a right held by the people as a single collectivity. Certainly the doctrine of popular sovereignty entitles a people to choose democracy but it also entitles a people to reject democracy. Consequently there is in theory, if not always in practice, a conflict between collective rights of self-determination and individual rights to democratic government. Every plebiscite which endorses a dictator is a simple illustration of that conflict.

There is one more thing to be said about group rights and democracy. Traditionally, in democratic thinking, the 'demos' has been conceived as a body of individuals, but, since individuals often have identities and interests as members of groups, it has sometimes been suggested, particularly by pluralists, that the relevant actors in a democratic process are groups rather than individuals. If we accept that view, it does not follow, of course, that we should treat every group claim as a right, any more than we should treat every individual claim as a right. But where groups have special identities, for example as ethnic, cultural or linguistic communities, it is sometimes accepted that the political system should recognise and provide for those special identities, either in the form of constitutional rights or by way of informal understandings (Lijphart, 1977; Van Dyke, 1974, 1982). So, even if there is not a single collective right to democracy, there may still be societies in which the rights of groups figure importantly in the structure and working of the political system.

9 Some Doubts and Difficulties

Having examined a number of specific types of right, I now want to return to the general idea of rights and to investigate a number of issues that are common to rights, whatever their content, and which any theory of rights must confront.

The status of rights

How much moral weight should rights have? In the past, natural rights were often said to be imprescriptible, inalienable and indefeasible. A right was 'imprescriptible' if it could not be eroded by the passage of time; it was 'inalienable' if the right-holder could not divest himself of it; and it was 'indefeasible' if others could never rightfully override it or set it aside. Of these three alleged attributes of natural rights, it is indefeasibility that has most concerned modern writers on human rights. When people have said that a right is 'absolute', they have usually meant that it is absolutely indefeasible. An absolute right is one that is never justifiably infringed; it is a right that must be respected in all possible circumstances.

Should human rights be regarded as absolute? Should all rights be regarded as absolute? Given the special moral status that rights have, there is clear reason why we might feel inclined to answer yes. We have already seen how rights place limits upon consequentialist reasoning. If rights can be removed or overridden when they come up against competing considerations, that may seem to imperil their very character as rights. More especially, it is part of the purpose of human rights to provide guaranteed safeguards for individuals – particularly against the abuse of political power. What sort of guarantees would we possess if the right to a fair trial or the right not to be tortured were not absolute? Can we feel secure knowing that these rights might be set aside for the 'public good' or in the 'national interest'? What government that violates human rights does not claim some such justification for its actions?

It is easy to sympathise with these sentiments and life would often be more straightforward if all rights possessed an absolute status. Confronted with a right, we would know that we ought always to do what that right required of us. The trouble is that this uncomplicated appraisal of rights will sometimes yield outcomes that seem morally wrong. Consider the standard sort of example used to illustrate this point. I have promised a friend that I shall be at his house for tea at 5.00 pm. My friend can be said to have a 'right' that I should do what I have promised him I shall do, viz. present myself at his house at 5.00 pm. However, on my way to his house, I cross a bridge and hear the cries for help of a man who is drowning. I am a good swimmer and I can easily jump in the river and save him. But if I do, I shall not reach my friend's house until after 5.00 pm. Should I keep my promise and leave the man to drown, or should I break the promise and save his life? If promises yield rights and if all rights are absolute, I should leave him to drown. Yet no-one is likely to find that an acceptable conclusion.

Could this be the wrong conclusion only because more than one right is at issue in this example? The drowning man, as well as my friend, might be said to have a right – the right to be saved. So, in diving into the river and making myself late for tea, I am still honouring a right. But, if we see the situation in that way, I am then confronted with two rights which make conflicting demands upon me. I cannot honour both, so both rights cannot be absolute which, in turn, means that not all rights can be absolute. But suppose that we fight shy of saying that the drowning man has a 'right' to be saved. Even then, we are likely to feel that, all things considered, I ought to save him and break my promise – which is to allow that rights can sometimes be justifiably overridden not only for the sake of other rights but also for the sake of other sorts of moral concern.

The right at issue in this example is, of course, a fairly trivial one. No significant harm is likely to follow upon my being late for tea. If the right at issue were a human right, we might be much less ready to see it overridden. But similar dilemmas can arise in relation to those much more significant rights. Amongst the rights listed in the UN Declaration is the right not to be tortured. Few who accept the idea of human rights are likely to challenge that right. Yet it is not difficult to think of circumstances in which it would be put very much to the test. Suppose, for example, that a terrorist has planted a bomb which is likely to kill hundreds of people. The terrorist has been captured but refuses to say where the bomb is. There is good reason to believe that torturing him will get him to reveal the location of the bomb and that will enable hundreds of innocent lives to be saved. Should he be tortured or should his right not to be tortured be given an absolute status in spite of the human costs that involves?

For virtually every right that one might assert it is possible to think of circumstances in which there is a plausible case for setting that right aside. The apparently uncompromising character of rights is one thing that has brought the whole rights approach to politics into bad odour. This was one reason why Edmund Burke took exception to the rights proclaimed by the French Revolutionaries:

'The pretended rights of these theorists are all extremes; and in proportion as they are metaphysically true, they are morally and politically false. The rights of men are in a sort of middle, incapable of definition, but not impossible to be discerned. The rights of men in governments are their advantages; and these are often in balances between differences of good; in compromises sometimes between good and evil, and sometimes, between evil and evil. Political reason is a computing principle; adding subtracting, multiplying and dividing, morally and not metaphysically or mathematically, true moral demonstrations.' (1910, pp. 59–60)

As so often, Burke's language is more eloquent then clear, but it is easy enough to understand the gist of his complaint. Government decisions call for a delicate balance of competing considerations. One interest will compete with another, the pursuit of one good might require the sacrifice of another, we may be able to avoid one evil only if we endure another, and so on. To suppose that the conduct of government can be dictated by a simple catalogue of absolute rights is morally naive and politically dangerous.

It is not only the critics of rights who have recognised this difficulty. It has also been acknowledged by the friends of rights. Drafters of bills of rights have often been aware that the rights that they enunciate may come into conflict with other legitimate considerations and may sometimes rightly give way to those other considerations. That has led them to build qualifications into their declarations of rights, but those qualifications have then seriously obscured the status and scope of the rights that they have announced.

Consider, for example, article 9 of the European Convention on Human Rights. That asserts that everyone has the right to the freedom 'to manifest his religion or belief, in worship, teaching, practice and observance'; but it then adds that that right shall be subject to such limitations as 'are necessary in a democratic society in the interests of public safety, for the protection of public order, health or morals, or for the protection of the rights and freedoms of others'. The Convention's assertion of the rights of freedom of expression (article 10) and of freedom of assembly and association (article 11) are subject to similar qualifications. There is nothing disingenuous in those qualifications. They simply betoken Burke's point that life is complicated and we cannot deal satisfactorily with its complications by focusing on one type of consideration to the exclusion of all others.

We therefore seem faced with an unfortunate choice of alternatives. Either we treat rights as absolutes, which has the merit of giving them an unambivalent status but which may also present us with thoroughly unsatisfactory moral outcomes and sometimes plain incoherence (when one right conflicts with another), or we accept that most, if not all, rights do not have an absolute status; but that threatens so to muddy the waters that it will cease to be clear what, morally, having a right amounts to.

There is no easy way out of this choice. A certain amount of 'specialness' is built into the very idea of rights, but the exact moral status that should be given to any particular right is a moral, not a conceptual, question and we should expect people to answer it differently. Nor is this conundrum unique to rights. A moral outlook cast wholly in terms of duties would present us with similar questions of whether one duty might conflict with another and whether some duties should be regarded as absolute. We can ask of any principle which is given fundamental moral importance – being just, keeping promises, telling the truth – whether there could be circumstances in which that principle would be justifiably set aside or overridden. However it may be that the question of 'weightiness' has come to be particularly associated with rights because people have looked especially to rights to provide them with security and protection. Although the road ahead is not clear, we can do a certain amount to clear a path through the thicket of considerations that surrounds this issue.

Conditional rights

Firstly, we can dispose of one way in which the possession of a right may be qualified which is quite separate from its moral 'weight' as a right. Suppose we enter into an agreement according to which you undertake to pay me a sum of money if I mend your car. My right to the money is then conditional upon my mending your car. If I mend the car, I am entitled to the money; if I fail to mend it, I am not. The question of the 'absoluteness' of that right – of whether there could be circumstances in which you would be justified in not paying me the money, even though I had mended the car – then remains to be argued. In other words, the moral status of that right is unaffected by the fact that my possession of it was conditional upon my mending your car. In that sense of 'conditional', a right can be simultaneously conditional and absolute.

Clearly rights which arise out of bilateral or multilateral agreements are typically 'conditional' in this way. Rights may also be conditional in that they are granted by rules which give people those rights subject to their satisfying certain conditions. Thus I may be granted a right to draw a welfare benefit conditional upon my satisfying certain criteria of need. In all of these cases, rights are conditional in a way that does not preclude their being morally or legally absolute.

One other significant way in which rights may be conditional is when their possession depends upon material circumstances. As we saw in Chapter 7, people cannot have rights to physical goods which do not exist. People cannot have a right to a standard of living which exceeds what can be achieved at that time. Nor can they have a right to a medical cure which does not exist. Human rights to socioeconomic goods must clearly be conditional in this way and, for that reason, it makes perfectly good sense to hold that, nowadays, human beings have rights to goods which they did not possess a century ago and that, in a hundred years time, they may have rights which they do not possess now. But, once again, the fact that the possession of these rights is conditional upon circumstances does not affect their moral standing as rights; that is a quite separate issue.

Prima facie rights

A right which is 'conditional' in the sense that I have just outlined is different from what has come to be described as a 'prima facie' right. The recognition that rights may sometimes be justifiably overridden has led to a widespread use of the phrase 'prima facie' in conjunction with rights.[1] Describing a right as 'prima facie' is a way of acknowledging that there may be circumstances in which that right would be justifiably overridden. Thus, if I have a 'prima facie' right to x, ordinarily it would indeed be wrong for me to be denied x but, extraordinarily, all things considered, that right may have to yield to some competing and more weighty consideration. That other competing consideration may be another right or it may be another sort of moral consideration.

Obviously there is scope for a right to be assessed as more or less 'prima facie' depending both upon the weight given to that right and upon the weight given to other rights and to other sorts of moral consideration with which it may come into conflict. There are limits to how 'prima facie' a right can be if it is to remain intelligible as a right. If rights yield too easily and too perfunctorily in the face of competing concerns, they will cease to warrant description as 'rights'. Some people claim that utilitarianism can never satisfactorily incorporate rights just because, in a society guided by that theory, rights would lapse so frequently and so casually in the face of the demands of social utility that they would lose their distinct character as rights (Lyons, 1984; cf. Flathman, 1984). But, although there must be limits to the negotiability of rights, there is now a very widespread willingness to accept that very many rights must be regarded as prima facie. For example, contemporary academic proponents of human rights are generally more reluctant to claim absoluteness for those rights than their predecessors were to claim absoluteness for natural rights.

Even so, there are philosophers who are deeply unhappy with the language of 'prima facie rights' (Morris, 1968, pp. 498–9; Feinberg, 1973, pp. 73–5; Melden, 1977, pp. 4–16). Their unhappiness stems from the fear that, if a right is said to be merely prima facie, that may imply that, when that right comes up against and yields to a conflicting moral consideration, the right itself simply disappears. A prima facie right would not then be one which might be justifiably overridden in special circumstances; for, in those special circumstances, an individual would cease to have a right, so that there would be nothing left to override. Thus Herbert Morris protests, 'It is seriously misleading to turn all justifiable infringements into non-infringements by saying that the right is only *prima facie*, as if we have in concluding that we should not accord a man his rights, made out a case that he had none' (1968, p. 499.) In order to cope with this understandable reservation about the language of 'prima facie rights', we need to distinguish clearly between there being merely a prima facie case for someone's having a right and her actually having a prima facie right. We must also distinguish between cases in which a prima facie right conflicts with, and is justifiably overridden by, another moral concern, and cases in which we simply encounter the limit or boundary of that prima facie right.

Consider first what we are to understand by there being a prima facie case for someone's having a right. Suppose we are weighing up various considerations in determining whether someone should be reckoned to have a right to x. Considerations a, b and c argue for a person's having that right and, in that respect, we might say that there is a prima facie case for her having a right to x. On the other hand, considerations d, e and f argue against her having that right. If d, e and f together are weightier than a, b and c, we shall conclude that the person has no right to x. In these circumstances it would be quite wrong to speak of someone's having a prima facie right to x. The most we can say is that there was a prima facie case for someone's having that right but, after all things were considered, that prima facie case turned out to be inadequate, so that the person was adjudged to have no right to x.

That is quite different from someone's having a prima facie right to x. In that case a person has a right to x even though we might encounter circumstances in which that right would conflict with other moral considerations and be justifiably overridden. In those circumstances the person still *has* a right to x, even though it is a defeasible right. If she had no right in those circumstances, there would be no moral conflict and no right to be overridden. Thus there is a difference between there being a prima facie case for someone's having a right and their having a prima facie right. Or, to express that distinction still more economically, there is a difference between someone's having, prima facie, a right and their having a prima facie right.

Lest this appear a distinction without a difference, consider the following case. A government introduces internment for the sake of national security. The threat to national security is sufficiently real and the benefits of internment are sufficiently certain to persuade us that resort to detention without trial is justified. Yet we are also to be heard holding that people have a right not to be imprisoned without trial. How then should we characterise the position of the internee? Suppose, having done our moral thinking, we conclude that the right not to be imprisoned without trial simply lapses when national security is threatened. In that case, during a national emergency the internee has no right – not even a prima facie right – not to be detained without trial and he suffers no 'wrong' in being interned. Suppose, however, that we reason differently. Suppose that we hold that people have a right not to be imprisoned without trial even during a national emergency. We might still reach the reluctant conclusion that, all things considered, including the severity of the threat to national security, internment is justified. However in that case we would have to allow that detaining people without trial infringes their rights and that internees suffer an injustice. All things considered, that injustice may be a justified injustice but it is an injustice nonetheless. Thus there is more to regret if we hold that, in an emergency, a right has to be overridden than if we hold that, in an emergency, people cease to have the rights that they normally have. In one case the internee is wronged, in the other case she is not and those different moral readings of internment are, for example, likely to affect our appraisal of whether internees ought to receive compensation for having been detained without trial.

Consider another example. One circumstance in which people are generally willing to allow that the right of free speech may be compromised is when its exercise is likely to result in a serious public disturbance. When a speaker is silenced in order to prevent a riot, what happens to his right of free speech? Does he cease to have that right, or does he continue to possess it even though, in the interests of public order, he is justifiably prevented from exercising it? If he is justifiably prevented from speaking, it may seem sensible to say that he has no right to speak. Yet, very often in these cases, the fault lies with the hearers rather than with the speaker. It is not that the speaker is saying something that he has no right to say; rather it is others who are responding to his speech in an improper manner. It is the audience rather than the speaker who are (morally) responsible for the disruption. Even so, the authorities may correctly believe that the only way that they can maintain order amongst the audience and protect life and limb is by silencing the speaker. In that case, it is quite appropriate to hold that the speaker had a right to say what he was prevented from saying, even though he was justifiably prevented from saying it.

In both of these examples the rights at issue are interpreted as prima facie rights. If the right not to be imprisoned without trial or the right of free speech were absolute rights, we could never justifiably detain people without trial, nor could we silence them in the interests of public order and safety. But treating rights as prima facie rights is still quite different from characterising the relevant circumstances as ones in which there is a mere presumption, a merely prima facie case, for people having rights which, on examination, they turn out not to have at all. Provided we remain sensitive to that distinction, there seems nothing exceptionable in the notion of prima facie rights.

Rights versus rights

Just how 'prima facie' should we expect rights to be? In particular, how tolerant should we be of the notion that rights can conflict with one another as well as with other moral concerns? It is easy to contemplate cases where such conflicts seem to arise. If we assert both a right of freedom of press and a right to privacy, or a right to choose one's associates and a right not to suffer discrimination, or a right to equal opportunity and a right to bequeath property, clashes between those rights seem inescapable.

The extent to which rights can conflict with one another will depend partly upon how prodigal we are in our assertion of rights. The more generous we are about the number and the scope of the rights that individuals have, the more occasion there will be for those rights to conflict. If virtually every significant interest a person has is made the subject of a right, we shall have to weigh rights against one another and allow them to override one another, regularly and perfunctorily, just as we routinely trade off competing interests against one another (cf. Waldron, 1989). In other words, rights will not only be 'prima facie', but 'prima facie' in a very high degree.

However the extent to which rights must come into conflict with one another is often greatly exaggerated. Frequently rights appear to conflict only because their scope has been inadequately defined. Consider, for example, 'the right of free expression' and 'the right not to be libelled'. Stated in those bald terms, we seem to have two rights which conflict with one another such that one of them – the right of free expression – must be only a prima facie right. At some point the right of free expression conflicts with, and is properly 'overridden' by, the right not to be libelled. But that appearance of conflict arises only because the boundaries of the right of free expression have remained wholly undefined. It is perfectly reasonable to hold that the 'expressions' which people are entitled to make are not unbounded. In particular, the freedom of expression to which people have a right does not include the freedom falsely to impugn the character of others. So it is not that, at some point, the right of free expression conflicts with, and has to be sacrificed to, the right not to be libelled; it is simply that the bounds of the right of free expression stop short of libel. There is therefore no conflict between those two rights.

Of course the same situation is open to different moral readings, as we have already seen. Where one person sees a right being overridden, another may see only a right reaching its limits. Consider the prohibition of racist speech. One person may see this prohibition as coinciding with the proper boundaries of the right of free speech. Another may see the right of free speech conflicting with, and being overridden by, the right not to be subjected to racial abuse and harassment. But, even allowing for the possibility of different moral interpretations, many rights theorists have been too ready to find conflicts between rights when greater attention to detail would have removed that appearance of conflict.

Part of the problem here is presentational. If a declaration of rights is to be popularly accessible and emotionally stirring, it has to be punchy and economical. It has to assert rights in a brief, pithy and easily assimilable form. If the statement of each right took several pages of detailed definition and qualifying clauses, it would lose its resonance. Yet, logically, there is no reason why rights must be formulated in a few simple words. Rights relating to freedom of expression or freedom of association or the fairness of trials, when fully articulated, might consume several pages of print. That, as I have said, might inhibit their utility in the rough and tumble of political argument, but it might also dispel the appearance of conflict between rights. If only rights were more fully defined, we might discover that they were entirely consistent with one another. Indeed we might suppose that the mutual compatibility of a set of rights *must* be a feature of a satisfactory theory of rights. If a theory yields conflicting rights, perhaps that indicates that there is something wrong with the theory. In a fully worked out moral or political theory all rights would be 'compossible' (Steiner, 1977a).

Is there any reason, then, why we should accept that rights will conflict with one another? Can there be genuine dilemmas of this sort or are those conflicts either apparent rather than real or merely symptoms of muddle-headed and inadequate theorising? There are two ways in which it remains difficult to eliminate the possibility of conflict between rights altogether. The first is really a matter of drafting – literally in the case of legal rights, metaphorically in the case of moral rights. In laying down rules and enunciating rights, it is difficult to foresee and to provide for all possible eventualities. It is therefore difficult to provide for all possible situations in a way that removes every possibility of conflict between rights. This applies not only to grand declarations of human rights but also to detailed statute laws. Legislators, however hard they try, still create situations in which people seem to have conflicting rights. Indeed a certain amount of 'openness' in legislative language is sometimes deemed desirable so that judges have scope to reach the best decisions in all the relevant circumstances rather than be forced by rigid rules to resolve a case in the 'wrong' way. Similarly there are limits to the comprehensiveness of our moral thinking. We can anticipate and take account only of so much. To demand that a moral theory yield a clear and unequivocal directive in every possible situation is to demand more than is reasonable.

The second reason why conflicts of rights may not be wholly eliminable is more substantial. In a society that was highly stable and in which everyone adhered to the rules, it might be possible to define a structure of rights that was entirely without conflict or dilemma. But our world is not like that and it is often because

people do violate others' rights that we ourselves are presented with
dilemmas concerning rights. Suppose, for example, that we ascribe
to individuals rights not to be harmed and rights to privacy.
Ordinarily those rights may co-exist without complication. Even so,
cases may still arise in which people's lives are threatened and in
which they can be safeguarded only by invading the privacy to
which others have a right (cf. Sen, 1982, pp. 7–12). What should we
do in those cases?

Suppose a murderous regime threatens the lives of thousands of
people. The only way of effectively putting a stop to that regime may
be by using violence which itself is likely to cause the deaths of many
innocent people, particularly if it involves bombing. What should we
do? Suppose a group has hijacked an aeroplane and threatens to kill
the passengers unless their demands are met. Should we save the
lives of the passengers by giving in to those demands? Or should we
resist the demands and sacrifice the lives of the passengers in order
to deter future hijackings which will endanger yet more lives and
which should be of no less concern to us simply because we do not at
present know precisely when they will occur or precisely whose lives
will be threatened? I have presented these dilemmas in a series of
'supposes', but they are all recognisable as real-life dilemmas. It is
often violations of rights of these sorts that present us with tragic
choices concerning individuals and their rights. As long as the
ordinary pattern of life is interrupted by those sorts of episodes, it is
difficult to provide wholly against conflicts of rights (cf. Sher, 1984).

If we are confronted with a conflict of rights, how should we
resolve it? That question is easily answered by those theorists for
whom rights are merely the subordinate ingredients of a goal-based
theory. Since rights are justified only as the instruments of goals, we
should resolve a conflict of rights in the way that is most conducive
to the goal that stands at the head of the theory. Part of the enduring
appeal of consequentialist moralities derives from their providing
overarching norms by reference to which competing values,
including rights, can be evaluated in relation to one another. But
how are conflicts of rights to be dealt with in a rights-based theory?
The reasoning which underpins such a theory might itself indicate
how the conflict is to be resolved. Thus, for example, Alan Gewirth
(1982, pp. 219–20) invokes his agency theory of rights to argue that,
if two rights conflict so that one cannot be fulfilled without
infringing the other, that right should take precedence which is the

more necessary for action. So, for example, if we should find that the right not to be lied to was at odds with the right not to be killed, it is the latter that should override the former. The greatest difficulty would seem to be faced by those theorists who assert a number of rights independently so that there is no hint of a common metric by which their relative significance is to be measured. For example, proponents of self-evident rights would seem to have nowhere to turn – except, perhaps, to self-evidence again – to find an order of priority amongst those rights (for example, McCloskey, 1985).

In general these sorts of trade-offs between rights go against the grain of rights thinking and it is worth repeating that they should be necessary only occasionally. The principles governing the form that these trade-offs should take amongst right-holders may also vary. One option is what Nozick has described as a 'utilitarianism of rights' (1974, pp. 28–30). In this approach the fulfilment of rights would itself become a sort of 'goal' whose attainment was to be maximised. Given inescapable conflicts between rights, we would seek to maximise rights fulfilment, or to minimise rights violations, in a way which would ape the utilitarian's endeavour to maximise aggregate utility or to minimise aggregate disutility. But that is not the only option. Remember that one of the rights theorist's stock objections to utilitarianism is that it is willing to sacrifice the interests of some individuals, without limit, for the sake of the interests of others, provided only that that maximises aggregate utility. A 'utilitarianism of rights' would be open to a parallel objection: it would be willing to have the rights of some individuals sacrificed, without limit, for the sake of the rights of other individuals, provided only that that maximised aggregate rights fulfilment. The rights theorist is unlikely to be indifferent to that objection and so is likely to prefer a more 'distributive' strategy. That is, if rights have to be sacrificed, he might be primarily concerned to ensure that those sacrifices are spread amongst the members of a society as equitably as possible.

Are there absolute rights?

Even if not all rights are absolute, it may still be that *some* rights are absolute. Gewirth (1982, pp. 218–33), for instance, argues that a mother has an absolute right not to be tortured to death by her son.

He tests the absoluteness of that right by arguing that it should not be infringed even if a group of political extremists had captured a nuclear arsenal and were threatening, credibly, to bomb a city and so kill thousands of innocent people if the son did not torture his mother to death. Gewirth's argument turns critically upon the claim that, even in these dire circumstances, the son bears responsibility for his own actions and not for consequences brought about by others. His duty is not to torture his mother and he is not at liberty to abandon that duty because others will perform some dire act if he continues to respect his mother's right. Nor should we think of the mother's right as in competition with the rights to life of the inhabitants of the threatened city. If the terrorists carry out their threat, it is not the son but the terrorists who are responsible for violating the rights of the city-dwellers. Hence the mother's right remains absolute.[2]

Gewirth is clearly correct to fasten upon the link between moral responsibility and consequences as something of central importance to the moral status of a right. As we have seen, rights limit consequentialist reasoning. Hence the duties imposed by rights cannot be entirely consequence-dependent. But the critical question for the absoluteness of a right is whether it should be upheld *whatever* the consequences. Arguments about the absoluteness of a right often turn into a sort of moral philosopher's game in which those who claim absoluteness for the right are challenged to maintain their position in the face of increasingly excruciating and improbable circumstances in which ever more lurid and unpalatable consequences follow upon the inviolability of the right. But is the difference between a right that may never be infringed and one that may virtually never be infringed really so critical? Suppose that we can think of extraordinary and utterly improbable circumstances in which a right of fundamental importance would finally have to yield. Of what significance would that be? None at all, except in those extraordinary and utterly improbable circumstances. So the search for rights which are absolutely and utterly indefeasible in every imaginable circumstance may be of limited practical value.

People have often been persuaded to forsake the idea of absolute rights because conflict and compromise seem inescapable features of the messy world of political practice. However, in some cases, the logic of absoluteness may work the other way round. That is, there may be reasons why a right which is not, in theory, absolute should nevertheless be treated, in practice, as though it were. Consider the case of torture again. Earlier I gave an example in which the torture of a terrorist might lead him to reveal the location of his bomb and so enable us to save hundreds of innocent lives. The point of that example was to suggest that there may be circumstances in which even the right not to be tortured should be set aside. But consider now the use actually made of torture in the modern world. It is easy to think of cases in which governments have used torture in morally grotesque and thoroughly unjustified ways; it is extremely difficult to think of cases where the resort to torture has been excusable. Given that state of affairs, granting governments even a limited licence to use torture would almost certainly do much more harm than good. So, in practice, the most prudent strategy might be to place an absolute ban upon the use of torture by governments even though, in principle, there could be circumstances in which torture would be justified. Thus appeals to the 'realities' of political life can sometimes argue for, rather than against, our treating some rights as absolute.

A right to do wrong?

If people have rights, whether prima facie or absolute, are they immune from criticism for the use they make of those rights? There seems nothing untoward in subjecting the use of rights to non-moral criticism. We may criticise someone for eating unhealthy food, investing their money unwisely or decorating their home tastelessly and yet accept that they have the right to do all of those things. But can we subject the use of rights to moral criticism? If people have a right to act as they do, it may seem that, morally, there is nothing else to say. However things are not quite so simple.

To begin with, it is easy to see how people may use *legal* rights in morally wrongful ways. People may be granted a legal right to do what they have no moral right to do, so that in exercising that legal right they would be committing a moral wrong. But even legal rights of which we approve are often open to misuse. Someone might, for instance, use the legal right of free speech to make gratuitously offensive remarks or to convey misleading information or to exploit people's emotions. There is a limit to how refined laws can be and, anyway, it is inappropriate to use the cumbersome machinery of law to eradicate every petty wrong. Thus the notion that people might 'abuse' their legal rights is not at all problematic.

It is also easy to contemplate circumstances in which someone might have a moral right to commit a legal wrong. What is more puzzling is whether there could ever be a *moral* right to commit a *moral* wrong (cf. Raz, 1979, pp. 266–7; Waldron, 1981, 1983; Galston, 1983). That suggestion sounds paradoxical and, clearly, there cannot be a moral right to commit every moral wrong. But might there be a limited class of wrongful acts which people have a right to engage in? Here we need to reintroduce the distinction between liberty-rights and claim-rights. For A to have the moral liberty-right to do x is for A to be morally at liberty to do x – to have no moral duty not to do x. For A to have the moral claim-right to do x is for A to have the moral right that others shall not prevent his doing x.

The notion that A can have a right to do wrong is most readily consistent with that right's being a claim-right. Suppose that A says something that he has no right (that is, no liberty-right) to say; it may still be incumbent upon others not to silence him. Silencing A may involve an act of assault, even if only a mild one, and A's speaking wrongly may be reckoned an insufficient reason for releasing others from their duty not to assault him. In that way, A may have a claim-right to say what he has no liberty-right to say. Even if A could be silenced without assault, for example, by pulling the plug on a microphone, there may still be reasons why others would have no right to do that. They may, for example, have a duty not to censor the statements of others. We may generalise that into the observation that, when individuals act wrongly, others may sometimes have a duty not to interfere with their so acting and, on those occasions, the offending individuals may be said to have a right (that is, a claim-right) not to be prevented from doing wrong.

Can we go beyond that and hold that A could have a moral liberty-right to do wrong? It may seem logically impossible to answer yes to that question. To have the liberty-right to do x is to have no duty not to do x and, if x is wrong, surely there must be a duty not to do x and therefore no liberty-right to do x. Yet even the notion of a liberty-right to do wrong is not wholly nonsensical. However, before investigating that possibility, it is best that we temporarily suspend the phrase 'the right to do wrong', since that makes the claim seem more perverse than it is. The claim sounds less paradoxical if we juxtapose rights to 'good' and 'bad' rather than to 'right' and 'wrong'.

Consider first cases in which someone uses a right in what we are likely to regard as an especially virtuous way. For example, we would ordinarily regard as particularly admirable someone who uses her right of self-determination to devote the whole of her life to relieving the suffering of others. We can praise those who lead such saintly lives without condemning those who do not. Such acts of self-sacrifice, we might say, are good to do even though people have a right not to do them, for they exceed the demands of duty. To that extent, then, there is scope for different moral appraisals of the ways in which people act, even though all of their acts remain within the range of what they have a (liberty-) right to do.

Consider now the obverse case, the sort of act that we would condemn people for performing but not praise for not performing (or, contrariwise, not praise for performing but condemn for not performing). Can people have a right to act in ways which fall below, as well as in ways which rise above, the line that divides vice from virtue? Suppose someone does me an unsolicited favour. For example, my next-door neighbour weeds my garden while I am away for several weeks so that it will not be overrun by dandelions and nettles on my return. My neighbour then goes away herself. Should I tend her garden while she is away? We may think that I have a right not to – I did not ask her to weed my garden while I was away and I have given her no undertaking that I shall weed her garden while she is away. Nevertheless we might still feel that I would be acting poorly if I did not return her favour, particularly if the effort involved was fairly modest.

Or consider a case in which a contract is involved. I have lent you money which you have undertaken to return by a certain date. I therefore have a right that, on that date, you shall return the money to me. However, before that date arrives, your financial circumstances take a turn for the worse. You will now be just about able to repay me on the agreed date but that will entail great hardship for you and your dependants. In those circumstances we might acknowledge that I still have a right to demand repayment but that, if I have no urgent need of the money myself, I really ought to extend the period of the loan.

Admittedly the distinction between acting viciously and failing to act virtuously is not always clear. If, for example, I refrain from contributing to a charity, am I acting badly or merely failing to act well? But the relevant point here is that we may find moral fault with the way in which people behave even though we accept that they have a right to behave in that way.

None of this shows that there *is* a liberty-right to act wrongly or badly or even a liberty-right to act with less than saintly virtue. But it does show that the notion of a right to do wrong (of the limited sort that I have described) is not incoherent. Moreover those who subscribe to the view that individuals have a right to a significant area of personal freedom may find it difficult to avoid this notion of a limited right to do wrong. Much of what people choose to do within that area of freedom may, of course, be a matter of moral indifference – neither good nor bad. But if individuals are given the freedom to form and express opinions, to begin and end friendships, to marry and divorce, to lead religious or irreligious lives, to act on their convictions, to dispose of their income as they wish, and to do all of the many other things that typically figure in the notion of 'personal freedom', it is unlikely that they will always do all of those things in ways which meet with our moral approval.

The limits of a morality of rights

While the notion of a right to do wrong serves to underline the special status of rights, it also indicates that rights are not co-extensive with morality as such. If we are open to praise or blame for the way we use our rights, rights themselves cannot provide the grounds for that praise or blame. Thus our conceptions of people's rights do not exhaust the range of our moral thinking and an attempt to think only in terms of rights would result in a severely attenuated morality.

We have already seen how there can be collective goods which cannot be factored into individual claims of right and that sometimes rights themselves have value only as instruments of collective goods. The natural partners of rights are duties, but even duties stretch beyond rights. As we saw in Chapter 2, duties to promote general goods – duties which are not owed to 'assignable individuals' – neither stem from nor give rise to rights. Consider too duties such as generosity, benevolence, mercy or kindness. These are usually characterised as 'imperfect duties' because they are duties which, by their very nature, do not answer to rights. For example, my giving you x can be an act of generosity only if you have no right to x; if you had that right, I would be acting justly rather than generously in giving you x. A morality which tied everything to rights could find no place for such imperfect duties.[3]

Sometimes acts of generosity and kindness are characterised as acts of supererogation rather than imperfect duty, particularly when they reach the heights of self-sacrifice that we associate with saints and heroes. Supererogatory acts are acts which it is good to do but not wrong not to do. They are acts which go beyond the bounds of duty. But since they exceed the bounds of duty, they also exceed what others can claim as matters of right, so that, again, the good of supererogation cannot be accounted for solely in terms of rights. Even so, the concept of supererogation remains tied to the morality of rights and duties in that we can identify a realm of good conduct which goes 'beyond' duty only if we can first identify a realm of duty. But much of our moral thinking is, typically, quite independent of rights and duties. There are many things that we may think we 'ought' to do which we would conceive neither as duties nor as supererogatory acts. For example, we may think that we ought to comfort someone who has suffered a bereavement or to clear the snow from an elderly neighbour's footpath or generally to strive to improve the lot of our fellow human beings without thinking of any of those things as duties grounded in rights or as discretionary acts of saintly virtue. The point is not that those acts could not, in their very nature, be either duties grounded in others' rights or acts of supererogation. The point is rather that they need not, and ordinarily would not, be conceived in either of those ways.

One area in which the limited scope of the language of rights is particularly apparent is that of close personal relationships. Consider friendship. Typically part of what we understand by that is the special concern for one another shown by people who are friends. But we would misrepresent the nature of that special concern, and the relationship from which it stems, if we tried to explicate it in terms of rights and duties.[4] Similarly the tissue of relationships that make up families at their best seems inappropriately described in terms of rights and duties. We think that the care and concern that the members of a family, ideally, have for one another should consist in something more than a punctilious regard for rights and duties. This does not mean that children have no rights in respect of their parents or, indeed, that parents have no rights in respect of their children. Clearly we can and sometimes have to think in those terms, but, typically, we resort to rights and duties in the context of families when something has gone wrong, when the love and care that ideally sustains family relationships has faltered or disappeared. As Kleinig observes, 'Unless there is love, care and concern for others as individuals, *in addition to* the recognition of rights, there remains a moral lack in interpersonal relationships' (1978, p. 46).

None of this argues against rights. It argues only that we should not attempt to say all that we want to say about how we should live and how we should relate to one another in the language of rights. A morality consisting of nothing but rights and their associated duties would not do justice to the varied and nuanced character of our moral thinking.

Individualism, egoism and community

Might the range of rights be reduced still further? If a morality consisting partly of rights is more attractive than one consisting wholly of rights, might a morality wholly without rights be still more attractive? Some have thought so. In some people's minds, rights have been associated with individualism and egoism and have therefore been thought incompatible with any truly communitarian ideal.

Rights may be said to foster individualism because they give moral significance and moral titles to individuals separately. They have therefore been condemned for promoting atomism, both in reality and as a moral ideal. In establishing safeguards for individuals, rights can seem to erect fences which separate and divide people from one another. A society of right-holders can begin to look like one whose members are invited to retreat to their individual moral territories and to live essentially private lives, rather than encouraged to think of themselves as members of a community characterised by a rich and closely integrated common life. These worries about individualism are sometimes accompanied by charges of egoism. Rights are alleged to foster egoism because they make claims on others which are grounded in the right-holder's own interest. Whereas duties, obligations and responsibilities are essentially other-regarding, rights are essentially self-regarding. Thus, if we encourage people to think in terms of rights, we encourage them to think about themselves. We enable them to cloak their naked self-interests in a garb of moral sanctimony. We do nothing to induce them to curb their selfish demands or to attend to the well-being of others. Rights, it is sometimes said, promote an unedifying and unhealthy self-centredness.[5]

These reservations about rights are to be found amongst the radical left as well as the conservative right. While many socialists have been eager to phrase their beliefs and demands in the language of rights, others have regarded that language as alien to the values and ideals of socialism. Marx, in particular, was scathing about 'the rights of man' declared in America and France. Not only did he think that these were part of the ephemeral bourgeois ideology thrown up by capitalism, he also deprecated them as manifestations of individualism and egoism: 'none of the so-called rights of man goes beyond egoistic man, man as he is in civil society; namely, an individual withdrawn behind his private interests and whims and separated from the community' (1971, p. 104).[6]

Sometimes people have suggested that we should respond to these objections by giving greater prominence to the rights of groups. Group rights, it is sometimes supposed, will provide a counter-balance to the atomism and egoism of individual rights. But that tactic is misconceived. If rights encourage fragmentation, group rights will encourage group fragmentation, the dissolution of a community into a number of separate and hostile factions, and that form of disintegration may be no more acceptable than social atomism; indeed, it may be more dangerous. If rights foster egoism, group rights will foster group egoism and, again, it is not clear that group selfishness is morally superior to, or practically more tolerable than, individual selfishness.

How, then, might rights be defended against these complaints of individualism and egoism? We must begin by accepting that some conceptions of rights are incompatible with some conceptions of community. Some conceptions of the nature and content of rights are highly individualistic, particularly those which stress the strictly negative character of human obligations, and these may encourage the weakening of social bonds. Likewise some conceptions of community, particularly those which stress hierarchy and inequality and those which 'lose' the individual in an organic unity, do not recognise individuals as beings with rights. But not all conceptions of rights are at odds with all notions of community.

It is sometimes said that when we ascribe rights to individuals we treat them as asocial beings. That is false. The whole point of providing for rights is to provide for human interaction. Robinson Crusoe may have had rights but they were utterly without practical significance while he remained alone. Rights provide for life in society. In addition, ascribing a set of entitlements to individuals *qua* individuals is quite consistent with acknowledging that human beings are fundamentally social animals whose well-being is inextricably tied to their social circumstances. Some rights, such as political, economic and social rights, presuppose a network of social institutions. But even the more traditional 'civil' rights are clearly directed towards regulating the lives of human beings in communities.

Historically rights have been used to break some social bonds, for example bonds of slavery and servitude, but generally the endeavour has been not to destroy societies but to change their character. The relevant issue is not whether we should sacrifice rights to community or community to rights; rather it is what sort of community we want there to be. The ascription of rights to individuals does not preclude community; it sets some of the terms of community and it is wholly consistent with a conception of human life as properly or ideally communal in character. All that the rights theorists want to insist is that there are ways in which a community is required to treat, or not to treat, its individual members. Nor need we think of those requirements as 'barriers' to community. They regulate rather than forestall social relations and, arguably, a community's provision for those rights should form part of what we understand by its 'common good' (cf. Finnis, 1980, pp. 210–18).

It is easy to understand why rights have attracted complaints of egoism. The spectacle of a pack of individuals baying for their 'rights' is not always a pretty one. Assertions of rights often come from people who seem to suffer from a form of moral tunnel vision which prevents their focusing upon anything but what they believe is owed to themselves. When rights are combined with a culture that makes a virtue out of the assertion of 'self' and 'identity', they can issue in a particularly vicious and divisive form of self-centredness. Even when rights do not assume this unpleasant aspect, there is a sense in which they remain conspicuously self-directed: generally my rights focus on my well-being; that is why I have them. There are some exceptions to that. One arises from promises or contracts involving third party beneficiaries: if you promise me that you will do something to benefit someone other than myself, I acquire a right that someone else shall be benefited. But that exception to the general self-directedness of rights is little more than a detail. More significant are rights which rely upon consequentialist justifications – rights whose ultimate justification resides, not in the well-being of the right-holder, but in that of society or humanity at large. However, if we want to give a fundamental status to at least some rights, we cannot resort to consequentialism for a comprehensive defence of rights against the charge of egoism.

How, then, might the rights theorist break this alleged link between rights and selfishness? In a number of ways. Firstly, we have seen that, when people have rights, the use they make of those rights remains open to critical appraisal. In no way do rights require people to act selfishly or place them beyond criticism if they do act selfishly. Secondly, we have also seen that rights typically figure in some rather than in all of our moral thinking. To allow that individuals have rights is not to allow that nothing should be of concern to them but rights. Thirdly, a comprehensive amoral selfishness is simply inconsistent with rights thinking. When we claim rights for ourselves as human beings or as citizens, logically, we must claim those same rights for all other human beings or citizens. Thus, when I demand or assert rights of that general sort, logically I cannot be making exclusively self-centred claims. In addition, if I conceive my rights as imposing duties upon my fellow citizens or human beings simply because they are fellow citizens or human beings, I must accept that I too must share in those general duties of citizenship or humanity.

Nor need I recognise and show concern for other people's rights only because that is a price I have to pay, reluctantly and grudgingly, for having rights myself. There is simply no good reason why a morality structured in terms of moral titles must be more selfishly motivated than any other morality. Indeed there are innumerable examples, both past and present, of people showing selfless concern for the rights of others.

The charge of egoism stems from a confusion of two quite separate propositions. One is that human individuals have a certain moral standing and a range of moral titles as human beings and that it is incumbent upon all of us to show the respect and concern for human individuals that that standing and those titles require. The other is that rights license individuals to behave entirely without regard for others. The second (false) proposition is not entailed by, nor even associated with, the first proposition.

Of course it remains true that a concern for the well-being of individuals is built into the morality of individual rights. But there is no reason why we should be apologetic about that. Are we supposed to give no moral significance to individual human beings? Are those who view rights with distaste, and who plead for community, really saying that its individual members should be enslaved or tortured or subjected to show trials or deprived of fundamental freedoms if their use in any of those ways would 'serve' a community? If so, few of us would want to join them. If not, it is hard to make sense of their unwillingness to ascribe rights to individuals.

It may be that one day we shall live in a world in which people are so well-disposed towards one another that insistence upon their rights becomes unnecessary. In such a world, the morality of rights may have been supplanted by an ethic of love which caters for all that rights demand and more besides. But, if that is the world we want, we should regard the securing of individuals' rights as a stage on the road to its achievement rather than an obstacle that stands in its path. That loving community should be understood as one which goes beyond, rather than one which removes, individuals' rights. People would still have rights, they just would not need to worry about them. Unfortunately, in the modern world, we cannot afford to be so casual; rights still need to be noticed and we should beware of ideologues, be they hectoring or silken-tongued, who seek to persuade us otherwise. The most disastrous and murderous political experiments of the twentieth century have provided ample notice that 'abolishing' rights does not expedite the journey to the promised land.

Human rights and cultural diversity

A feature of the world which is often associated with ideas of community and which is sometimes thought to embarrass proponents of *human* rights is cultural diversity. The world is characterised by different cultures embodying different world-views and systems of value. Yet the human rights theorist would have us believe that a single set of rights is possessed by humanity the world over. Does not the existence of cultural diversity belie that vision of a set of rights universal to mankind? Is the doctrine of human rights any more than an arrogant assertion by one culture that its values should take priority over and, if necessary, displace those of all other cultures?[7] Is the doctrine of human rights merely a new and insidious form of western imperialism (cf. Pollis and Schwab, 1979a)? That is a complicated question and we need to break it down into a number of distinct issues.

Perhaps the first question that needs to be asked is whether the mere fact of cultural diversity must embarrass a theory of human rights? In answering that question, we can begin by noticing a number of ways in which a doctrine of human rights can co-exist quite happily with cultural diversity. Firstly, 'cultures' are highly inclusive phenomena and the diversity of very many of their components need do nothing to perturb human rights theorists. Why should they be troubled by the existence of different forms of diet, dress, art, music, style of life, and the like?

Secondly, the rights theorist may be more than merely untroubled by this diversty. Freedoms of various sorts have always figured prominently in the human rights tradition. Thus, in living the form of life characteristic of their inherited culture people, may be doing just what the human rights theorist would insist that they are entitled to do. If we assert that human beings have a right of freedom of religion, why should we take exception to the diverse forms of religious belief and religious life present in the world? If people have a right of freedom of association, why should we be perturbed by the diverse forms of social organisation that humanity has adopted? The liberal tradition, in which rights thinking has been most firmly embedded, is one which has sought to accommodate and to celebrate human diversity rather than reduce all humanity to a single pattern of life.

Thirdly, it may be that human rights can be, and have to be, realised in different ways in different societies. Different circumstances may require the same general principles to be instantiated in different ways. For example, in a peasant society the right to education or the right to a fair trial may need to be provided for quite differently than in an urban industrialised society. It is important not to confuse a diversity of circumstance with a diversity of value. If a diversity of practice is simply a response to differences of circumstance, it need not embody any fundamental difference of value.

However, while there is something in each of these points, they evade the central way in which cultural diversity challenges human rights thinking. What if the beliefs, values and practices central to a culture are fundamentally at odds with those of a doctrine of human rights? What if a culture endorses slavery or gives fundamentally different statuses to people of different races or sexes or castes? What if it gives no recognition to the basic freedoms that usually figure in statements of human rights or prescribes forms of punishment that rights theorists would condemn as 'cruel and degrading'? There are some naturalistic versions of rights thinking for which the very occurrence of this sort of conflict must be an embarrassment. For example, a theory which alleges that it is 'self-evident' that individuals have rights, and also self-evident what those rights are, must have difficulty in explaining why the existence of those rights has not been evident to so much of humanity for so much of the time. There is also a tradition of rights thinking which holds that certain rights are so essentially a part of the human condition that, as a matter of fact, they will be recognised and provided for in the arrangements of virtually all societies. Clearly that sort of thinking will also be discredited if we discover that, on the contrary, there are major cultures in which these allegedly universal rights have remained unrecognised.

For the most part, however it is not the mere existence of different cultures that causes proponents of human rights to hesitate. After all, part of the very point of the ascription of rights equally to all human beings has been to challenge and to oust contrary ways of thinking. Is our conviction that slavery is wrong seriously threatened by the fact that there have been cultures which have viewed slavery as part of the natural fabric of life? Should the mere fact that many cultures have accorded different statuses to people belonging to different races dislodge our belief that people are entitled to neither better nor worse treatment merely in virtue of their racial origins? It would be very odd to hold that a set of moral convictions was discredited merely because they had not been held or acted upon by everyone.

The real reason for the human rights theorist to hesitate in the face of cultural diversity lies not in its mere existence but in the sense that there is something valuable, or at least something requiring respect and a measure of diffidence, in the cultures of others. Treating people in ways which have no regard for their own self-understanding and which compel them to conform to alien values goes against the grain of human rights thinking. Should we compel a society to respect 'rights' even though that notion is entirely foreign to its own culture? Can we really be content to destroy patterns of life which are characteristic of entire communities and which give meaning and coherence to the lives of their members merely because we ourselves believe that those patterns of life are somehow not 'rightful'?

Ironically the idea that people's cultural identities should be respected derives in large part from the same kind of thinking that underlies human rights. The human rights theorist holds that all human beings must be respected, which, in turn, entails allowing individuals to live according to their own chosen forms of life. In a parallel fashion, the champion of cultures holds that all cultures must be respected, which, in turn, entails allowing each culture to continue and to flourish in its own way. Indeed the case for respecting cultures can be stated in a way which brings it even closer to human rights thinking. Individuals, it may be said, are not asocial atoms whose identities and aspirations are wholly cut off from their social environments. Individuals' identities, perspectives and values are acquired from the cultures in which they develop. Thus respecting individuals entails respecting the cultures which are essential to the identities and forms of life of those individuals. In some measure the champion of cultures can be seen as simply appealing to human rights theorists to recognise the centrality of culture to people's lives and to recast their principles of equality and respect in a form which recognises that social fact. Respecting human rights and respecting cultural diversity may therefore be closer in spirit than the letter of each sometimes suggests.

It may also be that, once we have taken the cultural context of people's lives fully into account, the appearance of moral conflict – at least as it affects the fundamentals of morality – will prove to be no more than appearance. Moralities provide for social living and there may be certain norms that have to be accepted by any body of people if they are to live together in a single community. A doctrine of human rights might then be seen as a formulation of those common standards. What appear to be significant differences between cultures may be no more than different contextual expressions of a single set of norms (Milne, 1986).

As we have already noted, there is scope for holding that the same principles can be or must be instantiated in different ways in different circumstances. But that is not quite the same as the claim that I have just described: that the same moral principles can find expression in different cultural norms. That claim also has some plausibility, but it exceeds the limits of that plausibility to suppose that we can dismiss all significant moral conflicts as merely different particularised expressions of an identical set of principles. For example, the conventions governing what counts as 'civil behaviour' and 'good manners' vary considerably from one society to another. If we hold that all human beings have a right to be treated civilly, there is no problem in allowing that that right will require different conduct in different contexts according to different local conventions governing what counts as civil conduct (Milne, 1986, p. 138). But consider the cases of abortion and suicide. In some societies these are permitted, in others not. Milne (1986, pp. 126–8) also treats these as different contextual interpretations of the right to life, but that is much harder to accept. These look less like different local expressions of the same morality than *conflicting* understandings of what is morally permissible. More generally, if we make the universal cross-cultural acceptance of a norm a precondition of its being a human right, we are in danger of so diluting the content of human rights that they will cease to have point. If, for example, the doctrine of human rights has to be pared down so that it can accommodate the caste system and the imposition of religious and ideological uniformity (Milne, 1986, p. 167) we may begin to wonder whether it retains any moral and political significance.

Equally it is hard to see why, philosophically, a doctrine of human rights should be constrained in that way. If we are concerned with political practicalities, it makes sense to search for uniformity amidst diversity since it will be easier to achieve world-wide acknowledgement of a set of rights if those rights, or something like them, are already recognised by virtually all societies. But, morally, it is not obvious why our view of what is right should be constrained by what everyone, now or in the past, has regarded as right. In addition, if our concern is merely the practical goal of securing agreement on rights, we need concern ourselves only with finding common ground amidst the cultural differences that exist *now*. But if the claim is a philosophical one to the effect that human rights can consist only of rights that would be recognised in all cultures, those rights would have to be discoverable in all past as well as all present cultures – indeed in all *possible* cultures – and it is hard to be persuaded that there can be any such rights.

In truth, we have to recognise that a doctrine of human rights is a moral doctrine and not a set of anthropological generalisations (cf. Renteln, 1990). Given the fundamental character of human rights, it may well be that certain of them will be widely recognised and upheld. We should also be sensitive to the possibility that apparently conflicting beliefs and practices may really be no more than different cultural expressions of the same fundamental principles. But there is nothing inevitable about the embracing of human rights by all societies and proponents of human rights must therefore be prepared to confront opposing systems of belief and stand their ground. They cannot hold both that there are rights which all human beings have and that there are some human beings who do not have those rights.

Nor should the human rights theorist be too readily cowed by the invocation of cultural diversity. To begin with, the very representation of moral disagreements as conflicts between 'cultures' sets things up in a way which prejudges the nature of those disagreements. Cultures are evolved by particular groups of people at particular times. They are invented and developed by each group, even if not consciously so. Thus differences between cultures are merely differences between views of the world and ways of living that have been evolved by different sets of human beings. That suggests that they are all equally valid or perhaps all equally invalid. In that way, the idea of culture brings relativism with it. It does not describe the world in a 'neutral' way but comes heavily freighted with implications about the nature and the (lack of) foundation of human values. In addition, it is not always clear what is to count as a 'culture' and what is not. Is every system of value which is at odds with the idea of human rights to be considered a culture? Are Nazism and the beliefs of the Khmer Rouge 'cultures' or merely 'ideologies' – and what would be the moral significance of making that distinction? Why should some systems of value be open to critical examination yet not others?

Nor is the aspiration to universality unique to human rights thinking. Commentators on cultural diversity often treat cultures as if they made claims only on behalf of, and in relation to, those who are already encompassed by those cultures. Outside interference with a culture is then represented as interference with a people which is merely minding its own business and which has no concern with the world beyond its own cultural group. But that is simply a conceit held by would-be benign observers who look upon cultures from the outside. More typically cultures embody general views of how the world is, of man's proper place in it, and of how people ought to conduct their lives. That is especially true of cultures founded in religious faiths. Thus those who are within (what is described as) a 'culture' typically do not conceive themselves as mere bearers of a culture. From where they stand, they hold certain beliefs which they reckon to be true and therefore universally true. They do not subscribe to the logical nonsense that their beliefs are somehow true for themselves but not true for others. Thus it is quite wrong to represent the world as one peopled by moral relativists whose relativism is challenged only by human rights thinking. On the contrary, the world is in much larger measure one characterised by rival universalisms and, to that extent, it is grossly mistaken to suppose that moral diversity is uniquely problematic for theories of human rights.

None of these remarks is intended to suggest that proponents of human rights should regard themselves as licensed to treat opposing sets of values, or their adherents, with contempt. It behoves all of us to regard our beliefs with a degree of humility and, within the doctrine of human rights, there are powerful reasons for both tolerating and respecting diverse forms of life. Moreover, even when we confront a cultural practice which conflicts with human rights, there is a whole host of reasons why we should hesitate about intervening. The proponent of human rights does not have to be an insensitive boor. It is also worth reflecting upon how much of the opposition to human rights in the modern world, and what proportion of human rights violations, can be traced to the bearers of rightless cultures innocently pursuing their rightless lives. My guess is not very much. I suspect a much larger proportion of what would ordinarily be regarded as human rights violations are either mere abuses of power or consequences of ideologies which are every bit as western in origin as the doctrine of human rights. But, once all of those qualifications have been entered, the possibility of conflict between human rights and cultural traditions remains. Unless it is morally neutered, a doctrine of human rights cannot give its blessing to practices that it identifies as morally grotesque and inhuman merely because those practices are shrouded in the mantle of culture.

Conclusion

In the course of this book we have ranged over a large number of questions concerning rights. We have also seen how those questions have been answered in a variety of different and conflicting ways. Diversity is a feature of people's ideas about rights just as it is a feature of human cultures. Some debates about rights have been contests between the friends and the enemies of rights, but quarrels amongst the proponents of rights have been just as conspicuous and just as significant. How should the existence of those disagreements affect our thinking about rights? Can we take rights seriously if they are subject to doubt and dispute of this sort? Whatever we might think about the merits of opposing ideas about rights, does not the very existence of those opposing ideas do something to discredit all theories of rights and to undermine the practical aspirations of their proponents?

Dissensus does, indeed, pose a problem for rights but we should be careful to identify what sort of problem that is. The mere fact of disagreement does little to impair the *philosophy* of rights in general or of human rights in particular. There is in our world a measure of dispute about what, in general, is morally right, although sometimes there is less disagreement about what is right than about why it is right. Rights figure in that moral dissensus but the dissensus is in no way special to them. All of our moral notions attract controversy. What are our duties, what we ought to do, what sort of people we would ideally be, what we should consider just – all of these moral matters, and more besides, are subject to debate.

Sometimes this sort of disagreement is thought to be especially discreditable for rights, but it is difficult to understand why. There are, of course, traditions of rights thinking, such as ideas of self-evident rights, for which the fact of dissensus is philosophically threatening. But claims of self-evidence have not been confined to rights and anyway conceptions of rights need not be, and in this century generally have not been, wedded to claims of self-evidence. The fact is that rights merely share in a dissensus that infects morality in general and that discredits conceptions of rights neither more nor less than any other aspect of our moral thinking. So, if we scoff at rights because they are subject to dispute, we should scoff no less at the whole world of moral thinking. If we toss aside all talk of rights because there is disagreement about their content, we ought, in consistency, to toss aside all of morality. Philosophically, then, there is no reason for singling out the morality of rights as especially flawed or especially implausible because it is subject to debate.

The real problem that the fact of dissensus creates for rights is *practical* rather than philosophical. How can a society's conduct be governed by rights if those rights are subject to disagreement and uncertainty? Once again, this problem is not unique to rights. All of morality is practical in that it concerns what we ought to do and how we ought to live. Any aspect of morality is therefore practically problematic if it is characterised by doubt and dispute. But there is one way of providing for rights for which dissensus poses special difficulty. Generally, when we confront dissensus, we do not allow ourselves to be paralysed by it. There are still ways in which we can decide upon a course of action. In particular, it is part of the purpose of political processes to take diverse views and to produce decisions from them. But that way of dealing with dissensus is not uncomplicatedly available to the more ambitious aspirations for rights.

We saw in Chapters 3 and 4 that the traditional political purpose of natural or human or fundamental rights has been to tell those who wield political power what they may and may not do. That purpose has been to inform them that they must use their powers to uphold and to protect their citizens' rights and, more especially, that they must not use their powers in ways which violate people's rights. In that way, rights aim to limit the discretion available to governments and to political processes. There are some entitlements which must not be ignored or set aside by those who wield political power (including electorates) because, morally, those entitlements are founded upon something other than the largesse of political power and because, morally, they possess a significance which ranks above the purposes of those who exercise political power.

If that is the practical aim of propounding fundamental rights, how is it to be achieved? One commonly used strategy has been to take rights out of the ordinary political arena by giving them a special constitutional status. A set of rights is entrenched in a constitution and so rendered immune from the ravages of political power. Political power can then be exercised only within the constraints imposed by those constitutional immunities. But if that strategy is to be both appropriate and feasible, there must be a reasonable degree of consensus on the content of rights. If there is radical disagreement within a society over what rights people have, that disagreement has to be resolved and that process of resolution will place rights back *inside* the political process that they are supposed to constrain. Of course there may be ways in which a society can resolve disagreements about rights other than by resort to its ordinary political machinery. The point I am making here is simply that the attempt to provide for rights by taking them out of the political arena and by placing them beyond the reach of ordinary political decision making will be more difficult and more resented to the extent that significant numbers of people hold conflicting views about those rights. Thus, while disagreement about rights no more discredits philosophies of rights than disagreement about black holes discredits astrophysics, it does create problems for the ambitious project of providing for rights by excluding them from a society's ordinary political processes.

If we shift our focus from a single society to the whole of humanity, that practical problem is magnified. If human rights are to be recognised and implemented across the entire globe, they have to secure consensus amongst a much larger and much more diverse population and also across nation-states each of which is jealous of its sovereignty and independence. If the content of human rights is radically disputed, the attempt to impose any particular version of human rights upon all societies will seem little more than an exercise of power by some over others – an exercise of power that will be all the more resented because it will be conceived as violating the autonomy of societies and the sovereignty of their political systems.

Thus it is the high political ambitions that people have for rights that makes disputes about them especially troublesome. The greater the dissensus about rights, the more practically difficult it will be to establish them as fundamental entitlements which constrain what a society and its government may do. However, since we are now in the realm of the politically practicable, we should not exaggerate the reality of this difficulty. We have to deal, in practice, with what is the case rather than with what might have been the case. In practice there is not the radical and evenly distributed dissensus about every aspect of human rights that, in principle, there might have been. There may not be full world-wide agreement about any aspect of human rights, but there is at least very widespread acceptance of the idea of human rights and also a measure of agreement about their content. The UN's Declaration and other internationally endorsed statements of rights are testaments to those facts. Of course those documents typically phrase rights in very general terms which evade the detailed questions to which their rights give rise. Moreover the lip-service that people pay to human rights is not always reproduced in their conduct. But it is still significant that they feel constrained to acknowledge that human beings have rights, for, as Rochefoucauld observed, hypocrisy is the homage that vice pays to virtue.

If we turn to individual societies, whatever disagreement there may have been about rights has not prevented very many states from establishing constitutionally protected rights which have made a very real difference to the lives of their citizens. Dissensus about rights has not therefore been sufficient to prevent many societies from securing a special place for rights which removes them from the ordinary arena of politics.

However even when that way of providing for rights has been politically feasible, its wisdom has been questioned. Not everyone who is an enthusiast for rights is an enthusiast for constitutional entrenchment. Some argue that the effectiveness of rights depends less on constitutional forms than on political cultures. If concern and respect for rights is deeply engrained in a society's culture, that is protection enough. Nothing is likely to be added by constitutional documents. If, on the other hand, concern and respect for rights is absent from a society's culture, that lack of commitment cannot be made good by constitutional instruments. It is not paper documents and institutional forms that determine what happens in a society but the character of the people who make up that society, particularly its decision makers. If they have no concern for rights, constitutional protection will be difficult to achieve and may be ineffective even if it is achieved.

Another consideration which turns some advocates of rights away from constitutional entrenchment is the matter of their interpretation and application. Even if we can secure a measure of agreement on a bill of rights, those rights are typically announced in very general terms. If a right is formulated only in a general way, it will leave a number of questions still to be settled, such as where exactly its limits lie, what precise duties it entails, upon whom those duties should fall, what sort of practical measures satisfactorily provide for the right, at what point the right would be justifiably curtailed or overridden out of deference to other considerations, and so on. All of these are important questions. Who should answer them? Constitutional entrenchment normally means that they cannot be resolved by the ordinary political process, but that does not mean that they can remain unanswered. Somebody still has to answer them and that 'somebody' is usually a panel of judges. Are judges the best or the right people to decide upon those issues?

Many people think not, since these questions look like routine political questions; if they are political questions, surely they should be dealt with by democratically elected politicians. Judges should make judicial decisions and politicians should make political decisions. Of course we should not be too naive about that distinction. Judges cannot be mere ciphers; even when they administer ordinary laws, they cannot apply legal rules to specific cases without interposing judgements of their own. Nor need judges be worse interpreters or custodians of rights than politicians. It is often politicians who have the greatest incentive to compromise rights, so that they are not always their most trustworthy guardians. In some countries and on some issues, courts have had better track records as defenders and developers of rights than politicians. But there is no avoiding the fact that general bills of rights do leave large areas of discretion open to whoever interprets them and that that interpretation involves judgements of a moral and political rather than a strictly technical nature. That being so, some proponents of rights believe that the issues to which they give rise are properly dealt with by elected politicians rather than by unelected judges. On their view, rights should remain special but their specialness should be felt in the way that they are handled by politicians rather than in their not being handled by politicians.

Thus we have two models for the way in which rights should make their impact upon a society's political processes. One would remove rights from the political arena so that they are no longer at risk inside that arena and so that they limit what can be decided within it. The other would keep rights inside the political arena and, instead of looking to them to constrain political decisions from the outside, would intend rights to have their impact by guiding debate and decision making within that arena. Of course neither model need be adopted to the complete exclusion of the other. Not all rights are of equal importance and those who favour constitutional entrenchment are unlikely to want to provide for all rights in that way. Similarly those who are sceptical about constitutional provision might still allow it a limited role, if only a symbolic one. My concern here is not to resolve the question of which of these two models we should follow – indeed which is the more appropriate model, and in what measure, may vary from society to society – rather I have taken up these questions in order to make three general points about rights.

Firstly, disagreement is no more a feature of thought about rights than it is a feature of other areas of moral and political thought. Nor is disagreement any more of a problem for philosophies of rights than it is for other aspects of moral and political philosophy. If dissensus poses a problem special to rights, that problem is practical rather than philosophical in character. It arises from the special political role that we want rights to perform.

Secondly, institutionally we can look to rights to perform that special political role in different ways. We can provide for the special status of rights either by giving them a constitutional status which places them outside the ordinary political process or by allowing their special status to be felt inside that process. The first option has the merit of giving rights clear institutional recognition and protection but is more problematic the more rights, and issues relating to rights, are subject to dispute. The second option makes the handling of disputes concerning rights much easier since they can be resolved through the ordinary mechanisms of politics. But the price of that greater ease is that rights can be dismissed or set aside just as readily as any other matter that is subject to ordinary political decision making.

Thirdly, a distinction is to be observed between the matter of what rights people have and the matter of what institutions should be used to secure those rights. Thus we should not confuse (though people sometimes have confused) the general case for rights with the case for a particular form of institutional provision. In particular the case for rights is not exhausted by the case for bills of rights.

Although I have given much attention in this conclusion and in previous chapters to the difficulties that surround rights, I hope I have also managed to convey something of why rights matter. In some philosophical circles, the moral and political thinking associated with rights has recently become unfashionable. In particular the aspiration to ascribe rights alike to all humanity is now viewed in some quarters with a mixture of hostility and derision. But before we join in those smug dismissals, we should remember why it is that people have taken up the idea of rights. Outside the cocooned world of the academy, people are still victims of torture, still subjected to genocide, still deprived of basic freedoms and still dying through starvation. We should remember those people before we decide to forget about rights.

Notes

Chapter 1

1. For attempts to unsettle Hohfeld's analysis, see White (1984), Stoljar (1984), Stone (1963), Kamba (1974), Kocourek (1920), Goble (1935) and Radin (1938). For discussions sympathetic to Hohfeld, see Brady (1972), Perry (1977), Mullock (1971), Attwooll (1977), Dias (1976, pp. 33–65), Finnis (1972) and Wellman (1985).
2. Hohfeld gives 'duty' as the opposite of a liberty-right. However there is a lack of symmetry in this opposition. The opposite of the liberty-right to do x is not the duty to do x but the duty not to do x. Likewise the opposite of the liberty-right not to do x is not the duty not to do x but the duty to do x. Cf. Williams (1968, pp. 128–32) and Fitch (1967).
3. For examples of allegedly erroneous judicial decisions arising from the confusion of liberty-rights with claim-rights, see Hohfeld (1919, pp. 42–5) and Williams (1968, pp. 140–3). However these accusations of judicial error have proved controversial; see Hudson and Husak (1980), Perry (1980) and White (1984, pp. 67–70, 168–70).

Chapter 2

1. This is also implicit in Hohfeld's giving a 'no-right' (really a 'no-claim-right') as the correlative of a liberty-right. A has the liberty-right to do x if A has no duty not to do x. Hohfeld supposes that A's having no duty not to do x is equivalent to B's having no claim-right that A shall not do x. But that also implies that, if A has a duty not to do x (and therefore no liberty-right to do x), there must be a B who has a claim-right that A shall not do x. In other words, Hohfeld's analysis leaves no scope for A's having a duty not to do x which does not imply that there is a B who has a claim-right that A shall not do x.
2. MacCormick adds that, in this context, 'interest' or 'good' is to be understood as 'what is considered to be normally an advantage' rather than necessarily what proves advantageous in any specific case. Thus, for example, we would continue to speak of the right to inherit property even in a case where the relevant property was in such a state of disrepair that it was more of a burden than an asset (1977, p. 202).
3. The qualified beneficiary theory needs the qualification 'direct' as well as 'intended', as the following example shows. Suppose I undertake to give a regular sum of money to a married couple. They are then directly

228

and intentionally the beneficiaries of my undertaking; they can be said to have acquired a right to receive regular payments from me. However suppose that my real concern is not for the well-being of the couple but for their children; I have decided to give money to the parents in the expectation, and with the intention, that they should use it to benefit their children. The children can then be said to be the intended beneficiaries of my undertaking, but that is not sufficient to give the children rights to my payments, since my duty is a duty to – is directed to – the parents; the children stand in a merely contingent relation to that duty.

4. For an attempt, in my view unsuccessful, to accommodate these sorts of power within the interest theory, see MacCormick (1982b, pp. 166–7). It might be claimed that, if I have a right, I must also have an interest in that right's being respected (even though there may be cases in which that interest would be outweighed by another, competing, interest of mine – for example, my interest in being accorded my right to swim in rough seas may be outweighed by my interest in my life's not being endangered). But, even if we were to allow that I always have a prima facie interest in being accorded my rights, that claim could not be used to shore up the benefit theory, since the benefit it points to is logically separate from and consequent upon the possession of the right rather than definitive of the right itself.

5. Hart's view here contrasts with that of the celebrated jurist, John Austin, whose name is often associated with the 'will' or 'choice' theory. Austin describes duties which bestow rights as 'relative' duties since they are duties directed towards determinate persons. We can test whether a duty is of that sort, he suggests, by considering whether it would be capable of civil rather than criminal enforcement – whether its enforcement could be 'at the discretion or pleasure' of the person to whom the duty is to be performed (1911, p. 398). What he calls 'absolute' duties are directed to society at large and their enforcement must therefore be undertaken by the state rather than left to the discretion of private individuals. By contrast, the transgression of a 'relative' duty inflicts injury directly upon a determinate person and a legal system could therefore allow the injured party to choose whether action should be taken against the transgressor. However, as a test of rights, this 'choice' can be hypothetical rather than actual; it is designed only to indicate whether a duty is a 'relative' duty. Many such duties, although they could be the subjects of civil law, have, in fact, been made the subjects of criminal law, particularly in more developed societies, and their performance is not actually under the control of those to whom they are owed. Nevertheless, given that the performance of those duties could be under the control of those to whom they are directed, that, for Austin, is enough to indicate that they are 'relative' duties yielding rights. Consequently, unlike Hart, Austin holds that rights stem from criminal laws such as those proscribing murder, battery and theft, even though the right-holders can exercise no actual choice in respect of those laws. (Austin, 1911, pp. 398, 400–405, 501.)

6. Of these various characterisations of rights, it is the interpretation of rights as claims, or as claims of a particular sort, that has attracted most attention. For critical discussions of analyses of rights as claims, see Martin (1982), White (1982, 1984), MacCormick (1982b) and Halpin (1991).

7. The details of the way in which Bentham relates sanctions to legal duties are not without complication, on which see Hacker (1973) and Hart (1982, pp. 127–47). Bentham's follower, John Austin, also conceptualised duties, and therefore rights, by reference to sanctions (1911, pp. 343–6, 394–407). Austin sometimes spoke as though duties or obligations were conceptually separate from sanctions (for example, 'every right implies an obligation and a sanction', ibid., p. 344; 'It is only by conditional evil, that duties are sanctioned or enforced', ibid., p. 91). Yet he explicated being subject to a duty or obligation as being liable to a sanction or 'evil'. For example, in his famous statement of the command theory of law, he defined a command as 'a signification of desire' distinguished 'by this peculiarity: that the party to whom it is directed is liable to evil from the other, in case he comply not with the desire'. He then added, 'Being liable to evil from you if I comply not with a wish which you signify, I am bound or obliged by your command, or I lie under a duty to obey it'; '. . . command, duty and sanction are inseparably connected terms: . . . each embraces the same ideas as the others' (ibid., pp. 89, 91–2, Austin's emphases; see also ibid., pp. 443–57). Austin also tried to explicate moral rights and duties by way of sanctions (ibid., pp. 195–6, 286).

Chapter 3

1. Consequentialist theories have most commonly taken a maximising form; that is, they have defined right acts as those which maximise whatever is identified by the theory as the good state of affairs that ought to be brought about. Classical utilitarianism, for example, has taken this maximising form. However Slote (1985) has identified a form of consequentialism that would be 'satisficing' rather than optimising or maximising. This form of consequentialism would still judge the rightness of actions in terms of their consequences but it would require only that those consequences should be 'good enough' rather than that they should be the best possible consequences that could have been produced in the circumstances. However it is not clear that a consequentialism that is satisficing rather than maximising can avoid the conflicts with rights thinking that I go on to identify in this chapter, even though the less demanding nature of satisficing consequentialism may make it contingently less threatening to rights.

2. For discussions of what should be understood by 'utility', or what should be included in that concept, see Dworkin (1981, pp. 191–204), Griffin (1986, pp. 7–39) and Parfit (1984, pp. 493–502).

3. Utilitarians, while confining the raw material of social decision making to preferences, may seek to 'clean up' those preferences so that they remove the sub-optimal or distorting effect of preferences which rest on mistaken information, stem from erroneous judgements, meddle in the lives of others, and so on. The extent to which utilitarianism can allow the laundering of preferences is controversial. See, for example, Brandt (1979), Dworkin (1978, pp. 232–8, 274–7), Goodin (1986), Griffin (1986) and Harsanyi (1976, 1977).

4. Rights provide exclusionary reasons only when they give rise to duties. Thus, if we speak of mere liberties – mere absences of duties to the contrary – as rights, those are not rights which provide exclusionary reasons. The concept of an exclusionary reason helps to explain why a right retains its special status even when it is relatively trivial in content – as it might be, for example, in the case of the right acquired by the promisee that the promisor should run his promised errand. It is not the 'weight' of its content but its exclusionary character that gives the concept of a right its special status.

5. Notice that, in the right–duty relation, the right constitutes an exclusionary reason for the duty-holder rather than for the right-holder. That is, it provides an exclusionary reason for others, rather than for the right-holder, to act on; a right is not, for the right-holder himself, any sort of reason for action (cf. Waldron, 1981, pp. 27–9). In addition the duties generated by rights are only one of many sorts of exclusionary reason. All mandatory norms provide exclusionary reasons, including duties not stemming from rights, authoritative instructions, rules of thumb and decisions, as well as some non-mandatory norms and all prescriptions that are not norms (Raz, 1975, pp. 49–106).

6. I use the term 'rights-based' rather than 'right-based' to avoid confusion with the notion that a morality may be based upon a conception of 'the right' – the right thing to do or the right thing to be. A 'right-based' theory in this sense would belong to the family of duty-based theories rather than to that of rights-based theories.

7. In this tripartite classification of moral theories, 'goal-based' theories are to be understood as consequentialist theories which define right acts in terms of some best overall outcome for a society. A theory which recognises the significance of individuals' goals for individuals' lives can still be a rights-based theory. Cf. Dworkin (1978, pp. 90–94).

8. An exclusively rights-based political theory might be more defensible than an exclusively rights-based moral theory. That is, a rights-based position may be thought to provide adequately for the proper scope and use of political authority, even though a rights-based morality would not provide satisfactorily for the whole of life. Nozick is a good example of a theorist whose political position is rights-based but whose general moral philosophy is far too complex and subtle to be reducible wholly to rights (1974; 1981, ch. 5).

9. For an examination of various forms of rule utilitarianism, see Lyons (1965).

10. Rather than describing a view of the nature of the utility that we should aim to promote, the phrase 'rule utilitarianism' is sometimes used to describe the simple belief that adhering to established rules may be the most utile strategy for individuals to pursue. If that is all that is meant by rule utilitarianism, it is less clearly distinct from indirect utilitarianism.

11. Those who agree in urging the separateness of persons against utilitarianism do not agree about what that separateness itself requires, as is readily apparent from the conflicting political philosophies of Rawls and Nozick. Cf. Griffin (1986, pp. 230–1).

12. Frey (1980) argues against animal rights in just this way. He deploys a number of arguments but, briefly stated, his main argument against animal rights runs as follows. Let us work from the widely (though not universally) accepted premise that having interests is a necessary condition of having rights. To have interests one must have desires and to have desires, properly so called, one must have beliefs and be self-conscious (rather than merely conscious). But one cannot have beliefs or be self-conscious without possessing language. Animals do not possess language and so possess neither beliefs nor self-consciousness; consequently they do not have desires and so do not have interests; if they do not have interests, they do not have rights. (The same considerations lead Frey to place animals outside the scope of utilitarianism; 1980, pp. 131–8.) For an attempt to rebut Frey's argument and for a comprehensive defence of animal rights, see Regan (1983).

Chapter 4

1. Hobbes argued that, since individuals placed themselves under political authority to secure their own preservation, there were certain elements of their right of nature that they must be understood not to give up. These included an individual's right to resist those who 'assault him by force, to take away his life' and those who threaten him with 'wounds and chains, and imprisonment' (1957, pp. 86–7, 91–2). These natural rights of resistance were retained even when the relevant threats came from the sovereign (ibid., pp. 142–3). However it is crucial to Hobbes's argument that these continue to be understood as mere liberties. They were not claim-rights held 'against' the sovereign. On the contrary, the sovereign possessed the right to imprison or to kill any of his subjects; indeed those, like all of the sovereign's actions, were authorised by all of his subjects, including the subject whose life was threatened by the sovereign (ibid., pp. 112, 133, 139, 202–3).

2. Hobbes's right of nature was linked to his conception of natural law in that it described what men were at liberty to do under the law of nature. Thus how precisely one characterises Hobbes's right of nature depends upon how one interprets his law of nature – what it was that individuals were supposedly at liberty from. That issue has proved so

controversial that I shall pass over it. For purposes of the contrast I am making here, the crucial difference between the two thinkers is that Locke understood the laws of nature as a body of moral rules which bestowed a set of harmonious moral titles upon individuals and which provided for a naturally ordered mode of living. Hobbes's laws of nature, whatever their moral or religious status, consisted of a set of prescriptions instructing men how to escape from, rather than how to live harmoniously within, their natural condition.

3. For contrary views, see D'Entreves (1972) and Minogue (1978).

4. Aquinas himself made no such move from natural law to natural rights. While the language of rights is sometimes used in translations of Aquinas, there is disagreement amongst scholars about whether he himself possessed the concept of a right. This disagreement forms part of the larger argument over whether the notion of rights originated in the twelth or in the fourteenth century. See Tuck (1979, pp. 5–31), Finnis (1980, pp. 206, 228) and Tierney (1983, 1988, 1989).

5. Thus, for example, the 1793 version of the French Declaration included a right to education (article 22) and Paine in the last part of his Rights of Man elaborated a system of social security which he conceived a matter of right, not charity (1969, p. 265). However both of these rights were conceived as citizens' or 'civil' rights rather than natural rights (cf. Paine, 1969, pp. 90–91; Raphael, 1967b, pp. 61–3).

6. There are philosophers who argue, contrariwise, that human rights encompass only rights held against states and governments (for example, Mayo, 1967, pp. 77–8; Martin, 1980; Wellman, 1978, pp. 55–6). Certainly, where human rights take the form of positive claim-rights, they are most frequently understood as claims to be met through the use of state machinery. In addition, states and governments often pose the greatest threats to rights, so that there is reason to emphasise that states and governments in particular must respect human rights. But neither of those contingent features of human rights provides adequate reason for holding that human rights impose duties only upon states rather than upon individuals and non-state organisations as well.

7. Frey (1980, pp. 7–14) and Sumner (1987) do not use the language of 'ideal rights' but suggest, in the same spirit, that we should interpret 'I have a moral right to x' as 'I ought to have a legal or conventional right to x' or 'my having a legal or conventional right to x is morally justified'. For criticism of their views, see Feinberg (1992). Not surprisingly, this way of interpreting 'moral rights' is most prevalent amongst consequentialists.

Chapter 5

1. For critical discussions of Gewirth's theory, see Regis (1984) and the symposia in Pennock and Chapman (1981, pp. 148–74) and in Ethics,

LXXXVI (1976, pp. 265–87). Gewirth has given various replies to his critics; see Gewirth (1982, pp. 67–78) and Regis (1984, pp. 192–255).

2. Scanlon (1984) moves some way towards this solution. He rejects the utilitarian's use of subjective preferences as the basis for the evaluation of outcomes and substitutes 'an ethically significant, objective notion of the relative importance of various benefits and burdens' (p. 138). Thus he would include fairness and equality in the catalogue of ends which are to be valued in their own right (ibid., p. 142). He would also include in those objective benefits the ability of individuals to control what happens to themselves, which ability is typically a major concern of rights (ibid., pp. 139, 145, 148–50). Sen (1982) also argues for a 'goal rights system' which incorporates rights in the state of affairs by which consequences are to be evaluated.

3. For analyses of the right to private property and discussions of the issues that surround it, see Reeve (1986), Waldron (1988), Becker (1977) and Ryan (1984).

Chapter 6

1. However there is not a simple one to one relation between freedoms and immunities. A may be empowered to require B not to do x, in which case B is not immune from a requirement not to do x. However, as long as A does not exercise that power, B remains free to do x. That is why people can be said to enjoy freedoms even under a legislature that possesses unlimited powers and in relation to which, therefore, individuals enjoy no immunities.

2. I use 'duty' here not as an unqualified synonym for what we ought to do, but in its more specific sense as a particular sort of 'ought', such that it is necessarily true that my having a duty not to do x entails my having no liberty-right to do x. Thus what I say here does not exclude the possibility that we can have a right to do what we ought not to do. See further the section on the 'right to do wrong' in Chapter 9.

3. For general accounts of the idea of autonomy, see Lindley (1986), Young (1986) and Dworkin (1988).

4. Some writers prefer to limit 'being autonomous' to what I have described here as the 'internal' dimension of autonomy. External circumstances would then affect not whether one was autonomous but only the 'exercise' of one's autonomy. (cf. Lindley, 1986, pp. 68–9).

Chapter 7

1. In his later work Rawls has refined and narrowed his definition of primary goods; see Rawls (1993, pp. 106, 178–90).

2. I understand the right to personal security to mean the right to be protected from murder and assault rather than merely the right not to be murdered or assaulted.

3. International co-operation to realise economic, social and cultural rights is enjoined by the UN Charter (articles 1, 13 and 55), by the Universal Declaration of Human Rights (articles 22 and 28), and by the International Covenant on Economic, Social and Cultural Rights (articles 2 and 11). In particular article 11 of the ICESCR commits the State Parties to the Covenant, 'recognizing the fundamental right of everyone to be free from hunger', to taking measures 'to ensure an equitable distribution of world food supplies in relation to need'. On the other hand, article 2 of the ICESCR – (along with article 2 of the International Covenant on Civil and Political Rights – ICCPR) states that 'All peoples may, for their own ends, freely dispose of their natural wealth and resources without prejudice to any obligations arising out of international economic cooperation . . ..'; and article 25 provides that 'Nothing in the present Covenant shall be interpreted as impairing the inherent right of all peoples to enjoy and utilize fully and freely their natural wealth and resources.'

4. This issue is considered at greater length in Jones (1990).

5. For arguments which link welfare rights to civil and political rights – though not always quite as simply as I have suggested here – see King and Waldron (1988, pp. 425–31); Daniels (1975); Gutmann (1980, pp. 122–9, 190–202) and Plant (1985).

Chapter 8

1. Whether the sort of theory developed by Rousseau is properly described as rights-based depends upon which of its elements is given primacy. If the driving idea is the autonomy of individuals, it can be seen as rights-based. But if primacy is given to the attainment of a good which is general to the body of citizens, that would be what I have described as a decision-centred (goal-based) argument.

2. In practice, of course, it has often worked the other way round; that is, a group of individuals has often derived a sense of nationhood from its being marked off from 'outsiders' by its political boundaries and by its subjection to a common political authority. Thus, in reality, the claim of traditional nationalism has often been inverted - it is not the identity of a nation that has set the boundaries of the state but the existence of the state that has created a sense of national identity.

Chapter 9

1. This use of the qualification 'prima facie' derives from the moral philosopher, W.D. Ross (1930, ch. 2). Ross himself uses the phrase 'prima facie' in conjunction with duties, ought, and right and wrong but not in conjunction with rights. However his analysis of the relation between rights and duties implies that there must also be prima facie rights.

2. Gewirth seems to use the mother-son relationship for its emotional effect rather than because it is crucial to the logic of his argument. That specific case is subsumed by his more general thesis that 'All innocent persons have an absolute right not to be made the intended victims of a homicidal project' and that right, in turn, stems from the general principle that 'agents and institutions are absolutely prohibited from degrading persons, treating them as if they had no rights or dignity' (1982, p. 233).

3. However we should also note that some acts of imperfect duty are possible only because their authors possess rights. For example, my giving you x can be an act of generosity only if I myself possess a right to x. Many virtuous acts depend for their character upon their authors having rights which they refrain from claiming or exercising. See Tomasi (1991).

4. For an attempt to integrate rights into friendship, see Meyer (1992).

5. Even some of the advocates of rights insist that rights are, in their very nature, competitive and adversarial; see, for example, Wellman (1985).

6. For argument about the compatibility of Marxism with rights, see Lukes (1982, 1985), Cornell (1984), McBride (1984), Tay (1978), Keat (1982), Waldron (1987, pp. 119–36) and Kain (1988). On the more general question of the compatibility of socialism with rights, see Campbell (1983) and Bellamy (1990).

7. It might, of course, be thought equally arrogant and presumptuous to suggest that the values embodied in human rights are unique to western culture.

Guide to Further Reading

There are a number of general books on rights each of which handles the subject in different ways. Freeden (1991) is similar in scope to this book but contains rather different views about rights. White (1984) gives a close linguistic analysis of rights and of the concepts associated with them. The general books by Flathman (1976) and Wellman (1985) also give most of their attention to conceptual questions. Benditt (1982) and Thomson (1990) focus rather more upon the moral philosophy of rights.

Some useful collections of articles on rights are Melden (1977), Kamenka and Tay (1978), Waldron (1984), Paul, Miller and Paul (1984) and Nino (1992).

For conceptual analyses of rights, Hohfeld (1919) remains seminal. The most important contemporary statements of the interest theory of rights are those of Lyons (1969), MacCormick (1977, 1982a) and Raz (1986, ch. 7). Hart's (1967, 1982, ch. 7) is the most celebrated case for the choice theory; others who embrace that theory are Kearns (1975) and Sumner (1987, pp. 96–101). Feinberg's is the best known analysis of rights as claims (1966; 1973, chs 4 and 5; 1980)

For the morality of rights, Dworkin (1978, 1985), Mackie (1984) and Feinberg (1980) are important sources. Waldron (1984) is an excellent collection of some of the most important contemporary theories of rights. A number of philosophers have attempted to develop comprehensive moral theories of rights: Gewirth (1978, 1982), Melden (1977), Lomasky (1987), Nino (1991) and Martin (1993). Sumner (1987) argues a consequentialist case for rights. Meyers (1985) defends the idea of inalienable rights. Other books which are very important for the morality of rights, even though rights do not constitute their primary subjects, are Rawls (1971, 1993), Raz (1986), Finnis (1980) and Griffin (1986).

On the specific issue of rights and utilitarianism, Hare (1981) gives the best case for incorporating rights within a utilitarian theory. Seanor and Fotion (1990) is a collection of critical discussions of Hare's theory. Brandt (1979, 1983, 1984) is another important advocate for the accommodation of rights within utilitarianism. Other useful sources on this issue are Frey (1985a), Smart and Williams (1973), Lyons (1984), Sen and Williams (1982) and Gray (1984).

Many of the books on the morality of rights listed above include examinations of human rights. Some other books which examine the theory of human rights sympathetically are Donnelly (1985), Nickel (1987) and Cranston (1973). Milne (1986) and Renteln (1990) offer approaches designed to reconcile human rights with cultural diversity. For surveys of how the doctrine of human rights fares in the different cultures of different continents, see Pollis and Schwab (1979a) and Thompson (1980).

MacFarlane's study of human rights (1985) focuses on the details of the rights in the UN Declaration. Applications of human rights to specific issues and subjects can be found in Gewirth (1982), Campbell et al. (1986), Davies (1988) and Blackburn and Taylor (1991).

Brownlie (1992) collects together the most important international documents on human rights. Sieghart (1986) and Davidson (1993) are accessible sources on the international law of human rights. Alston (1992) examines the UN's machinery for monitoring and implementing human rights. Vincent (1986) gives a good account of the significance of human rights for contemporary international politics and Lawson (1991) is a comprehensive reference work for all aspects of human rights in the modern world.

The best history of the development of the idea of natural rights is Tuck (1979). Tierney (1983, 1988, 1989) challenges some of Tuck's and other scholars' claims about the historical origin of the idea of rights. Other useful sources on the history of rights are Shapiro (1986), Lacey and Haakonssen (1991) and Waldron (1987).

The general question of who or what can possess rights is considered in White (1984, ch. 6), MacCormick (1982a), Feinberg (1980), Harrison (1972) and Singer (1981). The literature on animal rights has grown rapidly in recent years. Frey (1980, 1983) argues against, while Regan (1983) argues for, the ascription of rights to animals. Two other important contributions to the debate are Clark (1977) and Leahy (1991). Not all defenders of animals give primacy to rights, for example, Singer (1976) and Taylor (1986). Some useful collections on the issue of animal rights are Paterson and Ryder (1979), Miller and Williams (1983) and Clarke and Linzey (1990).

The literature on freedom is vast and the reader should turn to Gray (1991) for a comprehensive survey of that literature. Rights to freedoms are important themes in Rawls (1971, 1993), Gewirth (1978, 1982), Raz (1986) and Lomasky (1987). The right of freedom of expression is scrutinised in Schauer (1982) and Barendt (1987).

Welfare rights are examined and, for the most part, defended in Plant et al. (1980), Weale (1983), Harris (1987), Moon (1988) and Goodin and Ware (1990). Cranston (1967a, 1967b), Raphael (1967b, 1967c), Watson (1977), Shue (1980) and Vincent (1986, chs 7 and 8) are important sources for the argument over human socioeconomic rights. Nozick (1974) is the best known modern exponent of natural property rights. General examinations of the right to private property can be found in Becker (1977), Ryan (1984), Reeve (1986) and Waldron (1988).

Some books which deal with normative issues concerning democracy of the sort that are considered in Chapter 8 are Cohen (1971), Singer (1973), Lively (1975), Nelson (1980), Graham (1986) and Dahl (1989). Some significant studies of group rights are Van Dyke (1974, 1982), Kymlicka (1989, 1992), Kukathas (1992), Crawford (1988) and Hannum (1990).

Sceptical treatments of the idea of rights can be found in Nielson (1968), Young (1978), Frey (1980), Nelson (1976) and Rorty (1989, 1991). The criticisms of natural rights penned by Bentham, Burke and Marx are conveniently brought together with helpful commentary in Waldron (1987); Waldron himself (1987, ch. 6) provides a well-crafted defence of rights against those and more recent criticisms. Some major examples of the contemporary communitarian critique of rights are MacIntyre (1985), Sandel (1982, 1984) and Taylor (1985). For feminist doubts about rights, see Gilligan (1982) and Hardwig (1984). Where Marx and Marxism stand on rights is considered in Lukes (1985) and Kain (1988), while the more general question of socialist rights is examined by Campbell (1983).

Bibliography

Alston, Philip (ed.) (1992) *The United Nations and Human Rights* (Oxford: Clarendon Press).

Anderson, Alan Ross (1962) 'Logic, norms and roles', *Ratio*, IV, 36–49.

Arnold, Christopher (1978) 'Analyses of right', in Kamenka and Tay (eds) (1978) pp. 74–86.

Attwooll, Elspeth (1977) 'Liberties, rights and powers', in Elspeth Attwooll (ed.), *Perspectives in Jurisprudence* (Glasgow: University of Glasgow Press) pp. 79–97.

Austin, John (1911) *Lectures on Jurisprudence*, Robert Campbell (ed.) 5th edn (London: John Murray).

Barendt, Eric (1987) *Freedom of Speech* (Oxford: Clarendon Press).

Barry, Brian (1965) *Political Argument* (London: Routledge & Kegan Paul).

—— (1982) 'Humanity and justice in global perspective', in Pennock and Chapman (1982) pp. 219–52.

Becker, Lawrence C. (1977) *Property Rights: Philosophic Foundations* (London: Routledge & Kegan Paul).

Beitz, Charles (1979), *Political Theory and International Relations* (Princeton, NJ: Princeton University Press).

Bellamy, Richard (1990) 'Liberal rights and socialist goals', in Werner Maihofer and Gerhard Sprenger (eds), *Revolution and Human Rights* (*ARSP*, Beiheft XLI) (Steiner: Stuttgart) pp. 249–64.

Benditt, Theodore M (1978) *Law as Rule and Principle* (Brighton: Harvester).

—— (1982) *Rights* (Totowa, NJ: Rowman & Littlefield).

Benn, S. I. and R. S. Peters (1959), *Social Principles and the Democratic State* (London: Allen & Unwin).

Bentham, Jeremy (1952) *Economic Writings*, Werner Stark (ed.) (London: Allen & Unwin).

—— (1962) *The Works of Jeremy Bentham*, John Bowring (ed.) (New York: Russell & Russell).

—— (1970a) *An Introduction to the Principles of Morals and Legislation*, J. H. Burns and H. L. A. Hart (eds) (London: Athlone Press).

—— (1970b) *Of Laws in General*, H. L. A. Hart (ed.) (London Athlone Press).

Berlin, Isaiah (1969) *Four Essays on Liberty* (Oxford: Oxford University Press).

Blackburn, Robert and John Taylor (1991) *Human Rights for the 1990s: Legal, Political and Ethical Issues* (London: Mansell).

Brady, James B. (1972) 'Law, language and logic: the legal philosophy of Wesley Newcomb Hohfeld', *Transactions of the Charles Peirce Society*, VIII, 246–63.

Brandt, Richard B. (1979) *A Theory of the Good and the Right* (Oxford: Clarendon Press).

—— (1983) 'The concept of a moral right and its function', *Journal of Philosophy*, LXXX, 29–45.

—— (1984) 'Utilitarianism and moral rights', *Canadian Journal of Philosophy*, XIV, 1–19.

Braybrooke, David (1972) 'The firm but untidy correlativity of rights and obligations', *Canadian Journal of Philosophy*, I, 351–63.

Brownlie, Ian (ed.) (1992) *Basic Documents on Human Rights*, 3rd edn (Oxford: Clarendon Press).

Buckland, W. W. (1945) *Some Reflections on Jurisprudence* (Cambridge: Cambridge University Press).

Burke, Edmund (1910) *Reflections on the Revolution in France* (London: Everyman).

Campbell, Tom (1974) 'Rights without justice', *Mind*, LXXXIII, 445–8.

—— (1983) *The Left and Rights* (London: Routledge & Kegan Paul).

Campbell, Tom *et al.* (1986) *Human Rights: from Rhetoric to Reality* (Oxford: Basil Blackwell).

Clark, Stephen R. L. (1977) *The Moral Status of Animals* (Oxford: Clarendon Press).

Clarke, Paul A. B. and Andrew Linzey (eds) (1990) *Political Theory and Animal Rights* (London: Routledge).

Cohen, Carl (1971) *Democracy* (Athens: University of Georgia Press).

Cohen, G. A. (1986a) 'Self-ownership, world-ownership, and equality', in Frank S. Lucash (ed.), *Justice and Equality Here and Now* (Ithaca: Cornell University Press) pp. 108–35.

—— (1986b) 'Self-ownership, world-ownership, and equality: Part 2', *Social Philosophy and Policy*, III, 77–96.

Cornell, Drucilla (1984) 'Should a Marxist believe in rights?', *Praxis International*, IV, 45–56.

Cranston, Maurice (1967a) 'Human rights, real and supposed', in Raphael (1967a) pp. 43–53.

—— (1967b) 'Human rights: a reply to Professor Raphael', in Raphael (1967a) pp. 95–100.

—— (1973) *What are Human Rights?* (London: Bodley Head).

Crawford, James (ed.) (1988) *The Rights of Peoples* (Oxford: Oxford University Press).

Dahl, Robert A. (1989) *Democracy and its Critics* (New Haven, Conn.: Yale University Press).

Daniels, Norman (1975) 'Equal liberty and unequal worth of liberty', in N. Daniels (ed.) *Reading Rawls* (Oxford: Basil Blackwell) pp. 253–81.

Davidson, Scott (1993) *Human Rights* (Buckingham: Open University Press).

Davies, Peter (ed.) (1988) *Human Rights* (London: Routledge).

D'Entreves, A. P. (1972) *Natural Law* (London: Hutchinson).

Dias, R. W. M. (1976) *Jurisprudence*, 4th edn (London: Butterworths).

Donnelly, Jack (1985) *The Concept of Human Rights* (London: Croom Helm).

Doyal, Len and Ian Gough (1991) *A Theory of Human Need* (Basingstoke: Macmillan).

Dworkin, Gerald (1988) *The Theory and Practice of Autonomy* (Cambridge: Cambridge University Press).

Dworkin, Ronald (1978) *Taking Rights Seriously* (London: Duckworth).

—— (1981) 'What is equality? Part 1: Equality of welfare', *Philosophy and Public Affairs*, x, 185–246.

—— (1985) *A Matter of Principle* (Oxford: Clarendon Press).

Feinberg, Joel (1966) 'Duties, rights and claims', *American Philosophical Quarterly*, III, 137–44.

—— (1973) *Social Philosophy* (Englewood Cliffs, N.J.: Prentice-Hall).

—— (1980) *Rights, Justice, and the Bounds of Liberty* (Princeton, NJ: Princeton University Press).

—— (1992) 'In defence of moral rights', *Oxford Journal of Legal Studies*, XII, 149–69.

Filmer, Sir Robert (1949) *Patriarcha and other Political Works*, Peter Laslett (ed.) (Oxford: Blackwell).

Finnis, John (1972) 'Some professorial fallacies about rights', *Adelaide Law Review*, IV, 377–88.

—— (1980) *Natural Law and Natural Rights* (Oxford: Clarendon Press).

Fitch, Frederic B. (1967) 'A revision of Hohfeld's theory of legal concepts', *Logique et Analyse*, IX, 269–76.

Flathman, Richard E. (1976) *The Practice of Rights* (Cambridge: Cambridge University Press).

—— (1984) 'Moderating Rights', *Social Philosophy and Policy*, I, 149–71.

Freeden, Michael (1990) 'Rights, needs and community: the emergence of British welfare thought', in Goodin and Ware (1990) pp. 54–72.

—— (1991) *Rights* (Milton Keynes: Open University Press).

Frey, R. G. (1980) *Interests and Rights: the Case against Animals* (Oxford: Clarendon Press).

—— (1983) *Rights, Killing and Suffering* (Oxford: Basil Blackwell).

—— (ed.) (1985a) *Utility and Rights* (Oxford: Basil Blackwell).

—— (1985b) 'Act-utilitarianism, consequentialism and moral rights', in Frey (1985a).

Galston, William A. (1983) 'On the alleged right to do wrong: a response to Waldron', *Ethics*, XCIII, 320–4.

Gewirth, Alan (1978) *Reason and Morality* (Chicago: University of Chicago Press).

—— (1982) *Human Rights: Essays on Justification and Applications* (Chicago: University of Chicago Press).

—— (1984) 'The epistemology of human rights', *Social Philosophy and Policy*, I, 1–24.

Gilligan, Carol (1982) *In a Different Voice: Psychological Theory and Women's Development* (Cambridge, Mass.: Harvard University Press).

Goble, George W. (1935) 'A redefinition of basic legal terms', *Columbia Law Review*, XXXV, 535–47.

Goldblatt, David (1976) 'Do works of art have rights?', *Journal of Aesthetics and Art Criticism*, XXXV, 69–77.

Goodin, Robert E. (1985) 'The priority of needs', *Philosophy and Phenomenological Research*, XLV, 615–25.

—— (1986) 'Laundering preferences', in Jon Elster and Aanund Hylland (eds), *Foundations of Social Choice Theory* (Cambridge: Cambridge University Press) pp. 75–101.

—— (1988) 'What is so special about our fellow countrymen?', *Ethics*, XCVIII, 663–86.

—— (1990) 'Relative needs', in Goodin and Ware (1990) pp. 12–33.

Goodin, Robert E. and Alan Ware (eds) (1990) *Needs and Welfare* (London: Sage).

Graham, Keith (1986) *The Battle of Democracy* (Brighton: Wheatsheaf).

Gray, John (1982) 'Spencer on the ethics of liberty and the limits of state interference', *History of Political Thought*, III, 465–81.

—— (1983) *Mill on Liberty: a Defence* (London: Routledge & Kegan Paul).

—— (1984) 'Indirect utilitarianism and fundamental rights', in *Social Philosophy and Policy*, I, 73–91.

Gray, Tim (1991) *Freedom* (Basingstoke: Macmillan).

Green, Thomas Hill (1941) *Lectures on the Principles of Political Obligation* (London: Longmans).

Griffin, James (1982) 'Modern utilitarianism', *Revue Internationale de Philosophie*, XXXVI, 331–75.

—— (1986) *Well-Being: Its Meaning, Measurement and Moral Importance* (Oxford: Clarendon Press).

Gutmann, Amy (1980) *Liberal Equality* (Cambridge: Cambridge University Press).

Hacker, P. M. S. (1973) 'Sanction theories of duty', in A. W. B. Simpson (ed.), *Oxford Essays in Jurisprudence*, second series (Oxford, Clarendon Press) pp. 131–70.

Haksar, Vinit (1978) 'The nature of rights', *Archiv für Rechts- und Sozialphilosophie*, Bd. LXIV, 183–202.

Halpin, Andrew (1991) 'More comments on rights and claims', *Law and Philosophy*, X, 271–310.

Hannum, H. (1990) *Autonomy, Sovereignty and Self-determination* (Pennsylvania: University of Pennsylvania Press).

Hardwig, John (1984) 'Should women think in terms of rights?', *Ethics*, XCIV, 441–55.

Hare, R. M. (1981) *Moral Thinking: Its Levels, Method and Point* (Oxford: Clarendon Press).

—— (1985) 'Rights, utility and universalization: reply to J. L. Mackie', in Frey (1985a) pp. 106–20.

Harris, David (1987) *Justifying State Welfare: the New Right versus the Old Left* (Oxford: Basil Blackwell).

Harrison, Frank R. (1972) 'What kind of beings can have rights?', *Philosophical Forum*, XII, 113–29.

Harsanyi, John (1976) 'Cardinal welfare, individualistic ethics and interpersonal comparisons of utility', in his *Essays on Ethics, Social Behavior and Scientific Explanation* (Dordrecht: Reidel) pp. 6–23.

—— (1977) *Rational Behaviour and Bargaining Equilibrium in Games and Social Situations* (Cambridge: Cambridge University Press).

Hart, H. L. A. (1961) *The Concept of Law* (Oxford: Clarendon Press).

—— (1967) 'Are there any natural rights?', in A. Quinton (ed.), *Political Philosophy* (Oxford: Oxford University Press) pp. 53–66.

—— (1979) 'Between utility and rights', in Alan Ryan (ed.), *The Idea of Freedom* (Oxford: Oxford University Press) pp. 77–98.

—— (1982) *Essays on Bentham* (Oxford: Clarendon Press).

Hobbes, Thomas (1957) *Leviathan*, Michael Oakeshott (ed.) (Oxford: Basil Blackwell).

Hohfeld, Wesley N. (1919) *Fundamental Legal Conceptions as Applied in Judicial Reasoning* (New Haven, Conn.: Yale University Press).

Honore, A. M. (1960) 'Rights of exclusion and immunities against divesting', *Tulane Law Review*, XXXIV, 453–68.

Hudson, Stephen D. and Douglas N. Husak (1980) 'Legal rights: how useful is Hohfeldian analysis?', *Philosophical Studies*, XXXVII, 45–53.

Jones, Peter (1980) 'Rights, welfare and stigma', in N. Timms (ed.), *Social Welfare: Why and How?* (London: Routledge & Kegan Paul) pp. 123–44.

—— (1982) 'Freedom and the redistribution of resources', *Journal of Social Policy*, XI, 217–38.

—— (1983) 'Political equality and majority rule', in David Miller and Larry Siedentop (eds), *The Nature of Political Theory* (Oxford: Clarendon Press) pp. 155–82.

—— (1985) 'Toleration, harm and moral effect', in John Horton and Susan Mendus (eds), *Aspects of Toleration* (London: Methuen) pp. 136–57.

—— (1989) 'The ideal of the neutral state', in Robert Goodin and Andrew Reeve (eds), *Liberal Neutrality* (London: Routledge) pp. 9–38.

—— (1990) 'Universal principles and particular claims: from welfare rights to welfare states', in Goodin and Ware (1990) pp. 34–53.

—— (1994) 'Bearing the consequences of belief', *Journal of Political Philosophy*, II, 24–43.

Kain, Philip J. (1988) *Marx and Ethics* (Oxford: Clarendon Press).

Kamba, Walter J. (1974) 'Legal theory and Hohfeld's analysis of a legal right', *Juridical Review*, 249–62.

Kamenka, Eugene and Alice Erh-Soon Tay (eds) (1978) *Human Rights* (London: Edward Arnold).

Kant, Immanuel (1948) *Groundwork of the Metaphysic of Morals*, in H. Paton (ed.), *The Moral Law* (London: Hutchinson).

Kearns, Thomas (1975) 'Rights, benefits and normative systems', *Archiv für Rechts- und Sozialphilosophie*, Bd. LXI, 465–83.

Keat, Russell (1982) 'Liberal rights and socialism', in Keith Graham (ed.), *Contemporary Political Philosophy: Radical Studies* (Cambridge: Cambridge University Press) pp. 59–82.

King, Desmond and Jeremy Waldron (1988) 'Citizenship, social citizenship and the defence of welfare provision', *British Journal of Political Science*, XVIII, 415–43.

Kleinig, John (1978) 'Human rights, legal rights and social change', in Kamenka and Tay (1978) pp. 36–47.

Kocourek, Albert (1920) 'The Hohfeld system of fundamental legal concepts', *Illinois Law Review*, XV, 24–39.

Kukathas, Chandran (1992) 'Are there any cultural rights?', *Political Theory*, XX, 105–39.

Kymlicka, Will (1988) 'Rawls on teleology and deontology', *Philosophy and Public Affairs*, XVII, 167–90.

—— (1989) *Liberalism, Community and Culture* (Oxford: Clarendon Press).

—— (1992) 'The rights of minority cultures: reply to Kukathas', *Political Theory*, XX, 140–6.

Lacey, Michael J. and Knud Haakonssen (eds) (1991) *A Culture of Rights: the Bill of Rights in Philosophy, Politics and Law – 1791 and 1991* (Cambridge: Cambridge University Press).

Lawson, Edward (1991) *Encyclopedia of Human Rights* (New York: Taylor & Francis).

Leahy, Michael P. T. (1991) *Against Liberation* (London: Routledge).

Lessnoff, Michael (1986) *Social Contract* (Basingstoke: Macmillan).

Lijphart, Arend (1977) *Democracy in Plural Societies* (New Haven, Conn.: Yale University Press).

Lindley, Richard (1986) *Autonomy* (Basingstoke: Macmillan).

Lively, Jack (1975) *Democracy* (Oxford: Basil Blackwell).

Lloyd Thomas, D. A. (1988) *In Defence of Liberalism* (Oxford: Basil Blackwell).

Locke, John (1960) *Two Treatises of Government*, Peter Laslett (ed.) (Cambridge: Cambridge University Press).

—— (1968) *A Letter On Toleration*, R. Klibansky (ed.) (Oxford: Clarendon Press).

Lomasky, Loren (1987) *Persons, Rights and the Moral Community* (Oxford: Oxford University Press) .

Lukes, Steven (1982) 'Can a Marxist believe in human rights?', *Praxis International*, I, 334–45.

—— (1985) *Marxism and Morality* (Oxford: Oxford University Press).

Lyons, David (1965) *Forms and Limits of Utilitarianism* (Oxford: Clarendon Press).

—— (1969) 'Rights, claimants, and beneficiaries', *American Philosophical Quarterly*, VI, 173–85.

—— (1970) 'The correlativity of rights and duties', *Nous*, IV, 45–57.

—— (1984) 'Utility and rights', in Waldron (1984) pp. 110–36.

McBride, William L. (1984) 'Rights and the Marxian tradition', *Praxis International*, IV, 57–74.

MacCallum, Gerald C. (1967) 'Negative and positive freedom', *Philosophical Review*, LXXVI, 312–34.

McCloskey, H. J. (1985) 'Respect for human moral rights versus maximizing good', in Frey (1985a) pp. 121–36.

MacCormick, Neil (1974) 'Law as institutional fact', *Law Quarterly Review*, XC, 102–129.
—— (1977) 'Rights in legislation', in P. M. S. Hacker and J. Raz (eds), *Law, Morality and Society* (Oxford: Clarendon Press) pp. 189–209.
—— (1982a) 'Children's rights: a test-case for theories of rights', in his *Legal Right and Social Democracy* (Oxford: Clarendon Press) pp. 154–66.
—— (1982b) 'Rights, claims and remedies', in M. A. Stewart (ed.), *Law, Morality and Rights* (Dordrecht: Reidel) pp. 161–81.
MacFarlane, L. J. (1985) *The Theory and Practice of Human Rights* (London: Maurice Temple Smith).
MacIntyre, Alasdair (1985) *After Virtue*, 2nd edn (London: Duckworth).
Mack, Eric (1990) 'Self-ownership and the right of property', *The Monist*, LXXIII, 519–43.
Mackie, John (1984) 'Can there be a right-based moral theory?' in Waldron (1984), pp. 168–81.
—— (1985) 'Rights, utility and universalization', in Frey (1985a) pp. 86–105.
Margalit, Avishai and Joseph Raz (1990) 'National self-determination', *Journal of Philosophy*, LXXXVII, 439–61.
Maritain, Jacques (1944) *The Rights of Man and Natural Law* (London: Centenary Press).
—— (1951) *Man and the State* (Chicago: University of Chicago Press).
Marshall, Geoffrey (1973) 'Rights, options and entitlements', in A. W. B Simpson (ed.), *Oxford Essays in Jurisprudence*, second series (Oxford, Clarendon Press) pp. 228–41.
Marshall, T. H. (1950), *Citizenship and Social Class and Other Essays* (Cambridge: Cambridge University Press).
—— (1981) *The Right of Welfare and Other Essays* (London: Heinemann).
Martin, Rex (1980) 'Human rights and civil rights', *Philosophical Studies*, XXXVII, 391–403.
—— (1982) 'On the theory of legal rights as valid claims', *Midwest Studies in Philosophy*, VII, 175–95.
—— (1985) *Rawls and Rights* (Lawrence: University Press of Kansas).
—— (1993) *A System of Rights* (Oxford: Clarendon Press).
Marx, Karl (1971) 'On the Jewish Question', in David McLellan (ed.), *Karl Marx: Early Texts* (Oxford: Basil Blackwell) pp. 85–114.
Mayo, Bernard (1967) 'What are human rights?', in D. D. Raphael (1967a) pp. 68–80.
Melden, A. I. (1977) *Rights and Persons* (Oxford: Basil Blackwell).
Meyer, Michael J. (1992) 'Rights between friends', *Journal of Philosophy*, LXXXIX, 467–83.
Meyers, Diana T. (1981) 'Human rights in pre-affluent societies', *Philosophical Quarterly*, XXXI, 139–44.
—— (1985) *Inalienable Rights: a Defense* (New York: Columbia University Press).
Mill, J. S. (1910) *Utilitarianism, Liberty, and Representative Government* (London: Everyman).
Miller, David (1976) *Social Justice* (Oxford: Clarendon Press).

—— (1978) 'Democracy and social justice', in Pierre Birnbaum, Jack Lively and Geraint Parry (eds), *Democracy, Consensus and Social Contract* (London: Sage) pp. 75–100.

—— (1983) 'Constraints on freedom', *Ethics*, XCIV, 66–86.

—— (1988) 'The ethical significance of nationality', *Ethics*, XCVIII, 647–62.

Miller, Harlan B. and William H. Williams (1983) *Ethics and Animals* (Clifton, NJ: Humana).

Milne, A. J. M. (1986) *Human Rights and Human Diversity* (Basingstoke: Macmillan).

Minogue, Kenneth (1963) *The Liberal Mind* (London: Methuen).

—— (1978) 'Natural rights, ideology and the game of life', in Kamenka and Tay (1978) pp. 13–35.

Moon, J. Donald (ed.) (1988) *Responsibility, Rights and Welfare: the Theory of the Welfare State* (Boulder: Westview Press).

Morris, Herbert (1968) 'Persons and Punishment', *The Monist*, LII, 475–501.

Mullock, Philip (1971) 'The Hohfeldian jural opposite', *Ratio*, XIII, 158–65.

Nelson, Wiliam (1976) 'On the alleged importance of moral rights', *Ratio*, XVIII, 145–55.

—— (1980) *On Justifying Democracy* (London: Routledge & Kegan Paul).

Nickel, James W. (1987) *Making Sense of Human Rights* (Berkeley: University of California Press).

Nielson, Kai (1968) 'Scepticism and human rights', *The Monist*, LII, 573–94.

Nino, Carlos (1991) *The Ethics of Human Rights* (Oxford: Oxford University Press).

—— (ed.) (1992) *Rights* (Aldershot: Dartmouth).

Nozick, Robert (1974) *Anarchy, State and Utopia* (Oxford: Basil Blackwell).

—— (1981) *Philosophical Explanations* (Cambridge, Mass.: Harvard University Press).

O'Neill, Onora (1989) 'The great maxims of charity and justice', in Neil MacCormick and Zenon Bankowski (eds), *Enlightenment, Rights and Revolution* (Aberdeen: Aberdeen University Press) pp. 297–312.

Paine, Thomas (1969) *Rights of Man* (Harmondsworth: Penguin).

Parent, W. A. (1974) 'Freedom as the non-restriction of options', *Mind*, LXXXIII, 432–4.

Parfit, Derek (1986) *Reasons and Persons* (Oxford: Oxford University Press).

Paterson, David and Richard D. Ryder (eds) (1979) *Animal Rights – a Symposium* (London: Centaur).

Paton, George Whitecross (1972) *A Textbook of Jurisprudence*, 4th edn, G. W. Paton and David P. Derham (eds) (Oxford: Clarendon Press).

Paul, Ellen Frankel, Fred D. Miller and Jeffrey Paul (eds) (1984) *Human Rights* (Oxford: Basil Blackwell).

Pennock, J. Roland and John W. Chapman (eds) (1981) *Human Rights* (*Nomos*, XXIII) (New York: New York University Press).

—— (1982) *Ethics, Economics and the Law* (*Nomos*, XXIV) (New York: New York University Press).

Perry, Thomas (1977) 'A paradigm of philosophy: Hohfeld on legal rights', *American Philosophical Quarterly*, XIV, 45–53.

—— (1980) 'Reply in defense of Hohfeld', *Philosophical Studies*, XXXVII, 203–9.

Plamenatz, J. P. (1968) *Consent, Freedom and Political Obligation*, 2nd edn (Oxford: Oxford University Press).

Plant, Raymond (1985) 'Welfare and the value of liberty', *Government and Opposition*, XX, 297–314.

—— (1991) *Modern Political Thought* (Oxford: Basil Blackwell).

Plant, Raymond, Harry Lesser and Peter Taylor-Gooby (1980) *Political Philosophy and Social Welfare* (London: Routledge & Kegan Paul).

Pollis, Adamantia and Peter Schwab (eds) (1979a) *Human Rights: Cultural and Ideological Perspectives* (New York: Praeger).

—— (1979b) 'Human rights: a western construct with limited applicability', in Pollis and Schwab (1979a) pp. 1–18.

Radin, Max (1938) 'A restatement of Hohfeld', *Harvard Law Review*, LI, 1141–64.

Raphael, D. D. (ed.) (1967a) *Political Theory and the Rights of Man* (London: Macmillan).

—— (1967b) 'Human rights, old and new', in Raphael (1967a) pp. 54–67.

—— (1967c) 'The rights of man and the rights of citizen', in Raphael (1967a) pp. 101–18.

Rawls, John (1971) *A Theory of Justice* (Oxford: Oxford University Press).

—— (1980) 'Kantian constructivism in moral theory', *Journal of Philosophy*, LXXVII, 515–72.

—— (1982) 'Social unity and primary goods', in Amartya Sen and Bernard Williams (eds), *Utilitarianism and Beyond* (Cambridge: Cambridge University Press) pp. 159–85.

—— (1985) 'Justice as fairness: political not metaphysical', *Philosophy and Public Affairs*, XIV, 223–51.

—— (1993) *Political Liberalism* (New York: Columbia University Press).

Raz, Joseph (1975) *Practical Reason and Norms* (London: Hutchinson).

—— (1977) 'Promises and obligations', in P. M. S. Hacker and J. Raz (eds), *Law, Morality and Society* (Oxford: Oxford University Press) pp. 210–28.

—— (1979) *The Authority of Law: Essays on Law and Morality* (Oxford: Clarendon Press).

—— (1984) 'Legal rights', *Oxford Journal of Legal Studies*, IV, 1–21.

—— (1986) *The Morality of Freedom* (Oxford: Clarendon Press).

Reeve, Andrew (1986) *Property* (Basingstoke, Macmillan).

Regan, Tom (1983) *The Case for Animal Rights* (London: Routledge & Kegan Paul).

Regis, Edward (1984) *Gewirth's Ethical Rationalism* (Chicago: University of Chicago Press).

Renteln, Alison Dundes (1990) *International Human Rights: Universalism versus Relativism* (Newbury Park, Calif.: Sage).

Richards, David A. J. (1982), 'International distributive justice', in Pennock and Chapman (1982) pp. 275–99.

Ritchie, D. G. (1895) *Natural Rights* (London: Swan Sonnenschein).

Rorty, Richard (1989) *Contingency, Irony and Solidarity* (Cambridge: Cambridge University Press).
—— (1991) *Objectivity, Relativism and Truth: Philosophical Papers*, vol. I (Cambridge: Cambridge University Press).
Ross, W. D. (1930) *The Right and the Good* (Oxford: Clarendon Press).
Rousseau, Jean Jacques (1913) *The Social Contract and Discourses*, transl. G. D. H Cole (London: Everyman).
—— (1968) *The Social Contract*, transl. Maurice Cranston (Harmondsworth: Penguin).
Ryan, Alan (1984) *Property and Political Theory* (Oxford: Basil Blackwell).
Salmond, John (1966) *Jurisprudence*, 12th edn, P. J. Fitzgerald (ed.) (London: Sweet & Maxwell).
Sandel, Michael (1982) *Liberalism and the Limits of Justice* (Cambridge: Cambridge University Press).
—— (ed.) (1984) *Liberalism and its Critics* (Oxford: Basil Blackwell).
Scanlon, T. M. (1984) 'Rights, goals and fairness', in Waldron (1984) pp. 137–152.
Schauer, Frederick (1982) *Free Speech: a Philosophical Enquiry* (Cambridge: Cambridge University Press).
Seanor, Douglas and N. Fotion (eds) (1990) *Hare and Critics* (Oxford: Clarendon Press).
Searle, J. R. (1969) *Speech Acts* (Cambridge: Cambridge University Press).
Sen, Amartya (1982) 'Rights and agency', *Philosophy and Public Affairs*, XI, 3–39.
—— (1985) 'Rights and capabilities', in Ted Honderich (ed.), *Morality and Objectivity: a Tribute to J. L. Mackie* (London: Routledge & Kegan Paul) pp. 130–48.
Sen, Amartya and Bernard Williams (eds) (1982) *Utilitarianism and Beyond* (Cambridge: Cambridge University Press).
Shapiro, Ian (1986) *The Evolution of Rights in Liberal Theory* (Cambridge: Cambridge University Press).
Sher, George (1984) 'Right violations and injustices: can we always avoid trade-offs?', *Ethics*, XCIV, 212–24.
Shue, Henry (1980) *Basic Rights: Subsistence, Affluence, and U.S. Foreign Policy* (Princeton, NJ: Princeton University Press).
Sieghart, Paul (1986) *The Lawful Rights of Mankind* (Oxford: Oxford University Press).
Singer, Peter (1973) *Democracy and Disobedience* (Oxford: Clarendon Press).
—— (1976) *Animal Liberation* (London: Jonathan Cape).
—— (1981) 'The concept of moral standing', in Arthur L. Caplan and Daniel Callahan (eds), *Ethics in Hard Times* (New York: Plenum Press) pp. 31–45.
Slote, Michael (1985) *Common-sense Morality and Consequentialism* (London: Routledge & Kegan Paul).
Smart, J. J. C. and Bernard Williams (1973) *Utilitarianism: For and Against* (Cambridge: Cambridge University Press).

Steiner, Hillel (1974a) 'The natural right to equal freedom', *Mind*, LXXXIII, 194–210.

—— (1974b) 'Individual liberty', *Proceedings of the Aristotelian Society*, LXXV, 33–50.

—— (1977a) 'The structure of a set of compossible rights', *Journal of Philosophy*, LXXIV, 767–75.

—— (1977b) 'The natural right to the means of production', *Philosophical Quarterly*, XXVII, 41–9.

—— (1987) 'Capitalism, justice and equal starts', *Social Philosophy and Policy*, V, 49–71.

Stoljar, Samuel (1984) *An Analysis of Rights* (London: Macmillan).

Stone, Julius (1964) *Legal System and Lawyers' Reasoning* (London: Stevens & Sons).

Stone, Roy L. (1963) 'An analysis of Hohfeld', *Minnesota Law Review*, XLVIII, 313–37.

Sumner, L. W. (1987) *The Moral Foundation of Rights* (Oxford: Clarendon Press).

Tay, Alice Erh-Soon (1978) 'Marxism, socialism and human rights', in Kamenka and Tay (1978) pp. 104–12.

Taylor, Charles (1985) 'Atomism', in his *Philosophy and the Human Sciences*, vol. II (Cambridge: Cambridge University Press) pp. 187–210.

Taylor, Paul W. (1986) *Respect for Nature* (Princeton, NJ: Princeton University Press.

Thompson, Kenneth W. (ed.) (1980) *The Moral Imperatives of Human Rights: a World Survey* (Washington: University Press of America).

Thomson, Garret (1987) *Needs* (London: Routledge & Kegan Paul).

Thomson, Judith Jarvis (1990) *The Realm of Rights* (Cambridge, Mass.: Harvard University Press).

Tierney, Brian (1983) 'Tuck on rights: some medieval problems', *History of Political Thought*, IV, 429–41.

—— (1988) 'Villey, Ockham and the origin of individual rights', in John Witte and Frank S. Alexander (eds), *The Weightier Matters of the Law* (Atlanta: Scholars Press) pp. 1–31.

—— (1989) 'Origins of natural rights language: texts and contexts, 1150–1250', *History of Political Thought*, X, 615–46.

Tomasi, John (1991) 'Individual rights and community virtues', *Ethics*, CI, 521–36.

Tormey, Alan (1973) 'Aesthetic rights', *Journal of Aesthetics and Art Criticism*, XXXII, 163–70.

Tuck, Richard (1979) *Natural Rights Theories: their Origin and Development* (Cambridge: Cambridge University Press).

Van Dyke, Vernon (1974) 'Human rights and the rights of groups', *American Journal of Political Science*, XVIII, 725–41.

—— (1982) 'Collective entities and moral rights: problems in liberal democratic thought', *Journal of Politics*, XLIV, 21–40.

Vincent, R. J. (1986) *Human Rights and International Relations* (Cambridge: Cambridge University Press).

Vlastos, Gregory (1984) 'Justice and equality', in Waldron (1984) pp. 41–76.

Waldron, Jeremy (1981) 'A right to do wrong', *Ethics*, XCII, 21–39.
—— (1983) 'Galston on rights', *Ethics*, XCIII, 325–7.
—— (ed.) (1984) *Theories of Rights* (Oxford: Oxford University Press).
—— (1987) *'Nonsense Upon Stilts': Bentham, Burke and Marx on the Rights of Man* (London: Methuen).
—— (1988) *The Right to Private Property* (Oxford: Clarendon Press).
—— (1989) 'Rights in conflict', *Ethics*, XCIX, 503–19.
Walzer, Michael (1983) *Spheres of Justice* (Oxford: Martin Robertson).
Watson, David (1977) 'Welfare rights and human rights', *Journal of Social Policy*, VI, 31–46.
Weale, Albert (1978) *Equality and Social Policy* (London: Routledge & Kegan Paul).
—— (1983) *Political Theory and Social Policy* (London: Macmillan).
Weil, Simone (1987) *The Need for Roots* (London: Ark).
Wellman, Carl (1978) 'A new conception of human rights', in Kamenka and Tay (1978) pp. 48–58.
—— (1985) *A Theory of Rights* (Totowa, NJ: Rowman & Allanheld).
White, Alan R. (1975) *Modal Thinking* (Ithaca, NY: Cornell University Press).
—— (1982) 'Rights and claims', in M.A. Stewart (ed.), *Law, Morality and Rights* (Dordrecht: Reidel) pp. 139–60.
—— (1984) *Rights* (Oxford: Clarendon Press).
Wiggins, David (1985) 'Claims of need', in Ted Honderich (ed.), *Morality and Objectivity: a Tribute to J. L. Mackie* (London: Routledge & Kegan Paul) pp. 149–202.
Williams, Glanville (1968) 'The concept of legal liberty', in Robert S. Summers (ed.), *Essays in Legal Philosophy* (Oxford: Basil Blackwell) pp. 121–45.
Young, Robert (1978) 'Dispensing with moral rights', *Political Theory*, VI, 63–74.
—— (1986) *Personal Autonomy: Beyond Negative and Positive Liberty* (New York: St Martin's Press).

Index